Doubly Chosen

Publication of this book has been made possible in part by the generous support from the Anonymous Fund of the University of Wisconsin–Madison and from the George L. Mosse / Laurence A. Weinstein Center for Jewish Studies, University of Wisconsin–Madison.

Doubly Chosen

Jewish Identity,
the Soviet Intelligentsia,
and the Russian Orthodox Church

JUDITH DEUTSCH KORNBLATT

THE UNIVERSITY OF WISCONSIN PRESS

The University of Wisconsin Press
1930 Monroe Street
Madison, Wisconsin 53711

www.wisc.edu/wisconsinpress/

3 Henrietta Street
London WC2E 8LU, England

1   3   5   4   2

Printed in the United States of America

Library of Congress Cataloging-in-Publication Data

Kornblatt, Judith Deutsch.
Doubly chosen: Jewish identity, the Soviet intelligentsia, and the
Russian Orthodox Church / Judith Deutsch Kornblatt.
p. cm.
Includes bibliographical references and index.
ISBN 0-299-19484-1 (pbk.: alk. paper)
1. Jewish Christians—Soviet Union—History. 2. Russkaia pravoslavnaia
tserkov'—Relations—Judaism—History—20th century. 3. Judaism—
Relations—Russkaia pravoslavnaia tserkov'—History—20th century.
4. Jews—Soviet Union—History. 5. Intellectuals—Soviet Union—History.
6. Soviet Union—Intellectual life—History. I. Title.
R158.K67 2004
281.9´47´089924—dc22
2003017446

To my parents, who bequeathed me, willy-nilly,
my Jewish identity,

and

To my husband and children, with whom that identity
has flourished.

Contents

Preface

The following study grows from a long-standing interest in Russian Orthodoxy. I came to my fascination with the Eastern Church through Russian literature, as did so many of the individuals interviewed here. Russian
culture, even modern Soviet Russian culture, is suffused with a worldview
that I began to realize is in many ways fundamentally different from my
own. When Feodor Dostoevsky wrote of the individual, of the collective,
the earth, and, yes, of God, he in fact meant something very different
from what I, an American, understand of those terms. A heroic individual is not that praiseworthy fellow in cowboy boots who strikes off on
his own into the new world of the frontier. Dostoevsky's hero, rather, goes
to the crowded and filthy Haymarket and bows down to kiss the dusty
earth. Only in this way might he reunite with Russia, with his fellow
human beings, and with the past.

I began to study the history, doctrine, and ritual of the Orthodox
Church in graduate school at Columbia University and as a special student at St. Vladimir's Seminary, where I learned about the early cult,
about its institutionalization in Byzantium, about it transformations in
the land of Rus', in Muscovy, and in the Russian Empire. I read the
thinkers of the Russian religious renaissance in the late nineteenth and
early twentieth centuries along with the better-known poets and prose
writers of the Silver Age, and learned how the ideas of Vladimir Solovyov
were taken into emigration after the Bolshevik Revolution by Nikolai
Berdyaev, Sergei Bulgakov, and a host of other religious thinkers and so-
called Sophiologists. And in Russia I witnessed first hand a flood of recovery of those thinkers, beginning underground and then openly during

glasnost and in the immediate post-Soviet society. *Sobornost'*, Sophia, *bogochelovechestvo*, and *vseedinstvo* became household words for me.

At the same time, through the very same years, my own Jewish practice intensified. The dual inquiry into Russian Orthodoxy and Judaism, into inherent Russian and Jewish values, into two worlds with highly developed rituals, highlighted for me deep questions of identity. What makes me a Jew? An American? A Jewish American? Or am I rather an American Jew? How am I connected to the people of Israel? To the land of Israel? To the history of Israel? On the other hand, how am I connected to Kiev, the original home of my grandmother, who spoke Russian and Ukrainian, but no Hebrew or Yiddish? What scholarly, or other, fascination did I find in the icons and liturgy of the Russian Orthodox Church? Was this an occupation, after all, for a good Jewish girl?

The prospect of a sabbatical in Jerusalem provided the impetus to write this study that looks, specifically, at the interface between the Russian and Jewish worlds about which I have thought so much. The coincidence of several conversations with Russian Jews who were baptized in the Orthodox Church led me back to Russia to interview other baptized Jews, then to New York, where many had immigrated, and then on to Israel, where still others had made a new home. When common themes about identity began to emerge from the interviews, I knew I had found, if not answers, then at least fresh perspectives on the questions I had posed about identity. As I began to speak about my conclusions, I met equal parts of skepticism and fascination from other Jews and other Americans, confirming my sense that a study of this albeit small group of baptized Jews had its place in our larger questions about Jewish, as well as Russian and Soviet identity. More and more individuals I met admitted to knowing Soviet Jews who had flirted with the Church, often suggesting that their knowledge was intimate indeed. In fact, the phenomenon is not at all obscure, and by no means esoteric. It has not, however, been studied before, whether because of a misplaced Soviet legacy of secrecy, a desire on the part of Russian Jewish émigré Slavists to establish a new identity as American scholars, or general squeamishness toward the topic of conversion.

I am often asked about my own squeamishness toward the subject. Would I have preferred that these Russian Jews did not seek baptism? Am I uncomfortable with their talk of Christ and Resurrection? Yes, as an American Jew committed to the Jewish tradition, I would rather that all Jews marry Jews, that all Jews bring up their children as Jews, and that all Jews understand Judaism as I do. But the Russian Jews I interviewed are not I. On matters of faith, I do not always see eye to eye with my own secular parents on the one hand, or with my religious brother-in-law living in Israel on the other. So much the more are my religious choices, my justification of faith and, most of all, my narration of identity different from those of my "clients," as one acquaintance playfully called the Russian Jewish Christians whom I sought to meet. Their choices relate to who they are, and to where and when they joined—and sometimes left—the Church, as well as to the society and culture in which they were raised. By listening to their stories, we can learn not only about them, but also about that society and how it arrived at where it is. And we can learn about ourselves, who made different, but not always more rational choices. Finally, we can also learn about a powerful interface of Christianity and Judaism, a theological and social moment not only of interest, but also potentially of great import.

I am particularly indebted in this study to several individuals, including Olga and Misha in the United States, Misha in Moscow, and Sergei in Jerusalem. I am thankful to the former two for their openness, and to the latter two, though they kept their personal cards quite close to their chests, for innumerable moments of revelation that they might not even have known they were providing. I do not know if any of these four new and old friends will see themselves in my conclusions, or find them to their liking. I can only hope that they, like my other readers, will understand the true specialness of their stories.

For research and critical help of all kinds, I would like to thank the following: Esperanza Alfonso, Michael Bernard-Donals, David Bethea, Chad Boutin, Rachel Brenner, Zvi Gitelman, Jean Hennessey, Stefani Hoffman, Ben Jens, Rabbi Kenneth Katz, Rachel Keren, John Klier, Marina Kostalevsky, Galina Lapina, David Polet, Dimitar Spasov, Roman Timenchik, Paul Valliere, and Matt Walker. In addition, I would like to thank the participants at several seminars, at which I was able to discuss the results of my research, including a faculty seminar and a Summer Institute at the University of Wisconsin Center for Jewish Studies, and the Mayrock Center seminar series at Hebrew University. My early teachers in Russian Orthodoxy—Richard Gustafson, Paul Valliere, and the late Father John Meyendorff—deserve credit for setting me on the path to this study, and for reconfirming my commitment along the way. Finally, I would like to thank Robert Mandel and all the members of the University of Wisconsin Press staff for their professionalism and sound advice.

Funding assistance was provided by an IREX Short-term Travel Grant to Russia; by the Vidal Sassoon International Center for the Study of Antisemitism and by the Department of Russian Studies at Hebrew University in Jerusalem, where I was a visiting scholar; by the Graduate School of the University of Wisconsin–Madison, and by a sabbatical from the University of Wisconsin.

∽

The greatest thanks, however, must go to my family. Although my parents teased me for wanting to go to Hebrew school ("You must think that Judaism is the study of Judy"), they were always more "Jewish" then they let on. ("Our kind don't go here," my blue-eyed mother surprised me by saying in the admissions office of a New England college, as we toured east coast schools my junior year in high school.) Equally important, they instilled in me a love of inquiry and an appreciation of culture of all kinds, and they actively encouraged my diverse interests from an early age. I only now, as a parent myself, begin to understand how difficult it must have been to see me off, again and again, on yet one more trip beyond the Iron Curtain, a suitcase full of toilet paper and peanut butter in tow. My children, Jacob and Louisa, endured my many absences as I traveled to the former Soviet Union, and spent five months with me in Israel, learning first hand about the differences between American, Israeli, and Russian Jews, both in the classroom and on the playground. There are some lessons they might not have wanted to learn, but, regardless, they are now who they are because of those experiences in Jerusalem. Marc, my husband and most exacting editor, lived through this project almost as closely as I did. I thank him dearly for his support, and for the Jewish home that we have made together.

Doubly Chosen

CHAPTER ONE

Introduction

Russian Jewish Christians

Vy —— veruiushchie? (Are you a believer?)
—Heard in Moscow in the mid-1970s

By undoing the concept of fixed, unalterable identities, conversion
unsettles the boundaries by which selfhood, citizenship, nationhood, and
community are defined, exposing these as permeable borders.
—Viswanathan, *Outside the Fold*

Everyone is against conversion to Christianity. Period.
—A religious Jew, New York 1998

A MEMORY HAS ACCOMPANIED ME NOW for many years. During
an extended visit to Soviet Russia in the Brezhnev era of stagna-
tion, on several occasions I was asked by acquaintances of only
a casual nature whether or not I believe in God. Why, I wondered, would
anyone on the streets of Moscow in the 1970s care about my personal
religious life? This had never been a topic of interest in the United States,
except, if ever, among close friends. Why there, and then, in the bleak atheist Soviet Union, should I hear the odd question: *"Vy —— veruiushchie?"*
What could they really be asking? It was clear that these Soviet citizens
did not care about my denominational affiliation, about which church
or synagogue I may attend, even whether I attend at all. Most had never
been in a house of worship. All were reared in an aggressively antireli-
gious society, and few to none had training in any organized religion.
Indeed, the question about belief had little to do with history, doctrine, or
ritual. Rather, I learned with a minimum of probing that Soviet citizens
asked about my religious feelings to determine whether I had within me

3

a spark of life, of energy, of idealism to counteract the mass skepticism and lethargy of their time. Did I believe in God meant did I have faith in the possible transformation of what they could only see as a vulgar and compromised world.

Another memory from the Soviet 1970s and early 80s: I asked an American friend who had just spent six months in Moscow whether he had made many Russian friends. "Yes," he answered, "but 'Russian' is a euphemism." In fact, the majority of his new acquaintances were not Russians, but Jews, labeled as such by the word *evrei* in the nationality category of their internal passports. The reasons behind the ethnic composition of my friend's friends were both simple and significant. Emigration for Russian Jews became possible in the 1970s, and it was largely Jews who had contact with visitors from abroad, whose relatives already in the United States passed on names and numbers to call, and it was Jews who had less to lose from open association with foreigners. They might be called in for questioning, as was done to many of my own acquaintances, but it would not have been the first time. And they could not lose the jobs or the privileges that many of them had already lost as they applied for permission to leave the Soviet Union.

This was still the time when Soviet children were taught about the evil American imperialists. Most educated Soviets refused to believe the propaganda about rampant exploitation and poverty, but unfortunately jumped to the opposite conviction, causing no small amount of disillusionment once immigrants came off the plane in New York. Many average citizens who stayed behind, not knowing what else to think, and having been taught to read only in black and white, believed the picture of total American oppression.

I remember meeting a group of Russian laborers through a dissident theater director who had been expelled from his professional union, and who avoided imprisonment on charges of "parasitism" by digging graves. (The communist Soviet Union prided itself on its ideal of full employment, although, as the joke ran, "They pretend to pay us, and we pretend to work.") The director wanted to film the reactions to me of "common Russians," for none of his fellow gravediggers had ever met a foreigner. As it turns out, they indeed half expected me to have horns, as well as a nuclear weapon in my back pocket, for they had read that all rich Americans want war. And if I was a white American, I had to be rich. At that time, the issue of my Jewishness did not come up, and I don't know what would have happened if it did. I also don't know what became of the underground film, but I do know that, if not for this Jewish director, whose dissidence resulted in an unfulfilled desire to leave the Soviet Union, I would never have met these "ordinary" Russian Soviet citizens, who lived in fear of the American enemy and of the consequences of association with one.

The mass emigration of Jews in the 1970s and 1980s, when foreign travel was still forbidden to most Soviet citizens, produced a great irony. In addition to the common economic and sometimes ideological reasons for emigration, and the desire to reunite with family that had already settled in the West, Russian Jews often wanted to leave for Israel, the United States, or other destinations because of fears of widespread antisemitism in the Soviet Union. The discrimination they had endured, although in fact rarely leading to violence, formed the fabric of their lives as Soviet citizens: unspoken university quotas, glass ceilings in the workplace, and, as I personally witnessed on more than one occasion, graffiti on doors, hate mail in newspapers, taunts by neighbors. But their ability to emigrate, granted sometimes only after long waits as "refusniks," caused yet more feelings of antisemitism, and the paradoxical confirmation among Russians and other Soviet national groups that, yet again, "the Jews get all the privileges."

A second irony, and one perhaps even more pertinent for the current study, is that the new immigrants, once marginalized as Jews in Russia, became marginalized anew among Jews abroad. Just as immigrants to Israel *(olim)* from the United States, England, and South Africa are all "anglos," the Russian-speaking *olim* from the former Soviet Union are all "Russians." Many *olim* themselves cling to their new/old identity. As Maya Kaganskaya, a Russian Jewish immigrant to Israel, told a researcher writing on the "Russians" in Israel: "The new immigrants from Russia have fled the new nationalism, but here they find no security, there is no earth under their feet. Some of them feel that Israel is their homeland. Others are alienated, so they fall back on Russian culture, work out a symbiosis between Russians here and the Russian mainland. There must be some sort of continuity."[1] The same holds true in America, where Russian Jews now tend to call themselves "Russians," an ethnic designation denied them in their old home.

A final observation on the Jews whom my university-educated friend met in the Soviet Union: During the period of mass emigration, as in most periods in the twentieth century, Jews comprised a disproportionate percentage of the so-called Russian intelligentsia. Therefore, the conclusions my friend drew from his interaction with his Jewish acquaintances, as well as the conclusions that this study will draw about Russian Jews in general, both grow from and reflect back on the Soviet intelligentsia as a whole. In the late Soviet period, the interest in faith as a mark of vitality among intellectuals, including Jewish intellectuals, coincided with the beginnings of emigration. As their gaze turned toward Israel and the West, it also turned inward in search of spiritual meaning.

Double Chosenness

Not coincidentally, the majority of my own acquaintances in Soviet Russia were also Jews. The one exception, or so I thought, was a close friend who regularly, and bravely, attended Sunday liturgy at one of the few working Russian Orthodox churches in Moscow of the pre-glasnost period, and who took me quietly to the baptism of one of her children. But this friend, too, turned out to be Jewish, and here was my first conscious encounter with a baptized Russian Jew, or, in the oxymoronic terminology of this study, a Russian Jewish Christian. Her internal passport read "Jewish," since both parents were Jews. But her mother and father, too, had joined the Russian Orthodox Church. Indeed, the more often I took notice, the more Russian Jewish Christians I found, both in Russia and in emigration. Why, I had to ask, did the search inward bring these intelligentsia Jews to Russian Orthodoxy (or *Pravoslavie,* "right faith"), either before or at the same time as their search outward brought many of them to questions of their Jewishness and emigration? Eastern Orthodoxy is not known as a particularly "intellectual" religion, or, to say the least, as a haven for the Jews. In fact, Russian Orthodox–Jewish relations have been fraught with tension for centuries; the discussion of the so-called Jewish question in Russia in the next chapter makes this abundantly clear. The thirst for belief among the intelligentsia during the final decades of the Soviet period must have been quite compelling, indeed, considering charges of antisemitism within Russian Orthodoxy and the discrimination many Jewish converts continue to feel from the official Church. As it turns out, these Jews often suffer both antisemitism and anti-Christian discrimination. As Pasha, a particularly reflective interviewee lamented, *Jews don't understand us, and Russians don't really accept us.*[2]

So, why there and then, by them? Why would educated Jews, brought up on the uncompromising doctrines of atheism and Marxism-Leninism, turn to the Russian Orthodox Church? Ultimately, I came to realize, this inquiry leads to larger questions about Jewish identity in general, and Russian Jewish identity in particular. Who are Jews, citizens of a particular country, who absorb the culture around them at the same time as preserving—but to what degree and in what form?—the ancient covenant of Israel? Is there a special message in the Russian, Soviet context, with its unique history and social/ideological makeup that can bring into relief perennial questions about Jewish identity? And what about questions concerning conversion, of theoretical interest to sociologists and of grave concern to social planners in the Jewish communities around the world? Are these Jews different from other out-converts from Judaism? Is it significant that these intellectuals knew virtually nothing of Judaism, from which they could convert? Can we call this conversion at all? On yet another front, I began to see that the investigation opens up theological questions about Russian Orthodoxy, and about its paradoxical attraction for Jewish intellectuals. Was there something that these Jewish Christians sought in the mystical, many would say irrational, texture of Orthodoxy, as opposed to both normative Judaism and most branches of Western Christianity? Or/and does Jewish participation in the Church in this modern period reveal fissures in that centuries-old, Orthodox face? In short, what could a study of Jews in the post-Stalinist Russian Orthodox Church tell us both about Jews and about Russians of that unique time and place and about Jews and Russians in general? Finally, on the broadest of levels, what can we learn about the border of Christian-Jewish relations from the stories recorded here?

To answer these questions, it will be necessary to contextualize the subjects of this study in a number of ways, for they belong, or perhaps only awkwardly belong, to any number of different social, historical, and religious groups: converts both to Christianity and from Judaism; the Soviet intelligentsia after Stalin; Russian Jews; Jews in all countries; and, in fact, young people everywhere who seek an alternative to the status quo. (Most, but not all, were in their late teens and early twenties when they became interested in the Orthodox Church.) This contextualization will take place in various places throughout this study, where appropriate, to understand the unique angles of this particular cohort. These Russian Jewish Christians are both like and unlike Jews in America and Western Europe of the same time, and certainly like and unlike other intellectuals who experienced the restrictive atmosphere of the last decades of the Soviet Union. Their main distinction is that they took the unlikely step, at least to most modern American eyes, of joining the Russian Orthodox Church.

To students of Russia, the choice of Orthodoxy may be more readily understandable than to most Americans, given what we know of the strong acculturation of Russian Jews and their sense of belonging to the great tradition of Russian literature, music, and art that many profess.[3] Especially for intelligentsia Jews, Russia is their motherland, as it was that of their Russian cultural forebears: Pushkin, Tolstoy, Dostoevsky. At the turn of the twentieth century, Russian language, Russian literature, Russian culture in general were entrance tickets into modernity in general. This was the time when a number of Russian Jewish intellectuals integrated into mainstream Russian culture, and the philosopher Lev Shestov (born Yehuda Leib Shvartsman) insisted that the messages of writers like Dostoevsky and Gogol are not Russian, but universal. Yet Shestov repeatedly wrote about "our" literature, "our" culture, "our" civilization, as in the section called "The Russian Spirit" in his book of aphorisms, *The Apotheosis of Groundlessness.*[4]

Many Russian Jewish writers of the twentieth century, trained in the Russian classics, felt more closely drawn to the culture of Pushkin than to that of Sholem Aleichem. The poet Osip Mandelstam, who converted to Christianity ostensibly in order to gain greater access to higher education, and who always felt ambivalent about his Jewish past, wrote in his autobiography: "All the elegant mirage of Petersburg was merely a dream, a brilliant covering thrown over the abyss, while round about there sprawled the chaos of Judaism—not a motherland, not a house, not a hearth, but precisely a chaos, the unknown womb world whence I had issued, which I feared, about which I made vague conjectures and fled, always fled."[5] Where he fled, of course, was into the Russian language and Russian culture on which he was raised, for the latter, he felt, participated in the broader culture of Western Europe in a way that what he called "tongue-tied" Jewish language(s) and traditions never could.[6] To return to the irony that Jewish immigrants become "Russian" once abroad, Naomi Shepherd found that, "All educated Russian immigrants, from the adolescents onward, will claim that what remains of their cultural luggage is Russian literature, by which they mean essentially the great novels of the nineteenth century and the poetry of the early twentieth century—much of it written by Jews. . . . Inevitably, those who write in Russian must look back on, draw on, that tradition. This is particularly true if they continue to write in Russian."[7]

Nonetheless, the choice of Russian Orthodoxy remains shocking to most Westerners who learn of it. The wave of Jewish baptisms here considered is indeed modest in comparison to the general population of Russian Jews who did not become Christian, and certainly in relation to new Orthodox believers of ethnic Russian descent, many of whom came to the Church in the same final decades of the Soviet era examined in this study. These Russian Jewish Christians have not changed the major course of the history of Russian Jews, or, so far, of the Russian Orthodox Church. Still, though the numbers may be small, in the thousands to tens of thousands, the significance of their stories is large in terms of the theoretical questions of religion and national identity they raise. Furthermore, the baptisms have continued after the fall of the Soviet Union, and, surprisingly for many, even in emigration. A number of Russian Jews who left their birthplace for New York, and even Jerusalem, have turned, in their new homes, to the Russian Orthodox Church.[8]

When asked why they joined the Church, the individuals interviewed as part of this study would usually answer that they found freedom in Christianity. Not all are overtly pious, although many have icons in their apartments,[9] and one in particular constantly fingered a small cross and liberally seeded his conversation with references to Jesus and the Church. In virtually all of the cases, I had no cause to doubt the belief of my subjects. No one in this wave of post-Stalinist conversions entered the Church for convenience—to avoid the *numerus clausus* for entrance into university or a profession, to obtain a residence permit outside the Pale of Settlement, to marry a non-Jew—as was sometimes done in the pre-revolutionary period.[10] My own great-aunt from Kiev converted before the Revolution—in her case to Catholicism, at the time an easier decision than baptism in the Orthodox Church—in order to marry her Russian Orthodox fiancé. On the contrary, entrance into the Church in the Soviet period brought danger, rather than convenience. What is more, no certificate of baptism could erase the word "Jewish" on my subjects' passports, nor could it undermine the conviction of most Russians that they could immediately spot Jews by their large noses or curly hair, and certainly by their names, even after three generations of intermarriage and the birth of an army of Jewish children named Nikolai, Tatiana, and Liudmila. Antisemitism could not end by conversion for these Jews and sometimes, as we will see, actually increased.

The choice of baptism into the Russian Orthodox Church, that is, into an institution with both national (Russian) and confessional (Eastern Orthodox) designation, is a brave act not only because of the hostile environment a Jew might find inside the Church, and not only because of the hostile environment in which the Church found itself during the Soviet period. It is a difficult choice even more so because it forces a Jew to confront his or her ethnic as well as religious identity. The confrontation is not always, or not initially, conscious. As we will see, a number of interviewees insisted that they had no "national" feelings whatsoever. Nonetheless, as we will also see, many underwent a kind of identity crisis or, at best, a sense of disjunction between various parts of their composite identity. Few emerged with no questions whatsoever.

Culturally Russian, ethnically Jewish, Christian by religious affiliation, Russian Jewish Christian refugees in the United States and *olim* in Israel take on added identities in their new homes as well. One man in his late forties, sporting ponytail, beard, and sandals, now works in the Greek Orthodox Monastery of the Cross, off Herzog Street in Jerusalem. Speaking with me inside the silent monastery walls, this soft-spoken man admitted that he probably would not have come to the Church if he had stayed in Russia. But in Israel he began to study Torah. And to ask questions. And, for whatever reasons, he began to believe that Christ, whose cross they say was taken from the wood of a tree in the very valley in which the monastery stands, was the *moshiach*, the messiah or anointed one of Hebrew scriptures. *It is not a contradiction to Judaism,* he explained, not knowing if he was speaking to a sympathetic or skeptical ear. *I came to Christianity through Judaism.* But why did he come to the Orthodox Church, I asked, and not to some other confession? *Because we are Russians. It wouldn't be natural to go to Catholicism, or something else. We are from Russia. There are lots of Russian Jews working here in the monastery. Look at that one over there. And others. All Jews.* Why did he come precisely to this monastery, I asked, in the heart of Jerusalem, a five-minute walk from the Knesset, three minutes to the Dead Sea Scrolls, housed in the Shrine of the Book? *Because of its antiquity. Because of the stones.* As I, with my training in literary analysis, "read" this story of a Russian Jewish Christian, I began to hear the interweaving of any number of different narrative voices. This displaced Jew desires to be connected to an age-old tradition, to a tradition at least as old as the stones that made the monastery, or as old as the tree that supposedly supported Jesus in his last hours, or even an ancient tradition that brought Jesus to Jerusalem in the first place. But the desire to belong, as we will see, is also paradoxically the desire to be different. Such a Russian Jew, no longer in Russia, but not fully in the Jewish state of Israel, might seek an identity that makes him both connected and special. My quiet one wants to be both at home and in exile, and feels, at least spiritually, that he has found a way.

For some Jews who had lived in non-Russian Soviet republics, the clash of different Jewish cultures intensified the clash of other national identities as well. Viktor, a Jew who grew up in a Russian-language home in Riga explained that, *it was difficult for me to become friends with so-called local Jews. Latvian Jews. They were a kind of clan. The majority of the Latvian Jewish community was destroyed during the war, but those who remained preserved some of the traditions. They knew Yiddish. And I felt alien among them.* What Viktor experienced as a schoolboy was the effects of his Russian acculturation, intensified under the Sovietization of Russia in the decade after the war. His family had completely lost the Jewish "affect," the Yiddish and Yiddishisms (not to mention liturgical Hebrew) that still lingered in Latvian Jewish families, and he felt himself to be more Russian that Jewish. Nonetheless, he clearly knew himself to be ethnically Jewish, and his family retained some affiliation as well; was it a coincidence that the school they chose for him was predominantly Jewish? There was no religion at home, however, and no concrete ties to a Jewish language or ritual.

Viktor continued his story, talking to me in Jerusalem, far from the Latvia of his childhood: *I recently bumped into one of my former classmates. Here in Israel. Almost all of the Jewish community from Riga came to Israel. Fairly early, in the 1970s. Anyway, she said a rather strange thing. She said that when I showed up in the school in the fifth grade, the students couldn't decide among themselves whether or not I was Jewish.* The students' questioning and Viktor's memory remind us to ask what makes a Jew "Jewish"? The answer, clearly, is multivalent, and complicated in the Soviet experience by both history and culture.

Viktor claimed not to have wanted to emigrate, but, when forced to for political reasons, and after a prison stay for supposed dissident behavior, chose Israel over Western Europe or the United States. Why? *As I said, I never had any intense national identity. I can say that I felt myself more Russian than Jewish. All the same I had a different reason. I had always envied the Latvians. I understood that they lived in an occupied country. . . . I sympathized with them. I sympathized with the nationalists there. Not that I considered myself to be one of them. No. But I understood the justice of their position. And I envied them for the fact that they lived in their own country. On their own land. I wrote in an article once that I didn't care which nation I belong to, but that if I were reborn, I would want to be born among my own people on my own land. I wanted what I didn't have then. In Latvia, the problem was doubled. It wasn't my own country as a Russian or as a Jew. And thus, I considered that if I were to leave, I would go to a country that I could, at least nominally, call my own. It wasn't as much a national feeling as a feeling of soil.*

At this point in the interview, Viktor let out a self-conscious laugh, no doubt realizing that his statement about soil might have been made by right-wing Russian nationalists today, or, likewise, by Dostoevsky and other Russian "pochvenniki" in the last part of the nineteenth century as well. ("Pochvenniki" were so-called people of the soil, or *pochva:* intellectuals who wanted to reconnect to the roots of Russianness, found, presumably, among the simple folk. Coincidentally or not, many *pochvenniki,* Dostoevsky included, also espoused strident antisemitic ideas.) The attraction to the Jewish land for this Jewish Christian was not, perhaps, purely "national," but it also wasn't simply "spiritual" or "religious." In fact, as this book will argue, the pull away and toward a Jewish identity, in Israel or elsewhere, takes place on the tense and uncharted frontier of both national *and* religious identity.

In recent years, Russians have been scrambling to define themselves in the chaos of post-Soviet life, and the question of the national Church takes on added poignancy, for Jews as well as ethnic Russians. As Russia today more and more allies itself with the Orthodox Church—it has become de rigueur for politicians to be photographed next to priests, and banners of the patron Saint George the Dragon Slayer adorn Moscow in the place where Lenin flags once flew—we must ask how much Russianness underlies Russian Orthodoxy, and, conversely, how much Orthodoxy underlies traditional Russian culture.[11] The answer is not simple. Indeed, the centuries-old tradition of Moscow as the "third Rome," that is, as the final guarantor of Christian faith, promotes an understanding of Russians as the "chosen people" who enjoy a special association with God. According to the Soviet dissident, Boris Shragin, the belief that "God himself endowed Russia with special virtue for all time,"

> is an ancient tradition of Russian Orthodoxy, which proclaimed itself for centuries to be more Christian than other Christianities. The special association of God with the Russian people, and then with the Russian state, is curiously analogous to the doctrine of the "chosen people," but, unlike Judaism, it excludes personal responsibility: to be a good Christian, it was only necessary to be and remain Russian.

All this has been described by authors far better versed in theology than I, among them, the great Russian philosopher Vladimir Solovyov. I am not suggesting, however, that all Russian religion was so crudely nationalistic. Indeed, it seems to me that the fault lies not with religion as such but with a weak and superficial form of religious faith. The deficiency of personal responsibility was not a result but a cause. Russia failed to develop such a sense because of its slowness to discover individualism and its corollaries—philosophy, art, and self-examination in general.[12]

Shragin was a Russian Jew who did not seek baptism, but who shared friendship and professional activity with many who did. In fact, I met my first Jewish Christians indirectly through him. As one interviewee remembered about the dissidents in the mid-1960s who would later split into Zionists, Christians, and/or liberal democrats: *They were all allies. In those days we were a minority of outcasts.*

In the statement quoted above, Shragin bemoans the uncertain distinction between Russian national and religious identity, derived, he believes, from a failure to adopt modern Western ideas of individual responsibility, and leading, according to him, to passivity and evil. By calling themselves "chosen," claims Shragin, Russians feel they need not investigate, and act upon, the unclear boundary between their destined spiritual essence and the accident of their ethnic birth.

A model for the interaction—positive or negative—of nationhood and spiritual chosenness, of course, can be found in Jewish history, as Shragin himself suggests. To what extent are the Jews a "people," whether defined in national or ethnic terms (the use of the terms ethnic or national here depends in part on where and when the Jews in question lived, with or without a state), and to what extent a religious or spiritual group? As one scholar of Jews and Christianity has suggested:

> The Jews . . . are neither a nation nor a religious community in the usual sense of these words, rather they are both at the same time in such a way as to make any distinction between these two concepts impossible. The nation is at its foundation a religious community, and the religious community is a nation. The Jews are a "covenant."[13]

As another Jewish scholar writes, "The crux of our problem derives from a single phenomenon—the dual nature of *Knesset Israel*, the Jewish

people. Jewry is, so to speak, both spiritual and material. It is a community as well as a communion, not only an *ecclesia* but a *polis*."[14]

The book of Genesis claims that God made a covenant both ethnic
(the Jewish "people" are all Abraham's family) and spiritual:

> When Abram was ninety-nine years old the Lord appeared to Abram,
> and said to him, "I am God Almighty; walk before me, and be blame-
> less. And I will make my covenant between me and you, and will mul-
> tiply you exceedingly." Then Abram fell on his face; and God said to
> him, "Behold, my covenant is with you, and you shall be the father of
> a multitude of nations. No longer shall your name be Abram, but your
> name shall be Abraham [that is, with the addition of the Hebrew letter
> "hay," signifying God]; for I have made you the father of a multitude
> of nations. I will make you exceedingly fruitful; and I will make nations
> of you, and kings shall come forth from you. And I will establish my
> covenant between me and you and your descendants after you through-
> out their generations for an everlasting covenant, to be God to you and
> to your descendants after you. And I will give to you, and to your descen-
> dants after you, the land of your sojournings, all the land of Canaan,
> for an everlasting possession; and I will be their God." (Genesis 17:1–8)

Presented with this proposition, Abraham presumably had a choice to
accept or reject the covenant, but his descendants, by their very family,
tribal connection, could not. They were eternally chosen; their ethnic or
national birthright became a spiritual legacy. Today, Jews of otherwise
very different ethnic makeup, and whether secular or religious, feel themselves as belonging to "am Yisrael," the people of Israel, the descendants
of Abraham through his chosen son, Isaac, and Isaac's son, Jacob, renamed
Yisrael. This study, at its heart, thus asks about this belongingness through
the relationship between religious and national identity. Russian Jews in
the Orthodox Church provide ample material for such an inquiry.

Jewish identity, as we know, is comprised of many elements, with religion being only one of them. The rise of modernity throughout the Western world caused a fracture in what may or may not have been a more
holistic sense of identity among more ancient Jews, but which certainly
had a less vexed relationship of its components. As we will see in the
next chapter, Russian Jews did not follow the lead of Jews in Western
European countries, or of Poland, who became citizens of those countries who simply professed the "Mosaic" faith. Nor did they become like

American Jews, who retained some ethnic "affect" (unlike Viktor, above), yet went through a process by which they became principally identified as American Jews by their synagogue affiliation. Instead, religion disappeared in twentieth-century Soviet Russia almost completely, and ethnic identity became defined, as we will see, largely from the perspective of the majority Russian culture.

As I began my interviews, I had assumed that baptism in the Russian Orthodox Church would finally make Jews feel more "Russian," that it would be an attempt, at least partially successful, to end any remaining marginalization in Russian society. Conversely, and perhaps perversely, I had posited that Jews who accept Christianity after having left a Russian environment, especially those having immigrated to Israel, or "made *aliya*," were searching for a way to remain "marginal," now feeling different (as Russian) among their own (Jewish) people. The majority of my interviewees, however, almost uniformly disproved these hypotheses. Instead, most Russian Jewish Christians I spoke with expressed a feeling of increased Jewishness after baptism, and their narratives of faith returned over and over to their Jewish identity. They acknowledged Russian cultural influences on their choice of Church, but now felt themselves decidedly, and specially, different as *Jewish* Christians. We might say that, in a sense, not their religious choice but their hereditary chosenness as Jews took on added meaning. Rather than lamenting, as the ironic Yiddish saying goes, that, "Thou hast chosen us from among all nations. What, O Lord, did Thou have against us?" these Russian Jews find a positive meaning in their new, hybrid identity. They feel now "doubly chosen."

It is this sense of double chosenness that distinguishes Russian Jewish Christians from other out-converts from Judaism, and also from other Russian Jews who did not join the Church. Like Abraham, we could say, the individuals interviewed in this study can claim that they are both chosen AND choosing. Skeptics might point out that the God who chose them is not the same as the one they chose, but those Jews quoted here, clearly, do not feel this way. Instead, chosenness is specialness and double chosenness is double specialness, despite its real risks. It paradoxically implies both belonging and distinction, a feeling that I earlier suggested motivated the soft-spoken Jew working inside the Monastery of the Cross. In a world of discontinuity and disruption, whether caused by Soviet repression or the dislocation of emigration, these individuals have found a way to feel at home as Jews, ironically while being Christian. The stories reported in these pages play, back and forth, with this great irony. It is a Soviet, but also, oddly, a very Jewish irony.

THE JEWISH INTELLIGENTSIA AND RUSSIAN RELIGIOUS PHILOSOPHY

Many of the Russian Jewish intellectuals who entered the Church, and this was, at least until now, largely an intelligentsia phenomenon, did so under the influence of the rediscovery of Russian religious philosophy in the late Soviet period. The works of religious thinkers from the early years of this century, including Vladimir Solovyov (1853–1900), Nikolai Berdyaev (1874–1948), and Pavel Florensky (1882–1937), had been suppressed for decades of Soviet rule, and emerged only slowly, and still underground, after the death of Stalin. As Marina remembered during an interview in her dimly lit, book-filled apartment, *I read an awful lot. We read Solovyov, Bulgakov, Berdyaev. No, not Bulgakov, I don't think. . . . I read through a lot. [Friends] had an open library. They were a kind of twentieth-century apostles. . . . They lent out the books for a night, a day. There was an unbelievable thirst for knowledge.*

Such reading was not without peril in the Soviet period. Mikhail Agursky came to faith in the early 1960s first through Russian religious philosophy: "My reading gradually led me to the desire to read something from religious philosophy, for which I had been prepared by the reading of Schopenhauer, Kant, and other thinkers. I was already familiar with the name of Vladimir Solovyov, but had no real notion about him." However, when Agursky would order religious books from the library (virtually no Soviet libraries had open stacks—to "protect" the reading public from "ideologically dangerous" books), he would "at the same time order some book on atheism, so I could always justify myself in case of questioning." He was, in fact, officially questioned on several occasions, and took to truncating the names of books he ordered, to leave off any words pointing to religion, or, in certain cases, to an ecclesiastic title of the author. Once, when he forgot his notebook in the library, he lived in fear of disclosure before he could retrieve it the next evening: "Through the whole agonizing day, I felt as though I had been thrown to wild animals, just like the early Christians. In general, I felt almost as though I were in the catacombs."[15]

For the Jewish Christians I interviewed, perhaps the most frequently cited influence from the history of Russian religious thought was Nikolay

Berdyaev, whose philosophy of freedom affected the Soviet intellectuals longing to escape the bleak restrictions of Soviet society. Marina admitted, *We were carried away by Berdyaev at that time. In general, he introduced the theme of freedom into our lives. We were rather obsessively focused on that issue. But our understanding of freedom actually didn't at all coincide with Berdyaev's. But at the time we didn't even notice.*

Berdyaev began his mature intellectual life as a Marxist, but became disillusioned with the relativity of Marxist ethics, and turned first to Kant as he made his way, through Nietzsche, on the path to the religion of his fathers. For him,

> Freedom is a primordial source and condition of existence, and, characteristically, I have put Freedom, rather than Being, at the basis of my philosophy. . . . The mystery of the world abides in freedom: God desired freedom and freedom gave rise to tragedy in the world. Freedom is at the beginning and at the end. . . . God is truly present and operative only in freedom. Freedom alone should be recognized as possessing a sacred quality, whilst all the other things to which a sacred character has been assigned by men since history began ought to be made null and void.[16]

Berdyaev emigrated from the Soviet Union in 1922, along with many leading intellectuals, and continued his philosophical work in Berlin, and then Paris. Assisted by the YMCA-Press, and the journal *Put'* (The Way) that he edited, and with a renewed connection to the Russian Orthodox Church in exile, Berdyaev can be said to have been one of the most influential writers who introduced the West to modern Russian Orthodox thought. In turn, he, as did Lev Shestov who also participated in émigré life in Paris between the wars, incorporated much of French existentialism into his religious philosophy, or, perhaps more accurately, recognized the correspondence of an existential worldview with his own emphasis on the *Ungrund* and freedom.

In addition to the attraction of the freedom philosophy of Berdyaev, a number of interviewees also cited the influential religious philosopher Father Pavel Florensky, who lived through the First World War and the Bolshevik Revolution, chose not to emigrate, and died, perhaps predictably, in the Gulag. He was known to some members of the intelligentsia for his scientific work, in which he studied the permafrost in Siberia, which was unfortunately his last, forced, place of residence. But his impact

extended well beyond his scientific articles; the fact that he continued
to wear his priest's cassock long after religion was discredited by the Bolshevik victors made him a symbol of spiritual strength to the freedom-
seeking generation that reclaimed his legacy several decades after his
untimely death. It was Florensky's esoteric writings on spirituality, on the
Church and iconography, that captured the attention of a generation
hungry for intimations of the spirit after Stalin's death. His credibility in
the scientific community only added to his attraction for the intellectuals who could not abandon the lessons of their university training, but
felt its inherent limitations as well.

Florensky's monumental work, *The Pillar and Ground of the Truth: An
Essay in Orthodox Theodicy in Twelve Letters,* reflects the aesthetic sensi-
bility of the symbolist poets who were his early friends, but describes not
an eternal divide between the "two worlds," but the mystical communion of those worlds through our innate experience of "ecclesiality." Both
his erudition (the treatise contains over one thousand footnotes, with references to books in some ten languages) and his antinomic thinking were
extremely attractive to a generation of intellectuals who rejected the black
and white doctrines of their rigid Soviet education. His belief in "God's
creative love," the Divine Sophia, appealed to their thirst for an active
experience of spirit.[17] Furthermore, his work in particular could appeal
to intellectuals straitjacketed in their institutes for Historical Material-
ism and Marxism-Leninism, for it celebrated the highly sensual ritual,
the materiality of Russian Orthodoxy not as a utilitarian end, but as the
incarnation of mystical Truth and as a sign of the possible deification of
creation. Icons, he explained, are not mere pictures on wood, yet the very
fact that they are made of the products of this world—wood, alabaster,
rabbit-skin glue, egg yolk, gold, linseed oil—is vital for their theological
significance. As he wrote:

> An icon remembers its prototype. Thus, in one beholder, it will awaken
> in the bright clarities of his conscious mind a spiritual vision that
> matches directly the bright clarities of the icon; and the beholder's vision
> will be comparably clear and conscious. But in another person, the icon
> will stir the dreams that lie deeper in the subconscious, awakening a
> perception of the spiritual that not only affirms that such seeing is pos-
> sible but also brings the thing seen into immediately felt experience.
> Thus, at the highest flourishing of their prayer, the ancient ascetics
> found that their icons were not simply windows through which they

could behold the holy countenances depicted on them but were also doorways through which these countenances actually entered the empirical world. The saints came down from the icons to appear before those praying to them.[18]

Not just a window, but a door, the flat, reverse-perspective of the icon becomes a true means for the incarnation of the Divine in our material, sensual world. How attractive this must have sounded to Soviets brave enough to read these words. Their gray world had meaning beyond it after all, and matter could be understood as a theological, not purely economic concept.

Indeed, the material senses are engaged, even bombarded in all aspects of the Orthodox Church service, as one daring enough to enter the doors of a church during the Soviet period would know. The incense, the icons in their glittering gold and silver "clothing," the beeswax candles, the multivoiced chanting, the dramatic structure of the service with its entrances and exits through the Royal Doors of the iconostasis that rises from floor to ceiling, all of these oddly combine to transport even the casual visitor out of rational, material contemplation. Thus aesthetics have a meaning in Orthodox theology, if a paradoxical, mystical one: the transfiguration of matter and simultaneous incarnation of spirit that makes heaven possible on earth.

The spiritual mentor of both Berdyaev and Florensky, and the modern Orthodox thinker who best describes this active interpenetration of spirit and matter, was the late-nineteenth-century religious philosopher Vladimir Solovyov. The inspiration for several generations of twentieth-century intellectuals and poets, Solovyov died five years before the first Russian revolution in 1905, although many believe that he predicted much of the bloody turmoil of the twentieth century, including the Russo-Japanese War, the various revolutions, and even the Nazi threat. It was his vision of the Divine Sophia that inspired the symbolist poets and religious philosophers, and his varied writings lie behind the baptism of many Soviet Russian Jewish Christians, as well. As Agursky wrote in his memoir, "Solovyov made a strong, and I would even say an inspiring impression."[19] Michael Meerson tells of a meeting in 1970, on the seventieth anniversary of Solovyov's death:

One was a convinced Marxist-Hegelian, won over by the dialectical rigor of Solovyov's exposition; his rationalistic mind accepted the Good

News of faith precisely through Solovyov's logic. Another came to Christian vision through Solovyov's religious aesthetic, having become acquainted with it during a period of youthful enthusiasm for theurgic projects for the aesthetic salvation and transfiguration of the world. A third was attracted by the universalism of Solovyov's understanding of Christianity and his criticism of national provincialism. A fourth, tormented by the history of Christian-Jewish antagonism that he had himself experienced, entered the Church thanks to Solovyov's interpretation of the historical mission of Judaism before and after the advent of the Saviour. . . .

Only God knows how many people in the past and the present are obligated to Solovyov for their conversion, how many he brought to the Church with his pen and witness of life, and how many more he will bring.[20]

It is worth pausing for a few moments on Vladimir Solovyov, for he, a Russian who was baptized as a child in the Russian Orthodox Church, nonetheless placed the Jews, Jewry, and Judaism centrally within his understanding of the world. The Christian philosopher studied both Torah and Talmud, and on his deathbed was heard reciting psalms in Hebrew. His interest was neither casual nor based purely on social concerns, although he did lobby for better treatment of the Jews within the Russian Empire. For the latter, he spearheaded the writing of a letter of protest in 1890, signed by over one hundred writers and intellectuals, including the popular writers Leo Tolstoy and Vladimir Korolenko, and he became an honorary member of the Society for the Advancement of Enlightenment among the Jews of Russia *(Obshchestvo rasprostraneniia prosveshcheniia mezhdu evreiami v Rossii)*. But his interest went much deeper; the Jews for Solovyov played a role in his central theological and philosophical categories, including the integration of the one and the many (the absolute together with the multiplicity of creation) in *vseedinstvo* or "all-oneness," and the organic reconciliation of matter and spirit, which he envisaged in terms of the incarnation and transfiguration of Christ. They also relate to his mystical visions of the Divine Sophia. The Jews, by their very character, and proven by the fact that they were chosen by God, reconciled for Solovyov the one and the many, general and particular, spirit and matter. Specifically, Solovyov wrote of the Jewish people as a model for the successful integration of national (he sometimes wrote ethnic, or even, as he wrote, tribal *[plemennoe]*) identity with religious calling, of the material fact of their peoplehood with their spiritual chosenness; they are a paradoxically "spiritual-national people."[21] For Solovyov, and why he might have been so interesting to the Jews of this study, the Jews in general are both chosen and choosing. God chose them as a people, and they chose God as their Spirit.

Furthermore, we must contrast Solovyov to most other Christian thinkers of his time, as well as to his own heirs in the Russian religious renaissance, who distinguished sharply between the Jews of contemporary Russia and Western Europe and those of the Bible, about whose unique relationship with God they read in the Old Testament. Various degrees of antisemitism and/or indifference promoted the widespread Christian interpretation that Jewish chosenness was abrogated with the coming of Christ, and completely betrayed by the rabbis of the Talmud. Even Berdyaev, as we saw often cited as an influence by Russian Jewish Christians, and who wrote an important essay on "Christianity and Antisemitism" that labeled Nazism as anti-Christian, claimed that "the Judaism which preceded Christ's coming, and that which succeeded it, are two distinct spiritual manifestations."[22] Solovyov, however, in his essay "The Talmud and Recent Polemical Literature Concerning It in Austria and Germany" (*Talmud i noveishaia literatura o nem v Avstrii i Germanii*, 1885), argued for the organic relationship of the Talmud to the Jewish people, both ancient and modern. And in *Jewry and the Christian Question* (*Evreistvo i khristianskii vopros*, 1884), he admonished the Christians around him for not acting "Christianly" toward the Jews, while the Jews, based on their adherence to the *mitzvoth* of the Torah, elaborated in the Talmud, continue to act "Jewishly" toward Christians. Perhaps, he conceded to his antisemitic readers, Jewish laws are wrong, but, "if it is bad to be true to a bad law, then it is much worse to be untrue to a good law, to a commandment that is unconditionally perfect," to the Gospels which they purportedly confessed.[23]

It is true that Solovyov was not a blind judeophile; as to be expected from his Christian worldview, he saw the highest fulfillment of the Jews' character to be found in their ultimate acceptance of their own son, Jesus, as Messiah. Even his most ardent promoter and collaborator in the Jewish community, Faivel' Gets, claimed that the philosopher best deserved the label of "righteous gentile," and that his love of the Jews was no different from his love of all people.[24] Regardless, Solovyov's interest in the Jews and in Jewish tradition and Judaic texts was sincere, and he believed that they and only they could provide the necessary spiritual-national element to reconcile East and West into the future Universal Church. Jewish intellectuals of his time and the next generation, including those who created the cultural basis of the new Zionist state, referred to Solovyov on numerous occasions, and his death provoked the publication of major obituaries in the Russian- and Hebrew-language Jewish periodicals of the time.[25]

Despite Solovyov's favorable assessment of the Jews and Judaism, and despite the attraction of Solovyov for many Russian Jewish intellectuals in the post-Stalin era, it goes without saying that not all Jews would define themselves in his terms. He was a nineteenth-century Russian, and an Orthodox thinker, who placed the Jews within his own Trinitarian worldview. The Jews of this study, despite their intellectual indebtedness to Solovyov, and despite the fact that in many cases the writings of Solovyov opened their eyes to a spiritual world for the first time, may very well feel their relationship in different terms. That is why it is important to hear their own stories, and why this study includes so many of their own words. Only through their stories can we learn how Jews who now place Russian Orthodoxy centrally within their own understanding of the world would speak about the relationship of national and religious identities within themselves. How do they understand themselves as part of the Jewish *people* and the Christian *religion,* something that to an American ear sounds discordant, if not outright impossible? To return now to the larger questions of this study, what do their self-definitions tell us about Russian Jewish identity? About late or post-Soviet identity? Does this tell us anything about identity in general? This is not only a history of a small group of people who took a surprising step in the decades following the death of Stalin. It is an analysis of their narratives, an analysis that takes us into religious studies, philosophy, anthropology, and sociology, as well as history.

The task I set myself then, quite simply, was to record the stories of Russian Jewish Christians, or, specifically, of Russian Jewish Orthodox *(pravoslavnye)* Christians. By analyzing the personal narratives of faith, I have tried to understand a larger narrative about the meaning of Jewish identity in Russia, and about why some Russian Jews turn to religion and become Russian Orthodox believers, despite traditional antisemitism in the Church. In the course of the answer, I have needed to determine what belief itself means for Soviet and post-Soviet citizens, and also for members of the intelligentsia in particular, and how that meaning might have changed throughout the four decades since the exposure of Stalinism, and the gradual opening of Soviet doors to the outside. As we will see, before emigration became a reality in the end of the 1960s and 70s, Russian Jews faced very different choices than did those only twenty years later.

STUMBLING BLOCKS

This study presents several difficulties for its potential audience(s), its subject(s), and for this researcher herself. The book is not aimed narrowly at readers who study Russia, particularly those interested in the Soviet intelligentsia, and in the role of Jewish intellectuals in defining Russian and/or Soviet identity, although I do think that it suggests important areas for further inquiry in those disciplines. But the book is aimed as much outside as within Slavic studies. In certain ways, the narratives collected here confirm what Gauri Viswanathan has written about conversion as dissent, as "an interpretive act, an index of material and social conflicts. . . . By undoing the concept of fixed, unalterable identities, conversion unsettles the boundaries by which selfhood, citizenship, nationhood, and community are defined, exposing these as permeable borders."[26] The Russian Jewish Christians I interviewed are clearly an example of the undoing of boundaries, and of the complexity of identity in the modern world in general, even if their stories of conversion differ in substantial ways from those of other converts.

I suspect that Jews with various interests will constitute a significant proportion of my readership, drawn to the subject as to an oddity in their midst. Jews, however, are notoriously suspicious of, if not downright hostile toward Christianity, in a way not true, for example, of their attitude toward Buddhism. For the latter, we can bring the counter example of a book popular among renewal-oriented Jews: *The Jew in the Lotus,* by the American Jewish poet Rodger Kamenetz. Kamenetz traveled with a group of Jewish rabbis and others to Dharamsala, India, in order to meet the exiled Tibetan Dalai Lama. As part of his mission, Kamenetz interviewed Buddhist believers whom he called JUBUs, Jews who had converted to the teachings of Buddhism. For Kamenetz, and I would suggest for the majority of his Jewish readers, the flirtation with Buddhism was an exotic fancy, and a nonthreatening way to think about spiritual renewal within one's own Judaism, as the book's subtitle indicates: *A Poet's Rediscovery of Jewish Identity in Buddhist India.* The same could not be true of a study of converts to Christianity. Kamenetz himself admitted as much: "Yet I don't think a dialogue with Christians could have led me to this place.

I had too many resistances there. I was too aware of how many times in the past Christians had killed Jews in the name of their savior. The beauty of dialogues with Buddhists, as several of us had noted, was they had no baggage with Jews."[27]

For some good and some less good reasons, Jews are usually threatened by Christianity. As one religious Jewish friend remarked after I had spent at least ten minutes explaining my research: *What's interesting about that topic? For a religious Jew it's a non-topic. Like euthanasia. Everyone is against conversion to Christianity. Period.* On the other side, one child of a Russian Jewish Christian reported hearing criticism of *vykresty*, or Jewish out-converts, at the time not understanding *what bothers them, what business is it of theirs?* Not all Jews I spoke with rejected the topic as categorically as my religious friend, and, in fact, many—religious and secular— were fascinated, never having imagined that Russian Jews, of all people, might have taken this step. For most, I suspect, the subject seems not only surprising, but also somewhat forbidden.

The second stumbling block in this study is the fact that many of the Jewish Christians themselves are reluctant to talk about the topic. This is especially true in Israel, where Jewish Christians who arrived under the Law of Return might fear revocation of their citizenship, or, at the least, suspension of the financial assistance to *olim*. Having heard that it was the spiritual home to a number of Russian Jews, I spent a morning at the beautiful Russian Orthodox Church of Saint Mary Magdalene on the slope of the Mount of Olives, in the Garden of Gethsemane, overlooking the back of the Old City in Jerusalem, only to be passed coolly from Arab to American to Russian nun. Finally, having been asked to wait for quite some time in the well-lit sanctuary, I was told categorically by a Russian-speaking nun that *Neither I nor anyone else can receive you,* and, at best, that I must first speak with the Mother Superior. No one, however, would point the Mother Superior out to me, much less take me to her. After volunteering that her husband is a baptized Jew and pointing to an older man, claiming that he is also Jewish, a young Russian worshiper smiled, but turned away with no answer when I asked for an introduction.

Even in Russia, many of my subjects wanted first to talk about my own relationship to faith before they would reveal their inner-held secrets. Many were ultimately put at ease only after hearing about my own "path of faith," although it did not involve baptism. The answer to the question, "*Vy —— veruiushchie?*" (Are you a believer?) apparently remains since the 1970s an important calling card.

Unfortunately, because of the reluctance of many Jewish Christians to identify themselves, as well as the lack of previous scholarship on the subject, I cannot know exactly how skewed my pool of subjects might be, nor the actual extent of the phenomenon of Jews in the Russian Orthodox Church. Some say there are tens of thousands of Jewish Christians in the Church. Others would play the number closer to several thousand. The dangerous nature of participation in the Church during the Soviet period prevented some baptized Jews from sharing their faith even with their spouses and children. When I asked the adult child of a Russian Orthodox priest why his parents had not had him baptized as a child, he reminded me that his father began to participate in the Church in isolation from and many years before his mother. By the time she was baptized, their sons were already teenagers, and the parents felt the difficult choice must be made on their own. Yuly explained: *It was an individual act. Not a collective act. I can't really explain it. Of course, it was nice for my parents to celebrate some holiday with me, but all the same. . . . The very fact that my father was baptized some six, seven, or more, maybe ten years before my mother. . . . It's not like Judaism, when "you have to convert, or whatever, in order to get married,"* he inserted in accented but idiomatic English, perhaps to drive home his point to this English-speaking interviewer, or, perhaps, because the idea was, indeed, alien to his culturally and linguistically Russian mind. *For them, it was an entirely different order of decision. What is more, and something we haven't talked about yet, was that at that time there was the so-called double standard of life* (again in English, this time because the phenomenon has been most extensively studied by Western scholars?). *It was understandable that even my parents, brave and open people, did not parade their Christianity. My father did not go to his scholarly institute to read lectures with a cross around his neck. [His religion] didn't have a public face or a public life. It's understandable that my parents, both teachers in an institute, didn't go to church in their own city. There was a feeling of "there is life here and there is life there,"* he concluded in English.

This sense of secrecy has held over well into the post-Soviet period. Subjects were sometimes reluctant to provide names of other baptized Jews in their community, and many have not kept track of one another as they leave for new parishes, new cities, or new countries.

And this brings me to the third difficulty of this study: my own sense that this is a private matter. Ironically, the issue of faith in Israel, and in Russia, is not as private as in the United States, or, rather, it is always as much political as individual (and thus the need to work so hard to

protect their privacy). When a Russian Jew I met in Jerusalem asked me
how I, personally, feel about the baptism of my subjects, and I answered
that I ultimately believe it is their own business, she responded with more
than a little contempt: *How very American of you.*

I have tried hard to respect the privacy of my subjects. One interviewee
is a well-known literary figure in Russia, whose work has sometimes involved Jewish themes. Although she told me that she is not ashamed of
her Christianity, she nonetheless does not want to be labeled a "Christian" writer. Another subject works in a Jewish day school in New York,
a third in a Jewish institution in Jerusalem, a fourth worked until recently
at a press that publishes Judaica. Most of my interviewees, especially in
Israel, fear anti-Christian discrimination from the Jews, as well as antisemitism from the Christians among whom they might wish to pray. As
one Russian Jewish Christian in New York proclaimed, perhaps with a
bit too much protest, *I am not scared. That is the reason I am in America.
Because I can say this openly. But in Israel, they might talk, but they will not
want to use their names.* (I chose not to use the real name of this American Russian Jewish Christian as well, despite his relative sense of safety.)

A final difficulty will be felt by all my readers, and that is the very in-
terdisciplinary nature of this study. Historians might miss a more detailed
historical context, when instead the flow of the study requires a return
to the subjects' own words. Empirical social scientists might question my
reliance on qualitative interviews, and find my appropriation of others'
quantitative studies not quite sufficient. Those interested in religion might
want an even more in-depth analysis of Russian Orthodox ritual and
belief that drew the Jewish intellectuals. But I have explicitly relied on
the individual stories themselves as they weave together into a larger narrative of identity, belongingness, and specialness.

BACKGROUND MATERIAL

In addition to interviews and contemporary narratives of the lives of Russian Jews, I have also been able to rely on scholarship on Russian-Jewish
identity in general and on the history of the Jews in Russia. Among the
former I include studies of Russian-Jewish writers by Alice Nakhimovsky
and Efraim Sicher, although these do not specifically address the question of conversion to Christianity, and by Gabriella Safran, who does.
Also on literary issues: articles by Mikhail Heifets. Valery Chervyakov,
Zvi Gitelman, and Vladimir Shapiro have made the most thorough study

to date of identity among contemporary Russian Jews from a social science perspective, surveying Jews both still within the former Soviet Union and in Israel and the United States. These studies, although not of Russian Jewish Christians per se, confirm many of my conclusions about Jewish identity in Russia, and will be cited where appropriate, providing statistical background for the analysis of the stories collected here. The scholarship on the history of Jews in Russia, as well as the history of the Church, is more extensive. There is extremely little previous scholarship on the attitude of the Church toward the Jews, however, as well as specifically on Jewish conversion. Some of the latter has been undertaken by the late Mikhail Agursky, and by historians Michael Stanislawski, John Klier, and Hans Rogger. Their conclusions will be discussed in the following chapter. I am aware of only two discussions in print of Russian Jewish Christians in specific, one a few paragraphs in an article by Benjamin Pinkus on Soviet Jews who embraced Judaism, and the other in Hebrew, as a small part of a book on the Russian Jewish *olim* by the Israeli writer Gail Hareven.

The relationship of the Jews and Orthodoxy in general was explored by the Russian religious philosopher Vladimir Solovyov in the late nineteenth century, as discussed above, and, to a lesser extent, by his followers in the first half of the twentieth century.[28] Some of Solovyov's writing on the Jews was published abroad in Israel and Europe during the Soviet period, although with little commentary. In terms of an understanding of Solovyov's understanding of the Jews, the names of former Soviet scholars Nikolay Kotrelyov and Evgeny Rashkovsky (who have edited recent collections of his essays) also come to mind. In recent years, Zoya Krakhmal'nikova, one of the interviewees for this study, has not only reprinted Solovyov, but has also begun to comment on his understanding of nationalism and spirituality. She is particularly concerned about antisemitism in the contemporary Church, manifest through its Great Russian nationalism. Specifically, she has attacked the comments of Igor Shafarevich, in his often-reprinted pamphlet *Russophobia*. Krakhmal'nikova is not alone in her reproach of the official Russian Orthodox Church in its treatment of the Jews, but her company is not large. On a more positive note, a short essay by Mikhail Agursky and Dmitry Segal explores, as the title indicates: "Jews and the Russian Orthodox Church: A Common Legacy— A Common Hope."[29] I must also note a collection of materials published in Moscow in 1994 called *The Orthodox Church and the Jews: Nineteenth and Twentieth Centuries. A Collection of Materials toward a Theology of*

Interconfessional Dialogue. This collection demonstrates that the uneasy relationship of the Church toward the Jews living in Russia was a concern for at least certain liberal thinkers since the partition of Poland at the end of the eighteenth century, when a large number of Jews became part of the Russian Empire. Its unnamed editors assert that the volume intends to "counteract the threat of the growth of antisemitism in the Church," and is addressed to anyone "who is interested in the problems of the interaction of Christians and Jews in the history of Russia and in perspectives for the development of these relations in the future."[30] The documents it contains clearly have bearing on the significance of Russian Jewish interest in Russian Orthodoxy examined below.

METHODOLOGY

Interviews for this study were conducted in Moscow, New York City, Washington, D.C., Jerusalem, and Haifa between September 1997 and May 1998, with the exception of two earlier interviews in Russia in 1993, and one later in August 2000. A research trip to Moscow on a related topic in 2003, after this manuscript was complete, produced more stories, not necessarily cited here, but which largely confirm the study's conclusions. Whenever possible, the interviews, lasting an average of one to one and a half hours, were taped and later transcribed. In other cases, notes were taken during or immediately following the interview. The majority of interviews were in Russian, and I translated as I transcribed. A few interviews conducted in English and one in Russian were transcribed by others, but checked against the tape by me as well. Thirty-five interviews of differing lengths were completed, including a few with Jews who were not baptized, but were either related to baptized Jews or who had some special interest in them.

The interviews were free ranging, but in the course of the hour I would ask about childhood associations with Jewishness and Judaism, whether or not they still feel "Jewish," and how Jewish family and friends reacted to their baptism. Questions were also geared to determine why a subject chose Orthodoxy, instead of another Christian denomination or, indeed, Judaism. For those who had left Russia, I asked about their decision to emigrate, and about how it felt to be a Jewish Christian in their new home. And, finally, I asked about their religious practice now. Some of the interviewees no longer consider themselves part of the Church, and many have greatly decreased their level of commitment. How they described their relationship to Orthodoxy now, as ex-Christians, or changed Christians, also had bearing on their narratives of faith. See Appendix A for an example of a complete transcript.

With one exception, all the subjects discussed in the following pages sought baptism in adulthood, so that Christianity was a choice rather than a family inheritance. (I have included the exception because I felt that the choices she made since baptism into the Orthodox Church relate to the general themes of the study, and because stories she reported about her baptized Jewish father reinforce the stories of other interviewees.) Because of the decision to focus on choice, I never interviewed the Russian Jewish Christian friend to whom I referred in the opening of this chapter. She became Christian as a child, and is bringing up her own children Orthodox as well, making them the third generation of Russian Jewish Christians in post-Stalinist Russia, and perhaps worthy of another study in the future. Do they know they are in any way Jewish? Do others in the Church treat them as Jewish because of their Jewish mother and grandmother? How do they feel about other Jews entering the Church? Are they conscious of national and religious identity issues at all? These questions will have to wait.

The sample was chosen largely by word of mouth, and I recognize that I therefore might have an over-representation of one view or another. But the study, based on a small number of in-depth narratives, does not pretend to be quantitative (again, I rely on data from the survey by Chervyakov, Gitelman, and Shapiro to support my conclusions), and I continued seeking out interviews only until the stories became repetitious, and I felt I had sufficient justification to speak about patterns, even on a small scale. In this way I follow Dominique Schnapper in her well-respected analysis of French Jewry. She writes: "The small size of the sample is justified by the fact that my analysis and interpretation are purely qualitative in nature." And:

Some readers may find that I have included too many excerpts from my interviews or that the excerpts are too long. The reason for this is that my interpretations are purely qualitative, and the excerpts serve as more than mere illustrations of the argument. They are the documents on which my analyses are based, and they are included in the text in the same way that statistical data are included in other kinds of work. Many citations have been cut out, and only those that seemed to me clearest and most significant have been kept. In making these cuts I noticed

that I often wound up keeping citations from only one or perhaps from
two or three interviewees. The reason for this is that, in reading a homo-
geneous set of interviews, I gradually evolved a sort of characteristic
group portrait, whereupon it became possible to reassemble the various
features that emerged from a number of interviews into a living composite. It often happened that a single subject, more lucid or articulate
than others in the same group, presented a livelier and clearer picture
of what remained confused and less vivid in other interviews drawn
from the same group.[31]

Most of the subjects interviewed for this study chose Christianity while
still living in Russia or one of the other republics of the former Soviet
Union. Several were baptized after immigration to New York, and at least
two entered the Church after making *aliya* to Israel. Their stories will be
treated separately when necessary. It is true that a large number of Russians in Israel today are attracted to Christianity, some because they are
in mixed marriages or are, themselves, fully Russian, but came to Israel
as spouses of Jews. Others, no doubt, first explore the Church because
of a kind of nostalgia for the Russian culture of their former home, and,
perhaps, from a sense of alienation from Israeli society, whether secular
or religious. Most Russians in Israel who are drawn to Christianity, however, do *not* join the Orthodox Church, turning instead toward various
evangelical or messianic Jewish groups in Jerusalem or elsewhere. The
Messianic Jews (sometimes called Hebrew Christians, in America often
known as Jews for Jesus) proselytize heavily to the new Russian Jews, with
numerous pamphlets, meetings, and Passover seders conducted in Russian.
In addition, the Christian Embassy in Jerusalem, a fervently Zionist,
fundamentalist group, devotes half of its activities to Soviet, and now
post-Soviet Jewry, providing logistical and financial assistance for Jews
who wish to immigrate to Israel. An acquaintance now living in Jerusalem recalled for me how warmly he felt toward these "missionaries" who
approached him in Moscow, and how he attended some of their church
services out of gratitude once he had arrived in his new home.
    The attraction toward or rejection of messianic Jewry on the part of
the Russian Jews in this study will be addressed at an appropriate point
in the coming pages. For its part, the Russian Orthodox Church does
not proselytize, perhaps because it still has so much of its own house to
put in order, perhaps because it does not really want Jews in its midst.[32]
The Jews who enter the Orthodox Church, then, do so with a large degree

of personal choice. They consciously enter an institution with a strong national identity, and an elaborate ritual tradition.

I have supplemented the interviews with discussions with non-Christian Jews in Russia, America, and Israel. Included as part of the study is also an interview with Father Daniel (Oswald) Rufeisen, known in Israel as Brother Daniel of the famous "Brother Daniel" Israeli Supreme Court case in the 1960s. Father Daniel was a Polish Jew who converted to Catholicism during World War II, and therefore his story does not fit the typical profile of subjects for this study on three counts: he was not Russian, not Orthodox, and not baptized in the post-Stalin years. The importance of the inclusion of his words will become clear in the following pages. Several books, articles, and samizdat pamphlets by Russian Jewish intellectuals, including two novels, provide additional voices on the subject.

Finally I have used as much previous research as possible on conversion, as well as on questions of ethnicity, nationalism, and identity to provide background and contrast for the phenomenon of Russian Jewish Christians. And certainly the work of historians and social scientists on the Russian intelligentsia in particular has helped put the path toward faith of my subjects—in some ways unique, in others not—in perspective.

STRUCTURE OF STUDY

Ultimately, it became evident that my subjects could be divided into two distinct categories, based on the years in which they were baptized: 1) the mid-1960s to early 70s—as the generation born in the last years of Stalin's rule grew into adulthood; and 2) the late 1980s and 90s—after the shattering effects of glasnost and perestroika, not to mention the exodus of a huge number of Jews from the Soviet Union. In both cases, the majority of the subjects were young adults at the time of baptism, and thus exactly a generational cohort apart. Some children of the first generation entered the Church as well, but I have excluded them from the study if their entrance came at too young an age to have involved consent, or possible dissent, on their part. Some children of the first generation consciously did *not* choose to become Christian, however, and this family dynamic interested me as much as that on the other generational extreme, solicited with the question: "What did your Jewish mother say?" (*This won't save you from the pogroms,* one daughter reported her mother to have said angrily.) Identity issues begin in the family, or so my early assumptions ran.

A third category for study would include those Jews who seek baptism in the Orthodox Church today, in the twenty-first century, now that Soviet culture has safely retreated into history. Such Jews, however, will not form a significant part of the current study. Many Russian Jews who take on Christianity today do not seek out the Russian Orthodox Church, and find themselves, as previous noted, in evangelical or messianic sects.[33] These groups continue to proselytize heavily among young Russian immigrants, both in the United States and Israel.[34] As a student of Russian Orthodoxy, however, I am interested here only in Jews who specifically joined the Orthodox Church, largely because of the Church's historical and contemporary association with Russian national identity. Some young Russian Jews who have remained in post-Soviet Russia are indeed becoming Orthodox, although I suspect their stories differ from those of the two generations I interviewed for this study. Their narratives will have to wait for future research.

A categorization that juxtaposes the 1960s and 1980s generations attends to the part of the narrative that describes the beginning of these Jewish Christians' path to faith. I examine these two generations in chapters 3 and 4, respectively, after a historical and contextual survey in chapter 2 of the Jewish question and Jewish identity in Russia, the United States, and Israel. A second categorization, discussed in a chapter 5, concentrates on the turns that path then takes, and on how the interviewees define their Jewishness and their Christianity today, at the time of the interview. The findings differ, depending on which section of the narrative we examine, although the conclusions I draw in chapter 6 depend on both analyses.

Whenever these Jews came to Russian Orthodoxy, and wherever they traveled—both spiritually and physically—after their baptism, their stories return over and over to the question of chosenness. To be chosen is both a privilege and a responsibility, however, and this study will conclude with a special sense of that responsibility. Again, chosenness is specialness for these Jews, and double chosenness is doubly special.

CHAPTER TWO

The Jewish Question in Russia

Separation of National and Religious Identity

It is not convenient to allow Jews to come with their goods to Russia,
since many evils result from them. For they import poisonous herbs into
our realms, and lead astray the Russians from Christianity.

—Ivan the Terrible, 1550

Maybe it was something genetic.

—Elena, New York 1998

T HE UNIQUE HISTORY OF THE Jews in Russia and Eastern
Europe establishes, at least in part, the context in which the Russian Jewish Christians of the late Soviet period can experience
their hybrid identity without the dissonance that it might create for
American or even Western European Jews. In the United States, as we
will see, Jews came to be considered largely a religious minority (even
absent, in most cases, of significant religious ritual), with certain marks
of ethnic identity to be sure, but decidedly not a national minority. In
the Soviet Union, Jews comprised, instead, a nationality. The complete
divorce of religious from national identity was not a simple process, and
had multiple catalysts both within and without the Jewish community.
The consequences of the creation of a Jewish nationality in the majority
Russian and Soviet states, however, were, and remain, far-reaching.

The Jews in Rus', Muscovy, and the Russian Empire

The Primary Chronicle of old Rus', also called *The Tale of Bygone Years* by its eleventh- and twelfth-century authors, tells the story of the formation of the Kievan state from the point of view of clerics within the ruling court. Although the voices are diverse, the central ideological message is consistent: the importance of Russian unity.[1] The call for unity under a single prince—so that the people of Rus' could be one—is paralleled in *The Primary Chronicle* by an assertion of oneness in creed. Such religious solidarity was a hope more than a fact, for the people of Rus' had been baptized for no more than one hundred years at the time of writing. Both Russian national and religious identity were still in formation. We read the following narrative next to the entry of 6495 (calculated from the assumed creation of the world, corresponding to the year 987 C.E.):

> Vladimir [reign 980–1015] summoned together his boyars and the city elders, and said to them: "Behold, the Bulgarians [Volga Bulgars, an Islamic Turkic people] came before me urging me to accept their religion. Then came the Germans [Western European Christians] and praised their own faith; and after them came the Jews [Khazars from the Caucasus and Caspian Sea area, who had converted to Judaism in 749 C.E.]. Finally the Greeks [from Orthodox Byzantium] appeared, criticizing all other faiths but commending their own. . . . What is your opinion on this subject, and what do you answer?" The boyars and the elders replied: "You know, O prince, that no man condemns his own possessions, but praises them instead. If you desire to make certain, you have servants at your disposal. Send them to inquire about the ritual of each and how he worships.[2]

The Primary Chronicle informs us that Prince Vladimir followed his boyars' advice and sent emissaries to the Muslims, who "worship in their temple, called a mosque, while they stand ungirt. The Bulgarian bows, sits down, looks hither and thither like one possessed, and there is no happiness among them, but instead only sorrow and a dreadful stench." The emissaries sent to the representatives of Western Christianity likewise "saw them performing many ceremonies in their temples; but we beheld no glory there." Only in Byzantium did Vladimir's men feel that "we knew not whether we were in heaven or on earth. For on earth there is no such splendor or such beauty, and we are at a loss how to describe it. We know only that God dwells there among men, and their service is fairer than the ceremonies of other nations."[3] Even today, anyone who enters an Orthodox church cannot help but be struck by the sensual nature of the space, with its icons, its hundreds of beeswax candles, its incense, and the chanted liturgy in several parts. The Orthodox ceremony is, indeed, "fair."

We do not know whether Vladimir sent a mission to a Jewish synagogue—there is no reference in *The Primary Chronicle*—but we do know that he accepted the Eastern Orthodox Christianity of the Greeks (Byzantines) in 988, and forced the baptism of all previously pagan subjects in his realm. The chronicler implies that the choice of Orthodoxy was largely aesthetic ("on earth there is no such splendor or such beauty"), reinforced by personal reasons (Vladimir's grandmother Olga had already converted), and cemented with miracles (including a cure for his blindness at the moment of baptism). Historical retrospection suggests that political and economic reasons might have been equally determinative. The Khazars, a tribe of Finnish-Turkish origins, had earlier developed into a stable commercial state and a minor political rival to Vladimir's Rus'. The rulers of Khazaria had chosen Judaism as their state religion several centuries before, apparently because there was no Jewish nation that could subsequently be a threat to political domination. It has been speculated that Judaism helped preserve the Khazar state until the twelfth century, even after the Russians in Kiev had established themselves as a more powerful commercial force, precisely because of the prophetic creed and the feeling of mission that the idea of the "chosen people" instilled.[4] Indeed, both Orthodoxy and Judaism would have provided the cultural independence that Vladimir sought, and the latter would have secured political and religious independence from the Church and states of the eastern Mediterranean as well, the reasoning that converted the Khazars. Vladimir avoided the Khazars, however, and by his decision united his people through the Orthodox religion, as well as allied himself economically and politically with the powerful Byzantine state.

This oft-repeated story of the origins of Eastern Christianity in Russia may well be apocryphal, but it does tell us much about the understanding of the relationship, or lack thereof, between religious and ethnic identity among the clerics who served as annalists in the eleventh century. Religion, whether Islam, Christianity, or Judaism, was a choice, not a family inheritance, and as such could serve as a political control laid over any given population's sense of self. This is how it was for the Khazars, who nonetheless were ultimately conquered and assimilated into the Christian Kievan kingdom, and this is how it was for the people of Rus' who became Orthodox. Only over time did the Slavic people of Kiev and, later, Muscovy, begin to equate their group identity with Christianity. Their self-understanding as specifically *Russian* Orthodox may still have been in flux at the time of the fall of Byzantium to the Turks in 1453, and perhaps as late as the establishment of the Moscow Patriarchate in 1588. By then, however, Moscow took on the role of preserver of Orthodoxy, the "third Rome" after the fall of both Rome and Constantinople (the "second Rome"), and, as the famous saying goes, "a fourth there shall not be."[5] The "chosenness" of the Russian *people* only slowly began to correspond to their *religious* identity.

One scholar of Russian nationalism finds Orthodox doctrine especially compatible with a fusion of the Church and national culture. Orthodoxy,

> while remaining a part of the Pan-Orthodox *Oikoumenie,* has become a national religion in every state by adopting the vernacular for its services and erecting an autocephalous [independent] structure within each national state, and also by virtue of *sobornost,*[6] which perceives the nation as a collective personality entrusted by God to the care and responsibility of the pertinent national Church. The Slavophiles had argued that owing to the meagreness of the pre-Christian Slavonic cultural heritage in general, and the Russian in particular, practically no other Russian identity existed except that given Russia by the Orthodox Church.[7]

Vladimir's choice thus united his people nationally as well as religiously. The particular brand of Russian Orthodox culture that grew, in fact a mixture of pre-Christian Slavic belief and Byzantine tradition (often called *dvoeverie,* or dual faith), became synonymous with the Russian *ethne,* and, after the establishment of a strong state under Ivan III (reign 1462–1505), with the Russian nation as a whole. At that point, Russian Orthodoxy came to be both *russkoe*—that is, the inheritor of the cultural riches of ancient Rus', and *rossiiskoe*—of the Russian state.

Yet the Russian state, whether centered in Muscovy, in St. Petersburg during the imperial period, or again back in Moscow in the Soviet period, was of course never purely Russian. The Empire incorporated many indigenous populations and neighboring peoples, often with very different ethnic and religious backgrounds. Tatars, Poles, Caucasians, Uzbeks, Germans, and many others integrated with various degrees of success into Russian society. Ironically, the great Russian nationalist of the Soviet period, Joseph Stalin, was actually Georgian. Khrushchev was Ukrainian.[8]

THE JEWISH QUESTION IN MODERN RUSSIA

Interestingly, Kievan sources demonstrate a remarkable lack of anti-Jewish sentiment at a time when the Western Catholic Crusades sparked murderous rampages through Jewish communities, and Jews were regularly accused of ritual murder in Western Europe.[9] This is perhaps because of the extremely small number of Jews actually present. Conflict with local Jews nonetheless began in the early Muscovite period, aggravated by the so-called Heresy of the Judaizers, reputedly begun by a Jew named Zecharia, who traveled to Novgorod from Kiev around 1470, decrying the Orthodox Church and converting several high Church officials. The movement, however, was actually of uncertain, and complex origins. What is clear is that some heretics were invited into the court in Muscovy by Ivan III, and were installed in Kremlin churches.[10] This was a period of the growth of sectarianism within the Church (as the Orthodox calendar was set to run out in 1492, ushering in, thought many, the Second Coming), and a time when some Russians were drawn to the Judaizers, in their search for an earlier, purer spirit of Christianity.[11] The Judaizers exploited prevalent spiritual unrest, setting themselves up as different and superior to the Church. Because the Judaizers were a vocal group heard deep in the Muscovite court, popular reaction against the Judaizing heresy filtered into growing public discrimination against all Jews. As John Klier has shown, the label of "Judaizing" became associated with heresy and dissidence in general. Even in the absence of real Jews, "the image of Jews, be they merchants or missionaries, crystallized into a personification as deadly enemies of the faith."[12]

Nonetheless, the comparatively small number of Jews in Russia did not become a real issue for Russian imperial policy until the three partitions of Poland in 1772, 1793, and 1795, and the consequent inclusion of a large population of Polish and Lithuanian Jews into the Empire. As Dubnow asks ironically: "What was to be done with the unwelcome heritage bequeathed by Poland," along with rich agricultural land and the culturally developed urban areas to the West?[13] The solution? The isolation of the Jews, formerly self-imposed in Poland in an effort to survive persecution, was reinforced in Russia by law. In 1791, Catherine the Great passed a decree that ultimately confined the Jews to the Pale of Settlement—

located largely in the old Polish-Lithuanian provinces that were absorbed into the Russian Empire—and the Jews' ethnic and religious status as "other," that is, non-Russian and non-Christian, was given an official stamp.

The subsequent reigns of Alexander I, Nicholas I, and Alexander II in the nineteenth century oscillated between attitudes of assimilationism and isolationism, both of which, ironically, could be manifest in either "benevolent paternalism" (Dubnow's term) or cruel oppression of the Jews,[14] the latter perhaps most evident in the policy of the conscription of Jewish children for twenty-five or more years of military service.[15] Under the policy, Jews were able to be drafted between the ages of twelve and twenty-five; young recruits served in special "cantonist" units until age eighteen, then began their regular twenty-five years of service.[16] Many young recruits were forcibly converted to Orthodoxy and those soldiers who survived the long exile returned to their communities virtual strangers.

The requirements for Jewish military service clearly disrupted traditional life among the Jews of the Russian Pale in the first half of the nineteenth century. Nonetheless, as the historian Michael Stanislawski admits, "When Nicholas I acceded to the throne of Russia in 1825, his Jewish subjects were living in blissful ignorance of Russian life and politics."[17] For the most part, the same was true of the average Russian's knowledge of his Jewish neighbors.

Gradually, however, the debate on the so-called Jewish question grew in intensity, first internally within the state bureaucracy, then, relatively freely, in the press. What to do with these resident Jews? Isolate them? Assimilate them into Russian culture? At best acculturate them? But can they ever be made "Russian"? If so, how? How to understand these odd, insular, and seemingly backward creatures inhabiting the imperial breadbasket? As a national minority among other minorities in a multiethnic empire? As stubborn believers in an archaic—some would say, along with one Jewish Christian interviewed for this study, "dead"—religion? To answer the question of their future, it became necessary to determine if the Jews were a national or a religious minority.

Traditional as well as new forms of antisemitism—or Judeophobia as it was called in nineteenth-century Russia—increased in the second half of the nineteenth century, so that the debates concerning the Jews were always more heated than those about the more remote Central Asian Muslims or the shamanist Siberian reindeer herdsmen or the independent-minded Caucasian mountaineers. Older Russian Judeophobia, which was based on medieval religious notions of Jews as deicides, slowly gave way to a newer, Western rhetoric of a modern Jewish conspiracy, bent on destroying all of Christian civilization.[18] While retaining their mysterious, "oriental" aura of old (including an association with sexual licentiousness), the Jews ironically acquired an association with the politically and economically imposing West, from whence had come these new forms of antisemitism. Thus, the destitute Jews living in the midst of Russian and Ukrainian peasants were accused of calculating the economic ruin of their otherwise innocent neighbors. Now the Jews, like the Slavophile depiction of Western Europeans, were shown to be corrupt, legalistic, and obsessed with the bloodless calculus of money. That the former passionate and bloodthirsty image never disappeared entirely is attested, of course, by the accusations of ritual murder as late as the Beilis Trial of 1911.[19] While coldly counting the ill-gotten gold of their gentile neighbors, the uncontrolled passion of the Jews apparently also required the blood of Christian boys for bizarre and exotic rites.

Nikolai Danilevsky, a major voice among the reactionary neo-Slavophiles in the last part of the nineteenth century (and ideological enemy of Vladimir Solovyov), believed that the Slavs were the true inheritors of the status of chosen people,[20] and some have speculated—although it is not a provable axiom—that anti-Jewish sentiment can be explained by the fact that a "newly proclaimed chosen people felt hostility toward an older pretender to this title."[21] The first generation of Jewish historians of Russian Jewry largely focused on religious prejudice as explanation for Judeophobia in Russia. Later scholars, however, have distinguished popular prejudice from official policy, the latter based more directly, and complexly, on questions of economics. The wheels of the Russian bureaucracy were many, and it was largely nameless officials, convinced of the dangers of Jewish exploitation on the Western model, who probably sealed the fate of the Jews in nineteenth-century Russia.[22]

Whatever the reasons for suspicion of the Jews in the second half of the nineteenth century in Russia, the Jewish question pressed passionately on Russian officials as well as intellectuals. John Klier has shown in great detail how the meaning of the Jews as a people and a religion within the Russian Empire was discussed heatedly beginning around 1858, "the first and last year of widespread Judeophilia in Russia," so that "by the end of the reign of Tsar Alexander II in 1881, it was one of the most contentious issues of contemporary debate."[23] Diplomatic defeat abroad, questionable economic success of the Great Reforms of the 1870s at home, growing corruption in the ecclesiastic establishment, and the importation of decidedly Western revolutionary ideology in the second half of the century all served to destabilize what had seemed to some to be a fixed Russian, and Russian Orthodox, identity among the subjects of the tsar. The problem must surely be the Jews, concluded many a Russian conservative. Liberals, too, focused on the Jews, for Russian treatment of this large population among them pointed to moral, or at least administrative failings of the Russians themselves. Changes of many kinds were in sight.

The debate in the Russian press was paralleled in the new Russian Jewish press, where:

> the Russian Jewish intelligentsia early on confronted the challenge of defining a Jewish identity—and identifying a role for Judaism—in modern Russian society. This search was complicated by the fact that the development of Russian national identity was itself in a state of flux, exemplified by the struggle between the Slavophiles and the Westernizers. How could one define a "Russian Jew" when there was, as yet, no satisfactory definition of a "Russian" *(russkii)* within the context of the multi-national *(rossiiskii)* Empire. As a further complication, other peoples of the Empire, especially the Poles and Ukrainians, who lived alongside Jews in the western provinces, were also engaged in a search for national identity.[24]

The Society for the Promotion of Enlightenment among the Jews of Russia, known as the OPE, organized in 1863 by privileged secular Jews intent on russifying Russia's Jews, moved gradually away from a policy of assimilation and toward questions of national identity and renewal. (It is this organization that made Solovyov an official member.) By 1880, the OPE had become the central institution of Jewish national social and cultural activity. But 1881, the year of Alexander II's assassination, was a watershed year in Jewish as well as Russian circles. The involvement of a Jewish student in the assassination was the ostensible spark to a series of bloody pogroms. The pogroms, in turn, inflamed a debate about the future of the Jewish people in Russia. As Jonathan Frankel reports,

> A revolution in modern Jewish politics took place in Russia during the years 1881–2. The inner turmoil engendered by the pogroms starting in April 1881 reached a climax in the months from January to May 1882, when the Jewish people appeared to be living in expectation of an imminent and massive emigration. The image of a new exodus, a going-out

from the land of bondage to a promised land, came to dominate, however momentarily, every aspect of Jewish public life in Russia.[25]

Millions of Jews, of course, ultimately chose to stay in their "land of
bondage," some joining revolutionary socialist movements in response
to what they saw as the oppression of both Jews *and* workers on the part
of the tsarist regime. The question of the identity of Russian Jewry was
posed most sharply at this time. Some in the workers' movement sought
to merge into the general socialist movement: "We were for assimilation;
we did not even dream of a special Jewish mass movement," remembers
one member of the Jewish Bund.[26] But full assimilation never became
possible, or even desirable for most Russian Jews. Other solutions were
sought.

Many of the so-called answers to the Jewish question in the nineteenth
century, both on the part of the Russian state and, of particular importance to us here, on the part of Jewish intellectuals of nascent enlightenment Jewry in the late imperial period (in particular the OPE), were
based on a theoretical separation of ethnic from religious identity that
had not previously been part of the Jewish experience, but would become
increasingly important in the twentieth century. There is no question that
Russian Jewry underwent radical changes beginning in the mid–nineteenth
century, promoted by Russian reorganization of schools and seminaries,
but even more directly influenced by internal religious and intellectual
trends traveling from the West. The Haskalah, or Jewish Enlightenment,
entered the Russian Empire against the backdrop of a century-old struggle between rabbinical Judaism and Hasidism. Enlightenment Jews in Russia did not immediately abandon tradition in imitation of their brothers
and sisters in Germany, but at least by mid-century,

> the new power of the maskilim [enlightenment Jews of the Haskalah]
> was matched, for the first time, with the security of numbers. From a
> handful of disjointed individuals clustered in tiny enclaves on the bor-
> ders of the Pale or in insulated anonymity in the largest cities, the
> maskilim grew to a well-coordinated movement of several hundred
> adherents, preaching their gospel to thousands of committed students
> throughout the Pale.[27]

Unlike the traditional or Hasidic Jews who comprised their parents'
generation, the *maskilim* sought some kind of integration into Russian

society, although all did not reach the desire for assimilation of the Bundist quoted above. And they came to no consensus on how, or in which direction, to shape the "new" Jews of the Russian Empire. Their debates ran parallel to those of the Russian officials. In the Russians' terms, if the Jews were "only" a people, they could be either assimilated into Russian society or granted equal minority status among other nationalities in the Empire. If they were "only" a religion, their faith could be allowed within limited strictures so as not to contaminate the dominant Orthodox faith, but its adherents should be considered Russians, just like the majority. Their culture and nationality could be Russian, with a few concessions made for eccentric ritual practices. Yet, to separate religious from ethnic identity was near impossible when all national categories were in flux, for the Jews as well as the Russians.

As Klier writes: "Ultimately there could be no consensus within Russian Jewry on the definition of Jews and Judaism because the Jews themselves were in the midst of a transformation about whose end result there was no agreement." Some, like this Russian Jew, writing in *Russkii invalid* in 1861, sought to make of Jews, "Russian citizens of Jewish descent": "Let the new generation, from the cradle, think in Russian, speak in Russian, feel Russian, and be Russian, body and soul." The idea was to become Russian in culture, but "hold firmly to the faith of our fathers," to make of the Russian Jews, along the model of Western enlightenment, "Russian citizens of the Mosaic persuasion."[28] But such an outcome did not materialize. The situation was quite the reverse, as we will see.

JEWISH IDENTITY IN AMERICA AND ISRAEL

According to the famous sociological study of American religion by Will Herberg, by the mid-twentieth century the "religious community" for Jews, as for Catholics and Protestants, began to take precedence over old ethnic lines as the "primary context of self-identification and social location":

> Formerly, religion had been but an aspect of the ethnic group's culture and activities; it was merely a part, and to some a dispensable part, of the larger whole; now the religious community was growing increasingly primary, and ethnic interests, loyalties, and memories were being more and more absorbed in and manifested through this new social structure. The religious community is fast becoming, if it has not already

become, the over-all medium in terms of which remaining ethnic concerns are preserved, redefined, and given appropriate expression.[29]

No doubt based on Herberg, Norman Roth concurs: "Jews are not a recognized ethnic minority; they are members of a religion."[30]

It is important for us to pause here and consider in more detail the self-identification of Jews in America in the second half of the twentieth century, for that group provides a crucial contrast to the identity of the Russian Jews of this study. I am a member of the former cohort, along with the majority of American Jews whose grandparents and great-grandparents emigrated from Eastern and Central Europe beginning in the end of the nineteenth century. The latter Jews, instead, are the heirs to those Bundists, maskilim, Mensheviks, or the masses of unpoliticized Jews who did not emigrate, and survived the Revolution, the Civil War, collectivization, Stalin's purges, and the Nazi invasion to then feel moved to join the Church in the decades following Stalin's death. It is true that Herberg in his study had a double agenda—one side explicit, the other hidden—that caused him radically to divorce Jewish religious identity from what might have been a more traditionally holistic one. He sought to understand the religious revival of his day that seemed to coincide paradoxically with growing secularization. He also attempted, or perhaps inadvertently succeeded, in legitimating the relatively small Jewish population of the United States as one of the three dominant social forces in American life. In the process, Herberg avoided discussion of other marks of what we might call cultural identity, the importance for example of "lox and bagel Jewishness," to American Jewish identity, of social action experienced as a "Jewish" value, and the continuing significance of Israel as unifying symbol for secular as well as religious Jews. Nonetheless, most later sociologists build on Herberg, and note trends in the Jewish community that largely replicate those in the majority Christian population of the United States; "Jewish" modifies a religion, not an ethnic group.

Despite the dominant influence of Herberg on contemporary sociologists studying American Jews, some of the latter are finding a more complex pattern in their subjects in which religious and ethnic identity continue to interact, as they did in virtually all earlier historical periods. This is the case in two recent studies by the sociologist Steven M. Cohen. One, a quantitative study of 1,005 American Jews, finds that religion carries an increasingly more significant role in their identification as Jews, in relation to a decline in Jewish ethnicity. He concludes that "younger

Jews are just as religiously committed, God-oriented, and ritually observant as their elders," while they are "considerably less ethnically identified than their elders. . . . Even when intermarried Jews are excluded from the analysis, younger Jews score lower on ethnic measures than older Jews."[31] Cohen's survey confirms Herberg's prediction about the direction of religious identification, for, although the researcher finds no growth in religious practice among young Jews, he demonstrates a decline in what had been for their parents the primary ethnic identification. In contrast to Russia in the late Soviet period, however, where no religion is present, we must note that both types of identification are still operative, and form part of the individualist, personalist catalogue from which American Jews today seem to create their "sovereign self."[32]

A second study, this one based on more than fifty in-depth interviews with "moderately affiliated Jews," provides a curious counterpoint to those studies that focus mostly on religious identity. Cohen and his coauthor, Arnold M. Eisen, conclude that their subjects "cling to a powerful Jewish tribalism: an ineradicable belonging which allows for considerable nonbelief and non-observance, and which eliminates the danger that these might otherwise have posed to Jewishness."[33] In this perhaps controversial conclusion, we see a strong emphasis on ethnic, rather than religious identity. Jewish identity is familial, hereditary; religion (Judaism) is merely a choice (as, we might say, in early Rus'), but Jewishness itself is inalienable. In an earlier study of American and Israeli Jewish experiences, Cohen cites Anthony Smith's definition of an ethnic community as a "culture-based solidarity," in which groups "betray a quasi-familial sentiment; even though the ethnic community subsumes many families and clans, it is, in the first place, an aggregate of such families and clans."[34] Although the conclusions of Cohen's quantitative and qualitative studies might seem to flatten each other out, for the purposes of our study they suggest that both ethnic and religious identity, along with possible other identity markers, continue to interact in American Jews, with religion perhaps defining the Jews vis-à-vis other groups in the larger American polity, but with ethnic affiliation continuing to provide a positive internal identity.[35]

A slightly different picture has emerged in Israel, where many Israelis feel that they are Jews simply by virtue of the fact that they are living in the "Jewish homeland" as a "people." They are now (again) truly a nation, although, as is evident on any street corner, Israeli Jews are composed of many ethnic groups. Secular Jews reject religion as the defining trait of Jewish identity, yet their calendar, their folklore, the history they teach in their schools, and of course their language are intricately entwined with an ancient understanding of Abraham's legacy.

In the early 1990s, the Guttman Institute of Social Science in Israel was commissioned to study a sample of 2,400 Israelis to assess Jewish identity along the secular-religious spectrum, although the ultimate report avoided a pure dichotomy of secular and religious by focusing on "levels" of religious observance. The results were surprising (and controversial) to some, for, "[i]n general, the report found, Israelis were far more traditional in their behavior and beliefs than had heretofore been imagined, and, in the words of the report itself, 'the rhetoric of polarization' within Israeli society between observant and nonobservant was exaggerated, at least from a behavioral point of view."[36] In other words, the Guttman report found that the majority of Israelis, whether "secular" or "religious," engage in some degree of traditional ("religious") practices and retain similar values and attitudes, including a commitment to Jewish continuity, the celebration of major holidays, and the performance of life-cycle rituals.[37] The level of at least some degree of Shabbat observance and observance of the dietary laws also turned out to be higher than expected, even among a majority of what would have been called "secular" Jews.[38]

Clearly, the relationship between religion and national identity, between Judaism and Jewry, remains intertwined in both American and Israeli societies, although to different degrees and with different emphases.[39] Cohen and Eisen, as we saw, unearthed a range of definitions of Judaism and Jewry in their interviews of American Jews. All subjects agreed on a crucial issue, however: "The one way to cease being a Jew is to convert to another religion."[40] The Israeli Law of Return confirms this opinion: all Jews are welcomed back to the Jewish homeland, and will receive citizenship and financial and other support as new immigrants, provided that they complete a questionnaire that includes a statement verifying that they have not accepted any other confession.[41] The parents of the former Israeli Minister of Absorption, Yuly Edelshtein, have both been baptized in the Orthodox Church, and could not immigrate to Israel as Jews. When asked in an interview for this study how he, who was then minister and Knesset member representing the Yisrael B'Aliyah party, feels about the immigration of baptized Russian Jews, he answered that: *it isn't a question of how I relate, but of how the Law of Return relates. You have to understand that there is a special point in the Law. If you come under the Law of Return, you need to declare that you are a Jew, or that you have taken on "Jewish Judaism"* (evreiskii iudaizm). *Then the Law clearly states, "and no other religion."*

The minister continued in the interview: *So, let's say, my mother, or my father* [who is an ordained priest], *too, would want to come to Israel. I would be very glad, but I could not provide them with grants and material support from the government. They could come here under regular "immigration law,"* he added in English. *They have a basis for that; they have relatives here. But as new* olim, *they wouldn't have the right. They could become citizens, but they would need a period of naturalization.*

In the minds of Israeli law and of American Jews, even only moderately committed ones, some kind of religious identification is thus the bottom line of Jewish identity. Core Jewish population is usually negatively defined as "an aggregate which reports no non-Judaic religious loyality."[42] In other words, for most Jews in America and Israel, Christian baptism negates Jewish identity.[43]

JEWISH IDENTITY IN RUSSIA

Russian Jewish identity in the twentieth century took a different path. The issue revolved symbolically, in large part, around language. And again, Russian imperial and later Soviet policy as well as Jewish intellectuals reasoned similarly. Let the Jews keep Yiddish, the language of their ethnic identity, but eliminate Hebrew, the obscure language of superstition. Or, on the contrary, let the Jews keep Hebrew, the mark of their religious peculiarities, but abolish Yiddish, in order to russify, acculturate, or even be absorbed into Russian culture. Klier points to the confused use of the Russian terms *sblizhenie* (rapprochement) and *sliianie* (merger) in the policy of both Russians and Jewish intellectuals. The former would imply preservation of Jewish national and or religious differences, the latter would lead toward full assimilation of Jews into Russian society.

Conversion of the Jews would be one possible method of assimilation, but, despite the fact that "more Jews converted to Christianity in the Russian Empire than anywhere else in Europe,"[44] mass conversion of the Jews never occurred successfully in Russia. The largest single group of involuntary apostates was the child recruits, forcibly converted in the imperial army. Other Jews who took on Christianity in the nineteenth century did so not because of official Russian policy, but rather because of a breakdown in the Jewish community itself. According to Stanislawski, voluntary converts included "(1) those seeking educational or professional advancement (whether or not they ever attained it); (2) the haute bour-geoisie; (3) the criminals; (4) the believers; and (5) the destitute and the desperate."[45] Regardless of the typology of apostates, it is clear that con-version could not constitute a satisfactory answer to the Jewish question in Russia, with over five million Jews, or 4.13 percent of the total popula-tion, remaining in the Empire as of the year 1897.[46] In fact, Russia at the turn of the twentieth century claimed one half of the population of all Jews in the world. Even today, after the departure of the generations of our grandparents and great-grandparents in the first two decades of the twentieth century, the mass genocide by the Nazis of many who remained, and the large immigration of Soviet Jews to Israel and the West, Russia still has the third largest diaspora population in the world. Only the United States and France are higher. Ukraine has the fifth, and Belorus', the sixth largest Jewish communities in Europe.

In contrast to the less significant effects of conversion on the Russian Jewish population, imperial efforts toward separation of religious and national identity made inroads into what had been in ancient and medieval times—and seems to remain at least to some extent in the United States—an unquestioned alliance. Those efforts continued even more successfully well into the Soviet period. Ultimately, the assertion of ethnic (called "national" by Soviet policy) identity took precedence over religious defi-nition, as religion was systematically repressed on all sides in the new atheist state. The Jews became nothing more than an ethnic category, in a way they had never before been in Russia or elsewhere. As Elena, a young, soft-spoken interviewee in New York admitted, *I always felt myself to be Jewish. My family was Jewish. All my friends (in Latvia) were Rus-sians or Jews. (We kept ourselves separate from the Latvians.) But I had no religion. Maybe it was something genetic.*

Since identity within the Russian Jewish community itself was in flux in the late nineteenth century, it would seem that "Russian Jewry [as a cohesive national identity] was partly, if unintentionally, a creation of the Russian state."[47] After the revolutions of 1917, Soviet officials—Jew-ish as well as Russian—attacked Zionism along with the use of Hebrew in favor of the creation of a specifically Soviet Jewish nationality, one national minority among many others in the multinational state. Reli-gion was fully marginalized in the debate. Stalin went so far as to create a "national homeland" for the Jews within the borders of the Soviet Union. Although many Jews did relocate to the Autonomous Jewish Region of Birobidzhan, five thousand miles east of Moscow, Stalin's vision to isolate the Jewish minority in its own land never came true. What did occur is that Jews remained a separate ethnic group scattered throughout the Soviet Union.

Despite the Soviet rhetoric of multinational brotherhood, antisemitism continued, so that, as Zvi Gitelman states, "Ironically, the two strongest forces for the preservation of Jewish national identity were the official classification of Jews as a nationality and social antisemitism. This left many Soviet Jews in an anomalous position: they were Jews officially and socially, but Russians culturally. They were acculturated without being assimilated."[48] They were Jewish, but not Jewish, Russian but not Russian. The Russian policies of separation of Jewish national and religious identity, ironically supported by the Jewish intelligentsia in the late imperial period and continued in the Soviet period, successfully allowed, or even required, Russian Jews to identify as "Jewish" without an association whatsoever with an earlier historical or religious meaning of the word. They had no language to mark them off from their neighbors, no ritual, and presumably only a common "Soviet" future.

To make matters worse, the Soviet classification of the Jews as a nation was not parallel to that of most of the other peoples of the Soviet Union: "The Jews are not defined as a nation, the highest category, which is the most stable and has the most developed sense of national identity. Nor are they classified as a people *(narod)*, the general term used for ethnic communities of different types. They are not even called a *narodnost,* the term used to refer to the minute groups living in Siberia and the Northern Caucasus. They are defined as a *natsionalnost* (nationality), a term of seemingly political significance, which reflects the authorities' desire to view the Jews as individuals, rather like atomised particles, and not as a united body with a feeling of national solidarity."[49]

Indeed, Jews actually had the political and constitutional status as a "negative nationality," as Benjamin Pinkus suggests, "a status that holds no rights, but only restrictions."[50] What preserved Jewish identity among most Soviet Jews was largely antisemitism, with its resulting "restrictions." A more complex identity that would include religion in whatever form was absent.

According to two recent surveys of several thousand Jews in three Russian and five Ukrainian cities, Gitelman and two Russian colleagues have shown that "Jews in the former Soviet Union (FSU) do *not* strongly connect the Jewish religion with being Jewish."[51] In fact, in contrast to the 1990 National Jewish Population Survey in the United States, in which

47 percent of Jews believe that Jews are a religious group, only 3 percent of Gitelman's sample in Russia and Ukraine say that practicing Judaism defines "being a Jew."[52] The items that drew the largest response to the question "What is the most important thing required of a person in order to be considered a genuine Jew?" were: "Be proud of one's nationality," "Defend Jewish honor and dignity," "Not hide one's Jewishness," and "Remember the Holocaust."[53] Jewish traditional practice (including kashrut, circumcision, synagogue attendance, keeping Shabbat), Jewish education, and knowledge of Jewish language were near the bottom of the list.

One question on Gitelman's survey is of great importance to this current study of Russian Jewish Christians. When asked the question "Which religious faith is most attractive to you?" 33.2 percent of the respondents in Russia in 1992 and 26.7 percent in 1997 responded "Judaism." Another 36.3 percent and 44.1 percent respectively answered "None." But over 13 percent in both years responded to the question with the answer: "Christianity." A number of these respondents, no doubt, are the Russian Jewish Christians of the current study, and/or Russian Jews who have or would consider baptism in the future. Furthermore, and perhaps even more significantly, in both years of the survey, only 30 to 39 percent of the respondents would condemn Jews who "convert to Christianity." Only 4 percent actually condone baptism, but a full 60 percent claimed that they would neither condone nor condemn Jews who become Christians.[54] The situation is obviously very different from that in the United States, where "the only way to lose this Jewish birthright is to choose a different religion for oneself."[55] In contemporary Russia, however, Jewish religion has virtually nothing to do with Jewish identity, and the adoption of Christianity does not seem to alter the core national identity as a Jew.

To aid the separation of religious and ethnic or national identity, modern Russian provides its speakers with two separate words: *evrei* and *iudei*. The former has an ethnic meaning: a member of *evreistvo*, (Jewry). The latter has a religious meaning: a follower of the laws and rituals of *iudeistvo* or *iudaizm* (Judaism). The two terms for "Jew" were not so distinct in the late nineteenth century, when the Jewish question was so hotly debated, so that Solovyov, himself, wavers in his usage, and a Jewish writer in 1881 needed to ask: "How can we more truthfully call followers of the mosaic law: *Evrei, Iudei,* or *Izrail'tiane*?"[56] Virtually all of the Russian Jewish Christians interviewed for this study announce that they are *evrei*, but decidedly not *iudei*. Whenever possible in this study, I will try to draw a distinction between Jewry and Judaism, between the identity of a Jew as part of an ethnic or national group and that of a Jew as adherent to religion.

A "RUSSIAN ORTHODOX JEWESS"

To summarize, although both Russian and English allow for two separate identifying categories—Jewry and Judaism—in fact the identity of the Jews has almost always and everywhere exhibited a tension between a political or ethnic nation and a religious community. Historically, Judaism *(iudaizm* or *iudeistvo)* has never been entirely separate from Jewry *(evreistvo),* for the Jews are defined largely by the body of laws—both spiritual *and* national—that formed them into a people. Traditionally, we speak of Jews as the chosen *people,* chosen by God for both a spiritual and historical mission. This ancient identification lingers, even among secular Jews. In English we wonder if Jews in the United States should be called American Jews or Jewish Americans, based on the level of their observance and/or their Zionist beliefs. This dual national identity is more pronounced in modern Russian, where the term Jewish *(evreiskii)* has only an ethnic meaning. One cannot logically be a Russian *evrei,* for one is either Russian or Jewish by nationality. One could theoretically be a Russian *iudei* (a Russian who follows the religious laws of Judaism, although this is rare if not nonexistent) or, certainly, a *evreiskii* Christian, or, more specifically for this study, a Jewish Christian member of the Russian Orthodox Church. Elena, who was cited above as feeling only a "genetic" link to the Jewish people, claimed *I am a* pravoslavnaia evreika, *a Russian Orthodox Jewess.*

Russian Jews, as a rule, see no problem with being Jewish Christians. This in large part explains the range of reactions I found as I began to speak publicly of my research into Russian Jews who had been baptized in the Orthodox Church; Americans and Israelis were in many cases shocked to discover this area of conversion that they had never considered. Russian Jews found little surprising about this small but nonetheless recognizable phenomenon. Some of their acquaintances in the intelligentsia might have been baptized, but with little public fanfare. Some of their cultural icons might have been as well, including the popular Odessan comic, Mikhail Zhvanetsky,[57] or Boris Pasternak, and the poet Joseph Brodsky, who reportedly was baptized as child, and never acclaimed publicly, but never repudiated his Christianity.[58]

As we will see in the following chapter, the Russian Jewish Christians themselves find their paths of faith to be fully understandable, given the Soviet society in which they lived. Political, spiritual, cultural, and personal influences arising in the post-Stalin period all conspired to lead them to the Orthodox Church.

One final note: Since 1932, Jews in Russia were identified as Jews on their internal passports under the "fifth point" (nationality). They took their passports with them as identity papers when applying for jobs, for higher education, for marriage licenses. Insofar as antisemitism played a role in the continuing identity of the Jewish people in Russia, this line alone was extremely significant. The fifth point was removed from passports as of October 1997. With religious and national identity successfully divorced in the former Soviet Union, it remains to be seen what effect the lack of existence of an official national category will have on Jewish identity in the future.

CHAPTER THREE

The Path of Faith

The 1960s Generation

Living in the Soviet Union, and always being bothered by the constant lie, you had the sensation that there must be a great deal that they are simply hiding. I was led to a sense of readiness, readiness to believe in something else. I didn't know what that something was, but the readiness was there.

—Osip, Jerusalem 1998

For those Jews in those days the fact that we were Christians was not an issue. Most of them had been in Stalin's camps. Christians were not enemies. They were all allies. In those days we were a minority of outcasts.

—Michael, New York 1998

Stalin's death brought forth a very acute crisis in Soviet ideology and in the spiritual body of the nation as well.

—Yuri Glazov, *The Russian Mind*

O NE COLD SPRING DAY IN 1993, the dissident religious author Zoya Krakhmal'nikova asked to speak with me about her latest project: the formation of an international association she called "A Christian Alternative to the Threat of Russian Fascism." Krakhmal'nikova is among those who rediscovered Solovyov for the post-Stalin generation, and she has come to focus more and more on the Russian philosopher's defense of the Jews. I was thus curious to hear how she would speak about what she saw as the current betrayal of Solovyov's values by Russian nationalists, both within and outside the Church. She took me into the study of the crowded apartment she then shared with her daughter's family, and, offering me a cassette recorder, began to tell me about her early years as a Christian, and her current attitude toward the official Russian Orthodox Church.[1]

Zoya, who is the mother of a good friend of mine in Moscow, had always been a forbidding presence, talking in whispered tones to cassocked clergy in one room as I chatted idly with her daughter about work or children in another. I realized that I knew next to nothing about her background. After some prodding, she revealed that she was born in Kharkov' in 1929 to Jewish parents that she characterized as "indifferent" to religion, although not exactly atheists. *We were Russian* intelligenty [members of the intelligentsia], she offered, as though this self-identification required no further explanation. Perhaps she was right, for in the decades surrounding the Revolution, as in the 1960s, 70s, and 80s explored here, Jews made up a disproportionately large percentage of the so-called Russian intelligentsia. In the effort to create a new, communal society with opportunities for all, many Jews, like Trotsky (born Lev Bronstein), abandoned not only religion, but also any markers of their past, individual or ethnic identity.

Zoya, the future dissident, received an advanced degree in philology and quickly joined the Soviet Union of Writers. Already an officially published critic, she began to participate in the Moscow dissident movement in the 1960s, however, and soon turned to Orthodox Christianity. Over time, she was influential in bringing a number of Russian Jewish intellectuals to the Orthodox Church, including her then-husband, the critic and writer Felix Svetov. Zoya was silent in the interview about details of the baptism, and when I returned to her in 1997, she was distracted and wanted mostly to provide me with contacts in Israel, where she had recently traveled. She had aged considerably, and I chose not to probe too hard.

Felix, however, related this story to me: *Zoya was the first* [in the group] *to be baptized. A certain friend showed up, several years younger than we are, a film director. He was a very talented man with a complicated history, who came to Moscow and for some reason became a believer. He didn't exactly come to the Church, though; his spiritual development was all very complicated. An individual. We had conflicts with him on this later. Nonetheless, he read a great deal, proselytized, and affected many people. He was a very strong missionary among us. Around that time, there was also a certain priest: Father Dmitry Dudko.*

Dudko, born in 1922, was first arrested and sent to the Gulag in 1948, as a daring student at the Moscow Theological Academy. After more than eight years in the camps, he was released and "rehabilitated" in 1956 as part of the post-Stalin cultural thaw, and was finally ordained in 1960.

But his liberal preaching again reached the attention of the authorities, both secular and ecclesiastic, and he began to suffer a round of humiliating relocations, dismissals, and arrests for "anti-Soviet activity." His international profile often saved him, but he returned to Moscow from his final incarceration in 1980 (on the eve of the Olympic Games) a broken man. Father Dmitry began to preach a reactionary platform, and many of his once-loyal followers, Svetov included, largely abandoned contact with him. His is a tragic story; having cultivated the generation that ultimately saw the dismantling of the Soviet Union, he succumbed to the pressures of the system he was fighting, and became a spokesperson for the very oppression he revealed.[2]

The dissident group around Dudko and cothinkers at the time was quite close, and consisted of a number of prominent writers and other intellectuals. Felix continued his narrative about the group: *Father Dmitry baptized all of us. First Zoya, then me, then little Zoya* [their only daughter], *and also many of our friends and acquaintances. He was a remarkable man. And later I myself helped baptize* [the famous poet] *Alexander Galich. Sasha* [Galich] *had a hard time coming to faith. He was a Jew, a member of the Russian intelligentsia, and the whole idea confused him quite a lot. Zoya proselytized frequently to him, but he could not quite come into the Church. Once, I remember, he had been drinking. He was a great fan of drinking, a beautiful "drinking artist." Zoya said: "Svetik, show Sasha your cross." And I showed him the cross. The very next day he went to the priest. He left here in 1974, I think. They* [dissident intellectuals] *all left in that year. The vast majority: Maksimov, Solzhenitsyn, Galich. In 1974.*

Despite his initial reluctance before baptism, Galich is quoted as saying the following about his new identity and his decision to immigrate not to Western Europe or America, but to Israel: "I am a Jew. A baptized Jew. . . . I took on baptism most of all because I believe in the word of God. I believe in Good. I believe that lack of faith is destructive and fatal. I believe in and proclaim my great ancestors the Jews Jeremiah, Ezekiel, Isaiah, Matthew, and John, those who wrote the best of all humankind's books and left them for the sake of that same humankind: the Bible and the Gospels. Do I want to go to Israel? It goes without saying."[3] Once he had arrived in the Promised Land, however, Galich apparently did not feel quite the same. As another acquaintance wrote about Galich's immigration to Israel: "Once he was already 'over there,' he wrote me a short note that stated that he could never get used to it 'there.' That's not surprising. He was from the very flesh of our life, of

Moscow, of our complex times, full of deep and eternal meaning."[4] No
doubt Israel turned out to differ too much from Galich's image of the
land on which Jesus and his apostles trod, not to mention from the intense
atmosphere of the Russian intelligentsia attracted to Christianity in
Moscow. As we will see in the next chapter, many baptized Jews felt an
acute identity crisis once in the land of Israel. The explanation suggested
by Galich's acquaintance covers only part of the story.

Zoya herself chose not to leave the Soviet Union in 1974 with many of
her fellow dissidents, and that year instead began a samizdat journal,
Nadezhda (Hope), published in Germany and smuggled back into the
Soviet Union for the small, but growing religious community. Publication ended with her arrest in 1982, which was followed by a year in prison
and four more in exile in Gornyi Altai, where she was joined by Felix,
also arrested for dissident activities. Over the years of our acquaintance,
she remembered me from visit to visit as the donor of a purple Williams
College t-shirt that she wore to tatters during her exile. At our interview
in 1993, over seventy years old and at the time a grandmother of three,
Zoya spoke softly, although with an impressive power and an almost
strident edge when discussing her fears for the future of Christianity in
Russia. She did not specifically focus on her Jewish origins, although her
concern over antisemitism in the Church of her choice labels her as a
"Jew" among her ultranationalist opponents.

Several minutes into the interview, Zoya pulled out a pile of antisemitic
newspapers she had collected since the late Gorbachev years—some of
which she called "dangerous," others "cannibalistic"—and related how a
publisher who marketed *Mein Kampf* in Russia had been arrested, but
quickly acquitted, while she, at the other extreme, was imprisoned and
exiled for years for the "crime" of producing a collection of Christian
teachings. Her pardon came only with Gorbachev's grace, and after an
initial refusal on her part to confess retroactively to any wrongdoing. But
Zoya's concern during our interview was not for the prudence of the legal
system, but for the Orthodox Church that she felt continually turns a
blind eye toward such unchristian attitudes. *What is most shocking about
these fascist publications I have collected?* she asked me rhetorically. *What is
most shocking is that they picture the swastika alongside the Orthodox cross, and
speak about the Church. There are hundreds of such newspapers in St. Petersburg and Moscow alone. But there is not a single Christian newspaper that is
prepared to argue with them.*

Zoya requested the interview with me in order to disseminate her ideas about antisemitism in the Russian Church, and her consequent fears for the future of a Christian Russia. I, apparently, was one of her few conduits to the West, even then, when the Soviet Union had fallen and Western culture was rushing into the vacuum. Propaganda, however, costs money, and even more now that capitalist ventures had taken over the market place. The lesson of the *Mein Kampf* story, after all, was ultimately as much about money as ideology. Who was more wrong, I asked, the publisher or the consumers? Zoya countered, justifiably, that this new entrepreneur could have chosen to market detective stories, which have proven very lucrative on the Russian market, but instead he chose Hitler. For her part, Zoya had neither money nor paper with which to propagate her fears for an Orthodox Russia that accepted Nazi ideology without an outcry.

With the recorder running and Zoya continuing to explain her desire to travel abroad and open a college for missionaries who would preach a Christian doctrine of tolerance, I looked over the document she offered on "A Christian Alternative to the Threat of Russian Fascism." At the same time, I began to listen for the pieces of her story that connect her disappointment with the Church to a more personal narrative. She, after all, had *chosen* the Church as an educated, thinking adult. What was she, a Jew, doing in a Church that she accused of acquiescence toward, if not actual Jew-hatred? How did she understand her place in the Church? How did she understand herself now, as a Christian, in relationship to the young Zoya, born of Jewish parents at the beginning of Stalin's atheist reign? As a member of the Russian Orthodox Church, did she see herself as Russian? Or did she divorce the national aspect of the Church from its religious identity? If she advocated an Orthodox Russia, could she remain a Jew in such a state? Did she have any remaining Jewish identity at all, ethnic or religious? How did she separate them? How did she relate them? Ultimately, what did it mean to her to be a "Jewish Christian," a term which for me, an American Jew, seemed, at best, an oxymoron?

I did not ask any of these questions during that first interview, but I eventually returned to her and to other Russian Jewish Christians to find answers that might be hidden in their personal narratives of faith. My meetings were all by word of mouth, and I passed from one small circle of devotees to another. When I would ask my subjects about their conversions *(perekreshchenie),* almost all would explain that they did not "convert," for in their understanding conversion implies the abandonment of one religious identification for the embrace of another. (The prefix "pere" in Russian means across or "trans," so that *perekreshchenie* means trans-baptism, from one confession to another.) Instead, they consistently used the term *obrashchenie*, meaning a turning toward or entrance into something new. Once, when I mistakenly had asked about Russian Jews who *perekrestilis'* after they made *aliya* to Israel (I had meant to say *krestilis'*, or "were baptized"), I received the following answer: *Yes, there are some, but precisely in the sense that they had "converted" (perekrestilis'). They left Jewry per se. It was an exit as much as an entrance.* As we will see, the reverse—a sense of entrance rather than exit—was particularly strong for the Russian Jewish Christians I interviewed, for they feel they, at best, have left an emptiness in order to enter into their first spiritually full existence.

ESCAPE FROM A SPIRITUAL VACUUM

My subject pool for this generation turned out to include two Russian Jewish priests who entered the Church in the 1960s: Fathers Pavel and Michael. The former was ordained and now serves in a parish in Russia, while Father Michael, although baptized well before his emigration, received his ordination from the Orthodox Church of America (OCA) only after settling in the United States, and now leads a congregation in New York City, itself with a significant percentage of Russian Jewish parishioners.

Father Michael is well-established in America—his house equipped with all the trappings of American technology—although he calls his parish "modest," having been reclaimed from virtual extinction some twenty years ago by his leadership and the influx of émigrés to New York. He has provided a spiritual home for Russian Jews, half-Jews, and non-Jews (intermarriage in the Soviet Union was as high as 73 percent, and has risen even more in the post-Soviet years),[5] who either joined the Church while still at home, or who now seek a kind of home away from home in Russian Orthodoxy. (A French journalist described Father Michael's parish rather picturesquely: "In a single move, he landed in Manhattan, where his temple prospers on 71st St., among the Jews of Christ and old Russian countesses."[6]) Because his parish is "liberal," as many of his parishioners agree, it feels a more welcoming haven to these Russian Jews than other Orthodox churches in New York belonging to the Moscow Patriarchate or the Russian Church in Exile, many with their long established *Russian* congregations.[7] As one young Russian Jewish woman who became Christian only after leaving her home in Soviet Latvia confessed: *I might not have chosen this religion if I hadn't come here. Father Michael is a strong influence. And this parish. There are no limitations here. It is very progressive. The "face" here is the most important thing. Everyone can be herself. If you believe, that is enough.*

Her mother, also baptized after immigrating to New York, concurred: *This parish is very good. It is very progressive. There is less tradition and more spirit. So, in Russia, you have to put something on your head. You have to wear a skirt, not pants. It is tradition. It is not connected with the Gospels, with religion. I think it might be possible to find a very good parish in Russia as well. In Moscow it must be possible. But here in New York, we travel two hours from Brooklyn, but we don't want to change. It is the only parish for us.*

Like the women in Father Michael's New York parish, most of Father Pavel's Moscow parishioners also travel long distances to pray with him, although out of, not into the city. He does not consider himself progressive, however, but rather, as he stated, "unprincipled," outside of any ideological dialogue. Father Pavel lives in relative poverty with his large family in a central Moscow apartment building that has been bought up by "New Russians" [nouveau-riche Russians—including Jewish Russians—who have become millionaires in the post-Soviet years]. The entrance was being fabulously renovated as I entered for our scheduled interview. Father Pavel's apartment, however, looked like it had not been painted since the 1950s, and every surface was piled high with clothing, books, and toys for his many children. He travels weekly to his parish, located about two hundred kilometers outside of Moscow; the majority of his parishioners, including many Moscow Jews, make the trip as well.

Father Pavel believes that he was denied a parish in Moscow for two reasons: *At the end of the seventies, there were two strikes against me in the eyes of the Communist authorities: that I had an advanced degree* [he is trained as a mathematician], *and that I was a Jew. The first barrier fell away after perestroika. As for the second barrier, it continues to have its place, although there are Jewish priests now serving in Moscow. Few. You could count them on one hand, but it is not impossible. I, however, do not have a pulpit here.*

Father Pavel's situation is similar to that of Father Georgy Edelshtein, who now serves in a small parish outside of the town of Kostroma in central Russia, and who happens to be the father of the former Israeli Minister of Immigration and Absorption under Netanyahu, Yuly Edelshtein. The story of the minister's Christian connection broke in the daily paper *Ma'ariv* in the summer of 1996 with pictures of a white-bearded Father

Georgy holding a large gold cross before his parishioners, and standing in front of a small wooden building in his village.[8] Loud headlines proclaimed: "Priest and father of Yuly Edelshtein, Minister of Absorption: 'I am a Jew who believes in Jesus.'" The Israeli minister himself was quoted in the article as saying, "That is the road which my parents chose; I respect them for it," but, "perhaps in the depth of my heart I wish that the situation were different." Edelshtein's embarrassment over what seemed like the beginnings of a scandal was mitigated by a visit in the summer of 1997 by his father, who was attending a Church conference in Jerusalem.

Although Father Georgy is not Jewish according to Jewish law *(halakha)*, since his father, but not his mother was Jewish, his son reports that their home had a decidedly "Jewish" feeling. Father Georgy's wife, whose mother *was* halachically Jewish, was also baptized. Yuly Edelshtein admitted reluctantly at an interview in his small, smoke-filled office in the Knesset that he, too, like much of the Jewish intelligentsia, had a *period of interest in Christianity* in his teenage years, and remembered thinking that Christianity *is even a kind of completion* [zavershenie] *of Judaism.* But the future minister instead became an ardent Jewish Zionist, and spent much of the 1980s as a refusnik and prisoner of conscience in camps throughout Siberia before being allowed to emigrate and join Natan Sharansky's Yisrael B'Aliyah party in Israel. When I asked about relations between the village priest and his Zionist son in the Gulag, Yuly smiled. *We had only the best of relations. Familial. Our relations weren't based on theological, theoretical conversations. As for the authorities, what could they do to me that would have been worse? They had already imprisoned me. All they could do was shoot me.* He laughed, then admitted seriously: *From my father's point of view, of course, it was something of a problem.*

Yuly's father, however, never hid his Jewish roots, and had chosen "Jewish" for the nationality listed on his internal passport. (Under Soviet law, children of mixed marriages could choose the nationality of either parent upon maturity.) *On the contrary,* claimed the minister about his father's national identity, *when he accepted a new position or employment, my father always made a point of saying that his name was Edelshtein. That way there would be no uncertainty, and no unpleasantness later if someone were to claim that he had not been up front about this point* [point five on his passport]. Significantly, in the *Ma'ariv* article that broke the story about the minister's father, the priest is quoted as saying, "I still feel myself to be a Jew."

Father Georgy became a priest in 1978, but had already been working at small jobs within the Church for several years. The Church authorities denied him a parish in Moscow not only because of his Jewishness, but also, as was the case with Father Pavel mentioned previously, because of his education: he had a higher degree in philology, with a dissertation on linguistic theory in the writings of the Fathers of the Church, and had served as head of his department at the institute where he taught. As Yuly explained,

> *At the end of the seventies, when he began to explore the possibility of ordination and started to work in the Church, everyone was afraid to have anything to do with him, since he was a Ph.D. I talked to him about the possibility of leaving* [the Soviet Union]. *I told him that there are seminars, institutes, scholarly projects in America, in France, elsewhere. He was a rather serious scholar, after all; he commanded a lot of respect. But he didn't want to leave. He decided that the true path for him was to become a priest in some little village. We had arguments about this. I said to him that he wouldn't find more than twenty old women* [in the village church], *and they wouldn't even understand what he is talking about in his sermons. They wouldn't understand his vocabulary. But he had an entirely different approach.*

And thus this Russian Jewish intellectual, Georgy Edelstein, traveled the difficult road to become spiritual father to peasants in the Russian hinterlands. For his part, Father Pavel in Moscow did not travel quite as far geographically, but an equal distance along the path of faith.

Meanwhile, Father Michael's path to the priesthood in the Orthodox Church of America was also strewn with difficulties, although of a different sort. He, too, grew up with a strong Jewish identity, even though he, like Father Georgy, is Jewish according to Soviet, but not Jewish law; his father, not his mother, was a Jew. In fact, his Russian mother had him secretly baptized at the beginning of the Stalinist antisemitic campaign, as he admitted,

> *for completely the wrong reasons. And I will tell you why. In 1949, Golda Meir came to Russia as the Israeli ambassador to the Soviet Union, and she had meetings with Russian Jews. After that came the beginning of the Stalinist antisemitic campaign. My father had the same name as the ambassador: Meerson* [Meir-son]. *He was saved, but only because his boss pressed him to take early retirement. Just months later, all the Jews who worked in*

that factory were imprisoned or killed. And I remember later that my mother took me to be baptized. But they never mentioned anything about it. They were not believers at all, so I did not understand why they did this. I only figured it out later: she was afraid. They were taking Jews. A lot of our friends disappeared, were exiled. So she thought this would save me. This was in 1953. The churches were already open when I was a little child [Stalin reopened many churches and relaxed legislation concerning the practice of religion during World War II, in an effort to increase patriotism and help the war effort],[9] *so why did she wait until 1953 if she wanted me to be a Christian? And it was never mentioned by anyone at all. I remember being surprised. No one told me anything. One day, she just didn't want me to go to school. "We'll go together someplace," is all she said. She took me to a church. The priest asked some questions and I answered. I was completely embarrassed. I didn't know what it all meant. And there was no follow-up. Only later did I figure out that it happened during the days and months of the case against the Jewish doctors.*

One of Stalin's last paranoid convictions was that his private physicians, mostly Jewish, were trying to kill him. His accusation began the case against the so-called Doctors' Plot that dragged many innocent Jews into a wave of antisemitism. *Some of the doctors were friends of the family,* explained Father Michael. *So she figured that maybe it would help. It was strange. Obviously, it didn't have any effect on me whatsoever.*

Father Michael's true entrance into the Church occurred only later, in 1965, at the age of twenty-one: *I went through the regular youth of our age: drugs, the typical sixties. And religion kind of took me out of it all. It was my way to get away from it.*

But to get away from what, precisely? And why go as far as ordination, I wondered, despite the significant obstacles? While I silently asked these questions, Father Michael continued his narrative of faith: *As soon as I became a member of the Church, I entered the underground. I hid from my parents.* The hiding, it seems, was as much to protect them as to escape their potential disapproval. As for the latter, Father Michael remembered with amusement, *the biggest opposition I had was not from my* [Jewish] *father, but from my mother, who had had me baptized.*

He explained what his life as an underground Christian was like:

In 1965 I joined the Church and left my house. . . . I was thrown out of the university twice. Working here and there in small-paying jobs left me with lots of free time. I tried to enter the seminary, but that was impossible because of my background—as a Jew, a dissident, a college graduate. And because I knew Alexander Men'. These things were all monitored by the KGB. Later, every six months I had to change apartments. And my parents' telephone was bugged.

I became afraid to stay in the Soviet Union. If I had stayed there in the Russian Orthodox Church, I would have to become more and more "Russian," because it is a very nationalist Church. Today's nationalism started at that time. It gave off little shoots. And I felt that it wasn't my way. And I felt more and more threatened politically. On the one hand, I left the Academy of Science and tried to enter the Church, but I failed completely. I was even rejected as an altar boy after three months of work at some small village church because of the local authority, because my case was not very "kosher," from their point of view. A fellow from the Academy of Science, a Jewish fellow. I realized that I was getting nowhere. And I was simply afraid that if I were arrested they could put me into a mental asylum. It had already happened in my early years, in 1963. They had diagnosed me as psychotic. I tried to get rid of the official diagnosis, but I couldn't, so I was simply afraid that if I were arrested I wouldn't go just to prison camp, but to this mental institution, where they destroy people completely.

Father Michael left the Soviet Union in 1972. Although he insisted that he had wanted to go to Israel, he was first invited to France because of his underground political and religious activities. He and a friend, who has since left the Church, had established a flow of religious literature between Paris and Moscow, a channel for samizdat publications in the West, and the import of literature back to the newly religious believers. *I lived in France for a year, but didn't like the life there. I felt very lonely. I lacked community, the fellowship I had had before. By a whirlwind of circumstances, I went to the United States, where I was a student for several years at St. Vladimir's Seminary,*[10] *and where I supported myself with a little journalistic writing.*

But the sense of loneliness continued, so that he traveled several times to Israel to see his former friends who had, for the most part, immigrated there. Finally, after graduation, he decided to stay in Israel for a longer period. He met his future wife, also a Russian Jewish Christian, and they were married as Christians on Cyprus, since the rabbinical authorities in Israel allow only halachically Jewish marriages.

But they could not settle in Israel. *I couldn't get ordained in Israel because of antisemitism in the Russian Orthodox Church in Exile. And the Church of the Moscow Patriarchate was too "official," too connected to the KGB.*[11] *The Greeks* [the Greek Orthodox Church, which has a large presence in Israel], *too, didn't want to deal with Jews in Israel.* Father Michael and his wife returned to the United States, where he was ordained in the Orthodox Church of America in 1978. The Church set him up with a pulpit in New York immediately, for they wanted not only to revive the dying parish on 71st Street, but to keep it "Russian" as well.[12]

These Jewish Christians traveled difficult roads as Jewish priests, and in the narratives I expected to hear stories of mystical calls to Christ and inner belief in the Gospels that initiated and sustained their faith. Instead of tales of a revelation on the road to Damascus, however, both Father Michael and Father Pavel spoke at length about the difficulties for intellectuals in the Soviet society in which they were raised: As Father Michael remembers:

> *It was an issue of how to maintain your difference. How not to be absorbed. To have the inner power to stay yourself. To stay a spiritual personality. Not to be completely engulfed. In this sense, the Church helped to support the human personality, the personality of the intelligentsia, for whom personhood is extremely important. Not to be completely dissolved into the aggressive Soviet mass. To withstand this aggressiveness of Soviet civilization. We were so threatened by this. From all sides. You need some kind of strength from within that gives you power to survive. And that is exactly what I felt in the sixties. It was the power that I found to stay myself. The pressure of this Soviet aggressiveness cannot be underestimated. You needed all the powers of your personality just to survive.*

The meaning of "personality" preoccupied many of the religious philosophers of the so-called Russian religious renaissance that took place in the two decades before the Bolshevik Revolution, and that was rediscovered by the 1960s generation after the collapse of Stalinism. Nikolai Berdyaev in particular, a thinker frequently cited as influential by interviewees, distinguished a mere individual (*individuum*, a foreign-loan word)—composed of separate, unintegrated parts—and a true personality—(*lichnost'*, from the Russian root *lik* for face, countenance, icon, or assembly), which is whole and free. According to Berdyaev:

> Personality . . . is a spiritual, a religious, category. Personality says that man belongs not only to the sociological and natural order but to another

plane of being, the spiritual. . . . Personality in general does not belong to the realm of natural law: it cannot be ranked in the hierarchy of the natural. It is rooted in the realm of the spirit. Its existence presupposes the dualism of spirit and nature, freedom and determinism, the individual and the social, the kingdom of God and that of Caesar.[13]

For the intelligentsia of the 1960s, who could easily read "Stalin" for "Caesar,"[14] the assertion of personality seemed especially crucial. One Jewish Christian of the 60s generation recalled his need for, as Father Michael had said, "the power to stay yourself," as we sat in the kitchen of my rented apartment in Jerusalem, sharing tea and *hamentaschen* on the Jewish holiday of Purim. This well-educated engineer spoke with numerous pauses, and asked for specific questions, since he found it difficult to reconstruct his path to faith on his own. Eventually, he revealed a search for self, for personality, at once deeper and more basic than even Berdyaev would claim:

> *I was driven by neither philosophy nor spirituality. . . . I would rather say that it was just something in my soul. There was no quick turnaround. Living in the Soviet Union, and always being bothered by the constant lie, you had the sensation that there must be a great deal that they are simply hiding. I was led to a sense of readiness, readiness to believe in something else. I didn't know what that something was, but the readiness was there.*

Speaking of Jewish intellectuals in general, Simon Markish, son of the Soviet Yiddish writer Peretz Markish who was murdered in Stalin's antisemitic campaign of 1952, wrote: "In describing such a person we should begin with the chief characteristic of Soviet man, which is his lack of any ideology." This lack is magnified for Soviet Jews: "Thus in the case of the Soviet Jew, the general mental vacuum is being supplemented and intensified by a powerful sense of rootlessness, precisely the complex named by Simone Weil as *deracinement*."[15] Ironically, the rootlessness of which Markish wrote, and which provided the interviewee just quoted with a "readiness" for belief in Orthodox Christianity, was at the base of Stalin's antisemitic campaign; Soviet Jews were accused of being "rootless cosmopolitans."

Jewish and Christian dissent did not initially feel so far apart. As Father Michael remembered: *My Jewish awareness started to grow around 1968. I was networking. From the same underground came the dissident movement and the Zionist movement. Discussions would take place in the same house. But the two movements had already split apart by the end of the sixties. I didn't hide the fact that I went to church. For those Jews in those days the fact that we were Christians was not an issue. Most of them had been in Stalin's camps. Christians were not enemies. They were all allies. In those days we were a minority of outcasts.*

Clearly, entrance into the Church was not a way for Father Michael to leave Judaism, or even Jewry. Indeed, he retained his Jewish name, and thus his tenuous connection to Golda Meir and the young Israeli state. Rather, it was a way to escape the "mental vacuum" of the Soviet Union at a time when physical emigration was impossible, a way to root oneself in a different, non-Soviet soil. He calls his choice "inner emigration." But if he was not leaving his Jewish roots, but rather looking to plant new ones where none had grown, why not become active in the synagogue, I wanted to know, as we sat in a small, windowless study in his darkened church on Manhattan's upper east side. I had come to speak with some of his parishioners one winter night after their Saturday evening service, and I then returned the next day for more interviews.

Father Michael speaks fluent English after many years in the United States, although with certain Russianisms that emerge, no doubt, from his memories: *Judaism almost did not exist. There was one synagogue* [in Moscow]. *And it was under the complete control of the state. The rabbi was afraid. It was not at all an option. It only became a possibility later in the seventies. Only with the possibility of Israel and the emigration. You have to realize that to be a Jew, or to be a Christian in those days, was the way of emigration. You don't participate in society. It is a way to leave Soviet society. So if you want to leave Soviet society, better to leave it for real. If you want to be a Jew, be a Jew outside of here. If you want to emigrate, where are you going to emigrate: inside or outside? In the sixties, there was no choice. To leave the Soviet Union was not an option. Just for some fearless freaks, just to jump in the ocean and swim somewhere.*

He laughed, perhaps at memories of acquaintances who did, indeed, take that freakish path.[16] *For me,* he continued, *as soon as I became a member of the Church, I entered the underground. My way was inner emigration.*

Yury Glazov, who participated with Father Michael in the turn toward religion in the sixties, wrote in his study of the post-Stalin Russian mentality: "Two striking phenomena are interwoven with the post-Stalinist development of the Russian intelligentsia: dissent and religious revival. . . . Stalin's death brought forth a very acute crisis in Soviet ideology and in the spiritual body of the nation as well."[17] But both Glazov and Father Michael, like a disproportionately large percentage of the "Russian" intelligentsia, were from Jewish backgrounds. The question still remains: Why did these Jews in search of a spiritual personality choose Russian Orthodoxy rather than Judaism?

In retrospect, a once-active Jewish Christian I call Yura believed that Jews *did* seek Judaism at the same time as Jews began to enter the post-Stalinist Church, although the numbers were quite small. Why was the latter phenomenon more compelling for him and others of his cohort? Maybe it was more available, he offered.

Anton, a Jewish professor who was friendly in the 1960s and 70s with many of the Jewish and non-Jewish intellectuals who joined the Church, doubted how much actual religious fervor these newly baptized Christians felt. About the poet Alexander Galich, he stated confidently that *it was* not *a question of Jesus Christ*.[18] About Nadezhda Mandelstam, the wife of the famous poet Osip Mandelstam, he claimed that she joined the Church *"in case" there is an after life,* but that *she had little connection to Judaism* to begin. For his part, the Russian-Jewish–once-Christian Israeli scholar Mikhail Agursky felt: "I simply had no Jewish alternative."[19]

"IT WAS EASIER TO BE ORTHODOX"

Judith, an elderly Russian Jew who lived through the late-Stalin and post-Stalin years, but who had never considered baptism, offered this explanation as she shook her head in mild disapproval: *It was "easier" to be Orthodox than to be Jewish. Perhaps even their grandfathers and their grandmothers themselves were unable to explain Judaism to them.* Judith's words echo those of an anonymous Jewish émigré inscribed in the Wiener Oral History Collection, a typescript deposited in the Jewish Division of the New York Public Library: ". . . it's easier to become religious in an [Russian] Orthodox way. Just because it's widespread and besides it's connected with the author Solzhenitsyn. It's [a] kind of cult or something . . . the tendency is to get some kind of religion. In a sense it's organizationally easier to do that. They do it. And besides Jewish religion demands more from you. . . . You must observe it, you know. It's easier to go to an Orthodox Church than to observe Judaism."[20]

Indeed, many Russian Jews never had any overt exposure to Judaism at all. A surprising number of those I interviewed began their narratives by saying that there was no "Jewish," that is, specifically religious *(iudeiskii),* feeling in their childhood homes. Nonetheless, many did relate early memories of a family connection to Jewish life *(evreistvo)*. For some, as for the young Elena, the connection was through Yiddish: *My grandparents spoke Yiddish, but it was lost by the time I was born. Still, I love Yiddish songs. I used to play them on my guitar for my Russian friends.* For others, childhood memories revealed the remnants of religious ritual, now meaningless to the young generation. Several described a grandfather or great-grandfather, with tattered prayer shawl and muttered blessings: *I come from a good Jewish family, a correct Jewish family,* Marina described her background as we talked in her kitchen, the makings of the evening's supper on the oilcloth-covered table between us.

> *I had a great-grandfather, who was ninety-three years old when he died. And I was seven. We spent a lot of time together. He loved me very much, and he was a man of faith* [veruiushchii]. *And now as I look back on it and can evaluate from this perspective, he was a righteous person. . . . He was kind and good and bright. He spoke Russian poorly, with a strong accent and with mistakes. He talked just like a character from a Jewish joke. . . . I remember these images from childhood. When he would pray, he would wear a* tallis, *and I would sit by the table and grab onto the fringes. That was my childhood pastime. He was a real, authentic Orthodox Jew. I remember very well how he would lie with me on the couch and tell me stories from the Bible and Jewish history. . . . When he told the stories, you had the feeling that he was telling stories about one of our relatives. That was the beginning of the 1950s. I am forty-three years old. . . . So, that was the time of the campaign against cosmopolitanism. . . . The hardest years for Jewish families, Jewish intellectuals, for Jewish medical families. My mother was a medic* [and thus at risk from Stalin's antisemitic actions concerning the Doctor's Plot].

These words spilled forth in a dark kitchen in the heart of Moscow, as their bearer—herself now a grandmother—chopped vegetables from the market. Was it the onions or the memories, I wondered, that provoked her tears? The subject was delicate, and I could only probe so far.

For some, however, these memories are not so warm. Felix Svetov writes in his *Opyt biografii* (Attempt at a Biography) that once his grandfather became terminally ill, his aunts organized a prayer *minyan* for him at their home: "Thirty or forty old men and women would fill up the house, toot on their tooters and shout gutturally. I was used to bringing friends home, . . . but here would be my grandfather, wrapped in his prayer shawl, muttering prayers. And my friends would ogle. So I stopped inviting them home, making up reasons why they couldn't come." For Svetov, with only negative feelings for this archaic ritual, the Jew who came to lay out the body of his late grandfather was archetypically "old, ugly, and dirty."[21]

Despite Russian Jews' scattered childhood memories, whether warm or embarrassing, a real connection to *iudeiskie* roots was lost for the post-Stalin generation. Father Michael explained:

> At that time, Judaism was not an issue at all. It simply wasn't practiced. It was repressed, or abandoned by the majority of Russian Jews who had entered the mainstream of Soviet life. Part of my Jewish family was very much assimilated. Assimilated within the Soviet structure. Soviet, not just Russian. Of course, many of their friends were Jewish. There was a sense of a Jewish community. There was a sense of Jewishness even without Judaism. But it was a life within the secular structure; in their own memory of Judaism, there were no religious overtones. My grandmother on my father's side was the granddaughter of a rabbi, and actually the grand-granddaughter of a great rabbi of Lithuania, who is mentioned in the Russian-Jewish Encyclopedia. But in her memory, Jewishness was more a sense of a way of life and of community, rather than anything religious. Or maybe it was just the loss of memory. When people secularize, they don't really remember.

Another interviewee admitted: *I grew up in an entirely atheist family. Nonbelievers. We had absolutely no traditions. Not Orthodox and not Judaic. We didn't even have Yiddish. An average Soviet upbringing.* It was this Russian Jew, Viktor, who had created some confusion among Latvian Jewish children in his new Riga neighborhood, as quoted in the introduction. He looked "Jewish." He probably even sounded "Jewish." But was he "Jewish" in the eyes of other Jews? Ultimately, what was the mark of his Jewish identity, if his family retained no Yiddish, no Hebrew, and decidedly no Judaism? He, himself, did not know.

Baptism for this generation was therefore not a conversion out of Judaism *(iudaizm)* at all, for they no longer had any connection to the Jewish religion. Rather, entrance into the Church meant departure out of Soviet ideology, or, rather, from the lack of ideology, from the "mental vacuum" of Soviet society. As Father Michael explained:

> In the beginning, the sense of spiritual emptiness after Stalin gave birth to both the political dissident movement and the religious question of the intelligentsia. The background was common. If we take the theocratic or ideocratic

communistic society of Stalin and the post-Stalin period, it had so much of perverse religion in it, that, when you leave, you look for any kind of religious substitute. You don't just walk out of it into secular liberalism. There would just be no way to get to it. Well, some people did, like [Andrei] *Sakharov, later, or Boris Shragin* [quoted previously]. *But for me and some others, it was a search for religious foundation, for spiritual foundation to get out of this system. . . . For me, I would say that my conversion helped save me from becoming a political terrorist.*

Another Jewish Christian spoke to me not of real incarceration, but of a *spiritual prison* in which the intelligentsia was trapped, and Glazov similarly compared "the life of the lie" lived by all thinking Soviet citizens to a "cellar":

After Stalin's death and especially after the brutal suppression of the Hungarian Revolution in 1956, many persons both old and young underwent a deep intellectual and spiritual crisis. All dreams of radical changes in society vanished. Life seemed meaningless and joyless. . . . One's own soul seemed a cellar which had not been washed or cleaned for ages and was full of cobwebs. The everyday need to lie, both in public and to one's self, drained life's resources and it seemed that the very air of the society had been woven into a lie.[22]

For the Russian Jews of this generation, who came to maturity in the decade following Stalin's death, and who felt trapped in Soviet society at a time before or only at the start of the emigration of the 1970s, the Church presented one of the few possibilities for escape from the cellar-like incarceration of their spiritual lives. They had no Judaism, so that entrance into the Church did not feel like a betrayal of an earlier religious identity. Baptism came to seem an almost logical step in the midst of an illogical and empty world.

THE POST-STALINIST "MISSIONARY TO THE JEWS"

Besides "inner emigration" from Soviet cynicism, a second, and equally powerful theme recurred in the interviews of the generation of Jews that was baptized in the pre-perestroika period: the influence of the charismatic Father Alexander Men'. Born a Jew, trained as a scientist, Men' came to represent for these Jewish intellectuals the best of all worlds. Once, when I had attempted to meet Father Alexander in the late 1980s,

I was told that he had become a "stadium figure," who could speak to whole crowds but, likely, not to me. At least one devotee has called him the "Soviet Billy Graham."[23] After Men's death, another follower wrote: "hundreds of people considered themselves his spiritual children. Thousands of people considered themselves his friends. I consider myself to be one of those thousands." Further, "It is impossible to count how many people the hands, the words, or the books of Father Alexander brought to the Church, to a meeting with Christ."[24] The popular preacher did, however, still have time for private interviews, as evidenced by the numerous ones he gave once glasnost had freed up his ability to speak broadly, and, certainly, he continued his individual spiritual counseling of parishioners and nonparishioners alike, despite his "stadium" appeal. Unfortunately, I was never able to reach him personally before his shocking murder in 1990.

The emphasis on Men' in the following pages does not mean to imply that he was the sole spiritual guide for the generation that came to faith in the 1960s. We have already heard about the influence of Father Dmitry Dudko on Svetov, for example, and Glazov places special importance on the popular work of Fathers Nikolay Eshliman and Gleb Yakunin for the "rebirth of the Russian intelligentsia" as a whole, which he examines in his book *Tesnye vrata* (Narrow Gates).[25] Men', however, had a consistent and enduring influence on the 1960s generation of newly baptized Jews, an influence, as we will see, that continued into the next generation. Furthermore, his name appears on the dedication page of a number of books by Russian and Russian Jewish scholars now in emigration. It is probably no exaggeration to consider him one of the shaping influences of an entire generation of Soviet and émigré specialists who helped bring contemporary Russian culture to the West.

Almost all the subjects interviewed for this study mention Men', describing either a meeting with him, the importance of his writings, or participation in a society established in his name. In 1997 I was able to attend a conference that is organized in Moscow every year on the anniversary of his death. Despite the official arrest of ordinary "hooligans" accused of his murder, most say today that the popular priest was killed by antisemites, probably ordered from within the Church. Participants in the conference were encouraged to make a chartered pilgrimage to his church and gravesite in Novaia Derevnia, and to his final home and the place of his murder in the village of Semkhoz. I for one was singularly unprepared for the intensity of feeling on the part of the mourners who walked along the flower-strewn path on the way to Men's grave, already seven years after his death. And I could not imagine how over three thousand worshipers had gathered at the small church to accompany Men's body on its last journey. The Moscow conference is not the only one held in his honor, so that Father Alexander's influence continues in the scholarly as well as spiritual sphere. In addition, his followers are becoming politically active, with one priest of his former circle holding a seat in the Duma in the 1990s.

It is possible that the figure of Men' explains in part the strongly Moscow-centered nature of the movement of Russian Jews into the Church. Although Jewish intellectuals did become Christians in other cities of the Soviet Union—I interviewed some from Riga, St. Petersburg, Kiev—the social contact with acquaintances traveling the same path and the personal influence of Men' all contributed to form a nucleus precisely in the capital. Even those living in other Soviet cities spoke to me of traveling to Moscow to attend Men's services or to speak with him at his church or in his home. The group of acquaintances was tight.

It is another question altogether what has become of these close friendships in the past thirty years. I honored subjects' requests for anonymity by not revealing their names to one another, but if I knew that two were acquainted, I would mention the other to learn more of their interactions or, sometimes, to open doors of communication by "proving" that I was already connected in the network. The proof often backfired, however, and my mention of a name would be met with silence or an angry, *Hmm, I don't know what has happened to him. . . .* The period of religious awakening was an intense time for most of these Jewish Christians, and ideological stances—not always religiously based—can ultimately divide as much as unite. *I don't keep up with so-and-so,* I would hear. *I don't know where she goes to church now. Or if she goes to church.* One well-known couple has split up, for personal reasons to be sure, but accompanied by recriminations about the betrayal of Christ, and worse. I bring this observation up now not to judge the changing patterns in Soviet and post-Soviet friendships, but rather to highlight the intensity with which the subjects of this study approached their lives in the period under investigation. Such intensity cannot always be sustained. When it was, however, it was often in the name of the personable, but equally intense Father Alexander Men'.

Alexander Men' (called Alik by his friends) was born in 1935 in the Soviet Union at the outset of Stalin's Terror, to two Jewish parents. Together with her sister, Men's mother became attracted to Christianity as a young adult, and had both herself and her infant son secretly baptized by a catacomb priest shortly after her son's birth.[26] She later baptized her second son as well. The young Alik, apparently quite precocious, felt drawn to religion throughout his childhood. His father, Vol'f Men', never entered the Church, and remained "a fiery Jew and even a Zionist, even prepared to give lessons in Hebrew."[27] Jewish identity was by no means absent from the Men' household or from the early education of the Men' boys. An acquaintance recently confessed to me how Alik's brother Pavel led the first Passover seder to which he had ever been invited, and Father Michael related this paradoxical story of Men's childhood:

> *He always had a strong sense of his Jewish roots. Actually he told me an interesting story, quite a paradoxical one. He told me that he remembered the day when the state of Israel was born and he named a particular date in 1948. His mother, who was by then a member of the canonical Church, had been very active in the Russian Zionist movement in the 1920s, when some of her friends managed to emigrate. But she stayed in Russia and married. His father, who never became a Christian, was always part of the Russian Jewish community. He was very much in love with his wife and he so to speak suffered her Christianity without really understanding what was going on. That was his "cross to bear." Nevertheless, Alik Men' was thirteen years old, a bar mitzvah boy, when Israel came into existence, and he told me: "I was terribly concerned with how I could contribute to the cause of Jewish survival. So I decided something very strange. Okay, I decided, I'll become a priest." And that very day he went to enter Moscow Theological Seminary. Obviously, he was not accepted; he was only thirteen years old. A boy. That was just about the time after the war that the Seminary was reorganized* [and the year the somewhat older Dmitry Dudko completed the Seminary and entered the graduate Academy, only to be arrested]. *So it is interesting that he connected the two things this way. It is obviously a bizarre way of thinking. But I remember this story that he told.*

Father Michael explained this odd logic somewhat more rationally in his short article, "The Life and Work of Father Men'":

Men' thought that if Jesus is the Messiah of Israel, the time for the people of Israel to acknowledge Him as such will eventually come. The emergence of the Jewish state was a sign. Living in diaspora, the Jews had to preserve their identity. The walls of uncompromising rabbinical

Judaism were absolutely necessary for the preservation of the people's existence. With the restoration of the Jewish state, the danger of assimilation would eventually disappear. The people, liberated internally from the fear of losing their national identity, would become ready to look at what Men' considered the earliest Jewish legacy—the New Testament. At this point the need for Jewish priests and preachers of the Gospel would be felt.[28]

The double "chosenness" of the Russian Jewish Christians apparently tied them tightly to Israel's ancient past as well as to its future. We will find arguments similar to the one Father Michael described above in chapter 5 of this book, although expressed with considerably less optimism. As we will see, some interviewees of this opinion feel that the time may be right to bring Jesus' teaching to the Jews because of the current instability, rather than security, of identity in contemporary Israel.

Father Michael continued in our interview to discuss Father Alexander Men's relationship to his Jewish roots: *He was very much aware of the Jewish roots; he paid attention to it in his writings, and also in his scholarly works. He once told me that he had his own files of various Jews in history who had chosen Christianity. So he was building some sort of tradition for himself.*

Avraham, who also knew Men' personally, remembered that *when you would speak with him, you would feel his Jewish character strongly.* This statement felt awfully close to pronouncements by antisemites, and I probed further. "How does one *feel* a Jewish character?" I asked. *He was a clear representative of the Jewish people. By his appearance.* (Agursky writes that "externally, he had the appearance of an orthodox rabbi.")[29] *By his humor. His view of life. He was a spiritual man, but very practical. That was obvious. You understand. Besides that, he was not indifferent to the Jewish people, as a Jew. Solovyov could feel that way as a Russian. But Men' felt it as a Jew. And he had a feeling for Israel as well. When you read his books, you will be surprised how a man who had never been here could have such a feeling for Israel. How he felt for the Jewish religion as though he had received his education within it. That is how he writes about it.*

By all accounts, Men's attraction to study began very early. As Father Michael told me: *He became aware of what he was going to do in his life when he was nine or ten years old. He started to write his first book,* The Son of Man, *when he was thirteen.* He would hide in a corner of his family's one-room apartment to read after his family had retired, and before they arose in the morning. According to a short biography in English: "By thirteen he was reading Kant. Soon after, by chance or providence, he came across the works of the exiled Russian religious philosophers and at the age of fifteen he found a copy of a book by Vladimir Solovyev [*sic*] in the flea market and began a life-long admiration for that visionary thinker."[30] Father Michael called Solovyov, to whom Men' dedicated his major seven-volume series, the Soviet priest's "primary teacher," and claimed that "[w]hat Solov'ev did as a philosopher, Fr. Men' attempted to demonstrate as a cultural historian of religion."[31] In general, Men's reading was voracious, encompassing works on Catholicism, the Church Fathers, the classical world, and the East. He claimed to know all of Dante's *Divine Comedy* by heart, and to reread it several times a year to keep his memory fresh.[32] And he followed the entire course of the seminary on his own before he turned eighteen.

There is absolutely no reason to doubt young Alik's precocity either in the spiritual or intellectual realm, and, certainly, an examination of his adult writings reveals an intellect of both depth and breadth. I myself saw his library, which included huge numbers of volumes on religious and secular history in a variety of languages. The frequent assertions in memoirs about Alik's early calling, however, say as much about the attitude of his fervent followers as they do about the actual prodigy himself, for it is a typical formula in the genre of a Saint's Life *(zhitie)* to assert that the young child had an unusual attraction toward books and learning. Father Men's figure was so attractive, and his end so abrupt, that it is perhaps to be expected that memories of him begin to take the shape of sainthood.[33]

Father Alexander Men' had a significant influence on at least two generations of atheist intellectuals. Perhaps with a bit of an overstatement, Richard Harries, the Bishop of Oxford, wrote: "His ambition was nothing less than fundamentally to shift the whole atheistic ideology of the Soviet intelligentsia."[34] With the right approach, this was not too difficult, for, as Glazov reminds us, "One has to live the life of an atheist for years—in one's maturity—to appreciate religion and its benefits."[35] Men' had that approach; as more than one interviewee admitted: *Men' opened the Church for people like me. For intellectuals, for youth, for Jews. And he kept it open as long as he lived.* Sadly, *it is precisely that he kept it open for too many that he was killed, you know.* In an obituary written shortly after the murder of the priest, Agursky called him a "passionate missionary, [who] tried to attract everyone to Christianity, but especially Jews. . . . For this, he was hated by many Russians as well as very many Jews."[36] Father Michael confers in his essay "The Life and Work of Father Men'": "The conservative Orthodox accused him of destroying the Russian church by being too ecumenical and tolerant toward other Christian confessions and other religions. Being an ethnic Jew, he also provoked open hatred among extreme Russian nationalist and fascist groups. Some zealots within Russian Orthodox quarters slandered him as a crypto-Catholic or a crypto-Jew."[37]

The hatred took some time to build, for Men' kept a fairly low profile in his early dealings with the Church.[38] His first interactions were with so-called catacomb priests who had not gone into exile, but did not recognize the Church hierarchy after 1927, when Metropolitan Sergii issued a declaration of loyalty to the Soviet state. His mother and he were part of the small circle of intellectuals around an even smaller handful of like-thinking priests who remained free of Stalin's Gulag. As a student, Men' continued his secular studies along with his religious education, and applied for entrance to the university in 1953. He was denied admission, however, because of his Jewish background, and instead entered the Institute of Fur in Moscow, later relocated to Irkutsk. Ironically, he was then denied permission to complete his studies at the Institute not because of his Jewishness, but because of his Christian activities.

Felix Svetov wrote of a similar paradox of discrimination in his semi-autobiographical novel *Otverzi mi dveri* (Open the Doors for Me). At this point in the narrative, the main character, a baptized Russian Jew, has just been fired from his job by his Jewish boss. When the boss questions his seemingly flippant response to the firing, the Jewish Christian answers:

> [I smile because] I remember that I have heard these same words once before, in the fifties on Sakhalin [in the Far East], when I was driven out of the press. And driven out because I, like you, am a Jew. Only then they drove me out because I am a Jew, and now they drive me out because I am an Orthodox Christian. And it was the same kind of press then and now, loyal to the Party, like our Constitution. It is amusing, isn't it?[39]

Men's followers among Jewish Christians assert that Jewish concerns continued to occupy Father Alexander after ordination in 1960, although he never wrote extensively about Judaism or the Jews. And there is disagreement among the testimony of interviewees about his feeling toward *aliya* to Israel. Some say he encouraged them to emigrate, others that he wished he could himself, still others that he never considered living in the Jewish state.

Following ordination, Father Men' first served in Alabino, about fifty kilometers outside of Moscow, and then in several other parishes in the Moscow region, during which time he graduated from the Leningrad Seminary (by correspondence) and received his master's in theology from the Moscow Theological Academy. He was installed in a large church in Tarasovka, just to the north of the capital, but in the late 1960s was removed to a humble wooden church in Novaia Derevnia, his last parish.[40] Moscow intellectuals, among them many Jews, continued to come to his church, sometimes out of curiosity, and later out of conviction.

Father Michael first went to see Father Men' at Tarasovka on a whim:

It was Easter night. I never had been to Alik's church before. Instead, I had been planning to go to some kind of wild party in Moscow. There was supposed to be drugs, and everything. And I had a bottle of vodka in my pocket. I had almost arrived at the party when something asked me, "Why are you going there? You already know what will happen. Why not try to go to an Easter service?" I had never been before, but I vaguely remembered that Alik's church was in Tarasovka. So I turned around in the Moscow subway and went to the Iaroslavsky train station. I was riding this train and didn't even know where the stop was. Then all of a sudden, when the train stopped at a particular station, I saw that the whole compartment got up and went out. I realized that they were probably going to this church service, so I followed the crowd. And it turned out that they walked through a field, and I saw this huge cathedral in the middle of nowhere. When I arrived, I saw it was full of people. I still had this bottle of vodka showing out of my pocket, and I had another thought: "Why did I come here?" It was so stupid and strange. And I decided to turn away. But just as I decided to turn, all of a sudden I saw Mikhail Agursky. He came out and said, "Oh, it's good you came. Let me take you to the choir loft. You'll see everything from there." So he took me by the hand, and brought me to the choir loft, from where I observed the whole service.

Agursky, whose father had been a major Jewish activist, was himself quite active in Men's circle at the time. He left the Soviet Union in 1975 after several years of refusal, however, already a scholar of both the Church and the Jews, and was offered a position as research associate at Hebrew University. According to his widow, Vera, he gradually distanced himself from the Church and was circumcised after coming to Israel. Vera, who is

Russian, was converted to Judaism about five years after settling in Israel, as were their son and daughter somewhat later. Even Agursky's Russian mother-in-law was converted to Judaism in Israel before her death. Vera discussed with me in an interview in May of 1998 that she felt a connection between national and religious identity, and thought that she should be "Jewish" *(iudeika)* in Israel. As for Agursky, he never rejected the *Church part of his life*, Vera claimed, while showing me numerous photographs of metropolitans and priests together with Melik, as his friends called him. But his published memoirs, *Pepel Klaasa* (Klaas's ashes), contain no mention of his baptism.[41]

Agursky's widow informed me that the editor of the memoirs removed all references to Church activities from the published version, although there had been quite a lot. In the afterword to the memoirs, however, the editor, Mikhail Gorelik, who had been a close friend of Agursky both in his youthful "Christian" period and his later "Jewish" one, asserts that the author, himself, excluded those references. As Gorelik wrote to me in private correspondence:

> I'm glad that you managed to get a copy of Melik's book. I once worked a fair bit on the manuscript. As for the Christian subject matter, it had already been carefully purged from the text by the author himself. (Why? is a separate question.) Still, certain fragments, of course, remain. A reader in the know will surely catch them. But the editor (that is, me) didn't specially remove them for any ideological considerations. Vera is not correct in that.
>
> It is different question that yet another manuscript existed on which the author had performed his subsequent surgical exercises. There the Christian theme has an important place. I must add that I found out about the existence of that (original) manuscript only when work on the book was already finished. The fact that it was finished delivered me from a moral dilemma: Should I take the full text, or should I fulfill the unambiguous desire of the author (although that desire was determined, most likely, by situational considerations)? That is the history of the book.

The omitted segments have been published only recently, following his premature death and presumably after the resolution of those "situational considerations" (his position at Hebrew University? his status as an *oleh*? his spiritual and/or intellectual distance from the Church?).

The newly published "Christian" sections reinforce the themes I heard in virtually all the narratives I collected from the generation of the 1960s, and not only the association with Men'. Agursky writes of a "spiritual thirst," as well as of, as we have seen, his entrance into the Church through Solovyov, Berdyaev, and other religious philosophers, who "came to his aid," and of his original distance from Judaism. "Other Jews who were searching found themselves in the same position. . . . I accepted faith not from people, who could have instilled in me confessional differences. I accepted it from Scripture itself, which contained no distinction between believing Jews *(iudei)* and those who had not yet taken on the new faith. . . . Torn from Jewish tradition, I had no conception of the fact that a Jewish religious alternative existed." Perhaps most poignantly, "I heard even about [Martin] Buber first through [Father Pavel] Florensky."[42]

Agursky died in 1991 in a hotel room in Moscow, where he had gone in an attempt to recover the body of his son who had tragically died on a mountain-climbing expedition in the mountains of the Soviet Union. As Vera confirmed, however, and I had suspected, Agursky had also gone to Russia this last time to investigate the unsolved murder one year earlier of his spiritual mentor, Father Men'.

Men' was crucial for Agursky, despite his assertion that it was not personalities, but Scripture that brought him to Christianity. For better or for worse, Men's charismatic personality as well as his writings drew intellectuals to an Orthodox worldview.[43] Agursky recalled him as "intelligent, clever, and dynamic," and credited him with the fact that "I came out of my religious solitude."[44] In the course of his mission, Men' baptized Nadezhda Mandelstam, the wife of the famous poet, Osip Mandelstam, as well as the poet Alexander Galich (despite the fact that Svetov earlier recalls this baptism in the course of his discussion of Dudko), and many others. As one interviewee in Israel recalls of his early years of faith in the Soviet Union: *I went with my friend to meet with Alexander. Alexander made a very strong impression, as he does on everyone. . . . The first impulse was really from the person of Men'.*

Men's reach was extensive, thanks to his publications and the publications on religious philosophy that he encouraged. Another interviewee, Viktor, wanted to tell me about:

> *other influential books I was given, the books of Father Alexander Men'. I was, it is true, never his spiritual son, although I was acquainted with him. . . . More than the influence of Father Alexander himself, although he*

was a remarkable man, an extremely attractive person, but more influential were his books, which I read before I ever met him. They opened for me some sort of orientation along the religious path of a human being. You could say they played an enlightening role for me. I can't say that I came to faith through his books. No. But they were a kind of religious enlightenment. Why? Perhaps because he writes simply, on the level where we found ourselves in those days. Of course we were completely untrained in religious history, and so forth. But it isn't only a question of simplicity. I was very close to his sort of universal point of view. Ecumenism. That was very interesting for me.

The recurring theme of his books underlines what Men' meant for his new flock. This generation of intellectuals had only forbidden books to connect them to a life that they had never known before the Revolution, or a life beyond the closed borders of the USSR. Books, particularly of poetry, fiction, and philosophy, took on a kind of sacred status, an otherworldly voice from beyond the grave, or prison, of Soviet society. Men's voice revealed for the intelligentsia, including many in the Jewish intelligentsia, the relationship between the word and The Word, between the knowledge they loved and a religious experience that had been absent for decades. And the spiritual word he brought them, as Viktor stressed above, was couched in the language of inclusiveness and universalism.

Father Men's ecumenical message attracted a number of Jewish intellectuals who may have otherwise felt excluded, especially since the Eastern Christian Churches are distinguished nationally: The *Russian* Orthodox Church, the *Greek* Orthodox Church, the *Serbian* Orthodox Church. But it was not just a question of universalism in Men's outlook that drew his university-educated audience. Jewish engineers, historians, and mathematicians were also attracted by Men's readiness to build a bridge between the Church and secular society, between science and religion: "This idea of dialogue with the world has stuck with me all my life," wrote the Jewish priest.[45]

A Jewish Christian with an advanced degree in history admitted: *I was influenced very much by a meeting I had with Father Alexander Men', and now I believe that probably without him I would not have been able to enter into work in the Church. . . . He amazed me as very much a thinking person. You see, I am an historian. And I saw that he, a priest, was much more aware, much more knowledgeable in all walks of history than was I.*

I also knew Father Men' at that time, recalled Felix. *He was a very free person. I would go to his services quite a lot, and was at marriages where he officiated. And I was at his home. And I even helped him baptize a number of people.*

Yet another member of the late Soviet intelligentsia, a writer, remembered the following about the period of her closest contact with Father Men':

> *Alexander Men' was unbelievably important for Moscow Jews. At the deafest, most difficult period, morally and religiously speaking, he was very attractive, and a huge number of Jews who in a healthy society would have used their so-to-speak Judaic energies—cultural and religious—would have felt themselves absolutely natural in the synagogue, they took on Christianity with Father Alexander out of simple spiritual thirst. Potentially, they were not his flock. Under different circumstances, Jews who would have been attracted to Judaism. . . . But Father Alexander simply received a flock that otherwise he might not have received. He had a huge quantity of young Jews that weren't destined to him, but for whom he built a wonderful life. Those people, who are already grown now, fifty years old, the children of Men's first work, it is a marvelous generation. In the second half of the twentieth century in Russia there were two such charismatic figures, comparable because of their influence, although in different spheres: Alexander Solzhenitsyn and Alexander Men'. . . . For the structure of our generation, not of the generation in general, of people who are cut off from culture, from true society—Alexander Men' played a colossal role. He was an apostle in the full meaning of that word. He continues to grow. A huge role.*

Recognizing this "apostolic" role for the intelligentsia, we can now see how it fits into the recurring themes for the generation of the 1960s. The Jewish intellectuals who came of age after Stalin's death experienced a spiritual thirst for something beyond Soviet reality (thus explaining the personal questions about my belief as late as in the end of the 1970s). In addition, they felt the lack of Judaism as an alternative (despite, and we will return to this, an acute sense of their "Jewishness"). And, finally, they experienced the personal and intellectual influence of Father Alexander Men'.[46] In some ways, then, this is a topic not about Jews, nor about Christians, but about the post-Stalin Soviet Union and the Soviet intelligentsia.[47] Sergei Averintsev, a well-known Russian intellectual called Men' "the man sent from God to be missionary to the wild tribe of the Soviet intelligentsia."[48] For the Soviet Abkhazian writer Fazil Iskander,

"He was Light."[49] For Nikita Struve, director of YMCA-Press in Paris, he was an "Apostle."[50]

The tribe to which Averintsev refers, comprised of both Jews and non-Jews, was ready for Men'. As the journalist Masha Gessen states somewhat cynically about the attraction of the Church in the 1970s in her book about the Russian intelligentsia: "With the generation of people who came of age in a religious state dying out, with religion consistently denounced by all official institutions, the once-powerful Church was well and firmly marginalized, which meant it also attained a certain romantic allure for the intelligentsia."[51] Glazov claimed that: "before the revolution, the Church and the intelligentsia lived in different eras, and could not possibly understand each other." The next generation of intelligentsia, however, witnessed Stalin's atrocities toward the Church and saw the murder of thousands of priests, which bestowed upon the latter a kind of martyrdom. A new life for the intelligentsia, however, did not truly begin until after the death of Stalin in 1953, with the first "flow of lava" with the writing of *Doctor Zhivago,* and the first signs of "pain and insult" emerging from the funeral of Boris Pasternak in 1960, himself a Jew who was attracted to the Orthodox Church.[52]

This story is also part and parcel of the study of the 1960s generation in America and throughout most of the Western world: the generation gap, political awakening, antiwar protests. Note Father Michael's several mentions of the drug culture that was pulling him in, even in the repressive Soviet 60s. Young Soviet intellectuals were particularly disturbed by the invasion of Czechoslovakia in 1968, coming on the heels of the internal suppression of dissident activity, the latter epitomized by the prominent trials of the writers Iuly Daniel and Andrey Siniavsky in 1966. As in the West, the Soviet 60s also saw a rebirth of spirituality. Young Jewish American intellectuals in the late 1960s and early 70s turned to transcendental meditation. They entered ashrams. They became JUBUs, like the counter-culture poet Allen Ginsberg. And some went to Israel. The Yom Kippur War of 1973 drew American recruits whose Zionism grew at least in part from a protest against their own bourgeois, and, some felt, spiritually or ideologically empty upbringing. My own protest took a few more years to flare up, but my husband, thankfully missing the draft and Vietnam by a year, took up transcendental meditation in high school in 1971, and seriously considered leaving college for the crucible of war in the "holy land" in 1973.

For their part, young Soviet Jews of the 1960s, dissatisfied with the world around and within them, had little to choose from but "inner emigration" in the Orthodox Church. Only later did Judaism become an option. And real emigration. In the meantime, Men's influence was electric.

As we conclude this section on Father Alexander Men', it is worth remembering what Father Michael had said about his own early years in the Church: *From the same underground came the dissident movement and the Zionist movement. Discussions would take place in the same house. . . . I didn't hide the fact that I went to church. For those Jews in those days the fact that we were Christians was not an issue. Most of them had been in Stalin's camps. Christians were not enemies. They were all allies. In those days we were a minority of outcasts.* Indeed, all the dissident groups began small and largely united. Vladimir Kormer's thinly disguised autobiographical novel, *Nasledstvo* (Legacy, in which "Melik" represents one of the first baptized Jews of this generation, Felix Karelin, and the young Father Michael, before his emigration and ordination, also has his part), describes the days and nights of heated debate in intellectual circles about Christianity and Russianness, about Judaism and Jewishness, about the Soviet Union and the West, and about young people of the time who flirted with the line between sanity and madness, between dissidence and danger. The outcome of the discussions was by no means preordained; the direction their dissident energies would take was not yet mapped out.

A Zionist from the time, Alexander Voronel', made an astute, but ironic comment about the Soviet dissident community: "The authorities themselves hastened to accuse the first dissidents of Zionism (thus showing them the way), when almost none of them had yet entertained such ideas."[53] Again, the result of the questioning of Soviet society and the search for meaning beyond the vapidity of Soviet reality that provoked the generation of the 1960s was not written in advance. Some Jews in the very early dissident movement began to investigate Zionism, although in some cases this was done in conjunction with interest in the Orthodox Church as an outlet for spiritual yearnings in the early to mid-1960s. Benjamin Pinkus, who researched the *hazara bitshuva* (return to Judaism) movement in the late Soviet period, asserts that "the young Jews who had played an important role in the Zionist movement in Moscow and other cities, such as Roman Rutman, Nathan Feingold, and Yeshayahu Averbuch," were also associated with the group of Jews who explored entrance into the Church. He quotes Rutman: "Many of my friends began to be baptized around this time. There was a neo-Christian movement afoot, and I myself was on the brink of being baptized."[54] This statement recalls a similar one quoted early by Yuly Edelshtein, the former Israeli Minister of Absorption. These men and women shared their questions openly, they shared their fear and sometimes the reality of prison camps and insane asylums because of their dissidence. Ultimately their paths began to diverge. Some, like Sakharov and Shragin, mentioned earlier, took the uncertain road of Western liberal ideals. Others became ardent Zionists. A very few "returned," ardently, to Judaism.[55] But, as we have seen, another important group of Jewish intellectuals in the late 1960s and early 1970s chose baptism in the Orthodox Church.

CHAPTER FOUR

The Path of Faith

The 1980s Generation

༄

I didn't understand the land of Israel, the people of Israel. It all seemed like a museum to me. A reliquary. But when I came and had a look, I saw that the museum was alive. And it was not merely alive. It was so alive that all the other lands by comparison seemed a museum.

—Seryozha, Jerusalem 1998

When I read the Gospels, I understood what it meant to be a Jew. This was the first Jewish book that I ever read.

—Boris, Jerusalem 1998

You know Moses' story about the exodus from Egypt? It became my history.

—Anya, New York 1998

THE GENERATION THAT CAME to faith as the Soviet Union was falling apart had much in common with the previous generation. Many mentioned to me the influence of Father Men', and of gathering in clubs in his name. And like Father Michael and the others quoted in the previous chapter, Russian Jews who were baptized in the 1980s describe their entrance into the Church not as a conversion out of Judaism *(iudeistvo)*, and certainly not as a departure from Jewry *(evreistvo)*, but rather as a response to the emptiness and confinement of the Soviet society in which they were raised. According to one Russian Jew who was baptized in the late 1980s, and now lives in New York: *It was an intellectual path in the beginning. The soul demanded freedom. I felt confined.*

Soviet intellectuals sought any outlet for escape. The freedom-seeker quoted above did not turn immediately to the Russian Orthodox Church, but told me that, *It all started with the study of Eastern religions.* His wife conferred in a separate interview: *My husband began to look for some sort of experience, for a way to express himself, for some kind of out-of-reality experience. At the time, it was dangerous to practice Judaism. So he went through Buddhism before he came to Orthodoxy.* In fact, many Soviet intellectuals—like their American counterparts—"went through" an interest in Eastern culture. Because of commercial as well as political reasons, the East opened up to citizens of the Soviet Union before the West did, and I remember the otherwise dowdy mother of an acquaintance practicing yoga in the late 1970s, and buying herbal remedies in small brown bottles with Chinese lettering from the almost empty Soviet-style pharmacy on the corner.

Yet another interviewee, Seryozha, traveled the "Eastern path," in his case through Hinduism rather than Buddhism, before coming to Orthodoxy. I recognized the very palpable lasting effects as I interviewed him in his modest home office on the outskirts of Jerusalem, where he practices homeopathic medicine surrounded by herbs and manuals on Asian medical procedures. He spoke of his path calmly, but rhythmically, almost poetically. As he explained about this period of searching: *I didn't have any special revelations, except that something was implanted in my soul, a small inkling of the fact that there is something higher than man. Something that watches man. . . . And so I came to Hinduism.* He practiced yoga for about a year and a half. *I chanted a mantra. I felt something. And in general, I didn't hurry to get anywhere. It seemed to me like it was some sort of holiday concert. Precisely a concert. It will finish, the curtain will close, and the real play will begin.* And, apparently, the play did begin, for Seryozha ultimately moved out of what he called the "impersonal" stage: *What I began to have was the feeling of a meeting with the All-Transcendent One as with a person* (lichnost'). *That was already a different step. That was the principal thought I had. That "It" is a* lichnost'. *The All-Transcendent One is not a something, but a someone. And He somehow participates in history.*

The sense of a personal God in history moved this interviewee toward the God of the Bible. For him, it was a natural progression of faith toward Orthodoxy, *connected to the fate of the Jewish people, and the fate of the Church, which for me are identical.* In the words of the Buddhist-leaning interviewee quoted above, *To escape the Eastern path, I was baptized.*

The desire for a world that transcends mundane reality, and the look eastward for it, do not distinguish the two generations studied here, any more than they distinguish Soviet Jews from many young Americans. The question of Jewish emigration, however, weighed much more heavily on the 1980s generation of Soviet Jews than on the earlier one, and it is here that we must look now for distinctions. Because of the possibility, and in many cases the reality of their emigration, confrontation with their own Jewishness plays a much larger role in the narratives of faith of these younger interviewees.

Yury Glazov, writing in the 1980s, recognized the differences in the generations: "Soviet reality after the death of Stalin, with its broken religious compartmentalization, is characterized by the Christianization of Jews in Russia, especially among the younger generation. By the early 1970s, hundreds of them had joined the Russian Orthodox Church. It may be, however, that the Jewish exodus to Israel since that time has altered the situation."[1]

For most in the early days of Glazov's Christian life, immigration to Israel was little more than a theoretical question. Glazov began to ponder it for himself in the early 1970s. He wrote in 1971:

> The Jewish question intruded. Maybe it was a sort of temptation, but even I began to think about leaving. Is it worthwhile to speak out in a country where they don't consider you their own? Is it worthwhile to sacrifice yourself—together with your children and dear ones—in a place where you are an alien *(inorodets)*, and no one wants to listen to you? . . . I hung thus in the balance for three years. I had to leave Russia, where they wanted to kill me. And all the same, what would I do in the West? In Israel, I'd have to draw myself in and talk about the greatness of the Jewish people with my blood brothers, who despise the humble son of Mary of Bethlehem. Should I leave the Russian language, Russian culture, which has become my own? Should I give up that which belongs to me by right, just because it seems to some people that I have no direct connection to that culture? Should I begin to learn a language that my distant ancestors spoke? No, there is not a drop of nationalism in me. Will I not be able to become like some wild Muslim, who suspects everyone else is an infidel? No, no, no.[2]

As though answering Glazov's questions in absentia, Father Michael described for me the first "convention" of a group of about fifteen Russian Jewish Christians, with a kind of retrospective chuckle:

> *[We were] thinking of building some kind of Judeo-Christian community. It was in an apartment. Alik was invited, and Agursky, and others. And*

their wives and children. We discussed whether it would be proper to emi-
grate to Israel. Whether we should go as a community to Israel. As a Chris-
tian community. I loved to give papers, so I gave a paper arguing that we
should not. Glazov also presented a scholarly paper on why we should stay.
Both papers provoked such indignation among the majority of the people that
we were labeled traitors to the general cause. I'm saying this because the two
of us who presented these papers were the first to emigrate. Glazov was the
very first.

By the 1980s, however, the situation was no longer theoretical, nor was emigration restricted to the "freaks" about whom Father Michael referred earlier, who were ready to jump in the ocean to escape. Many, if not most of the friends and relatives of the later generation of Russian Jews to turn to baptism had already left, and the average Soviet Jewish citizen had more and more access to material on Jewish life, culture, religion, and language by the 1980s. Over 1,215,500 Jews left the Soviet Union between 1968 and 1994, with the peak year in 1979. Almost one-tenth of the Jewish population of the Soviet Union left during the 1970s, with emigration continuing to this day. Of these, almost two-thirds have gone to Israel. As Zvi Gitelman points out: "Ironically, the USSR, which permitted no Zionist activity until the late 1980s and had no diplomatic relations with Israel for two decades, has supplied more *olim* than any other country in the world. People having origins in the USSR now constitute the single largest sub-group in Israel's Jewish population."[3] After the fall of the Soviet Union in 1991, the doors were fully open in both directions, and there is now a healthy tourist trade between Moscow and Tel Aviv. It is rare indeed for an individual or family to decide on *aliya* without having first visited, relieving anxiety and uncertainty. They know what Israel is like.

In the mid-1960s, however, most Soviet Jews knew next to nothing about their own religious heritage, and little more about the Jewish state of Israel. Israel and Judaism were far from their Soviet realities. News of the victory of Israel in the 1967 Six-Day War was therefore a surprise, and a wake-up call for many Soviet Jews' sense of Jewish identity, which had previously been confined to a point on their internal passports and antisemitism directed against them because of it. Father Michael and other Jewish Christians heard the call as clearly as those with no Christian interests: *There was a general rise of interest among Russian Jews in Israel, particularly in 1967. I remember that a friend of mine who was a painter*

came to my house and drew a map of Israel and of the new territories that
were acquired. That was the first time that I even heard of such a thing as the
state of Israel. Or, rather, I had heard of it, but it had never been a reality
before. Like there was some kind of America somewhere. Or Africa. But as a
reality, it only became to some extent palpable in the second part of the sixties.

Benjamin Pinkus, a scholar of Soviet Jewry, has underlined the role of
Israel in the creation of a new Jewish identity among Soviet Jews: "Although in our opinion this essentially negative factor [antisemitism] plays
the most powerful and decisive role because it is the driving force behind
the whole complex process of national awakening, there are also positive
factors at work here which influence many individuals. The outstanding
feature is the awakened identification with the Jewish people in general
and with the State of Israel in particular—the pride of belonging to a
people with a glorious past, a unique and specific culture, and a lofty
humanistic vision."[4]

The first moves toward opening Jewish emigration were made in 1966,
in reaction to incipient national movements in the Soviet Union in general, when Prime Minister Aleksei Kosygin announced that the Soviet
Union would do everything possible, "if some families want to meet or
even if some among them would like to leave us, to open the road for
them, and this does not raise here, actually, any problems of principle
and will not raise any." Still, virtually no one was allowed to leave. In
1968, emigration again became an official policy, "in order to contain the
slanderous statements of Western propaganda concerning discrimination
against Jews in the Soviet Union," and to "enable us to free ourselves of
nationally minded people and religious fanatics, who exercise a harmful
influence on their surroundings. The Committee of State Security [the
KGB] will be able to continue using this channel for operational purposes."[5] As Yaacov Ro'i, a scholar of Russian-Jewish relations, has pointed
out, "the Soviet leadership sought to kill three birds with one stone: to
rid itself of the main Jewish activists in order to nip the Jewish national
movement in the bud; to assuage public opinion in the West, where a
Soviet Jewry movement was steadily mounting and interfering with the
USSR's relations with the leading Western countries, first and foremost
the United States; and to use emigration for purposes of intelligence."[6]

But emigration was still extremely difficult if not impossible at that
time. Jerome M. Gilison, an expert on the Soviet Jewish emigration, explained the established procedure for applying to leave the USSR, which
continued well into the 1980s, by which an aspirant for emigration would:

request an invitation *(vyzov)* from a family member living in Israel. When the invitation was received the prospective emigrant would then request "references" from his workplace, and with these documents apply to the OVIR (the Soviet emigration office) for an exit visa. This procedure made it necessary for the applicant to reveal emigration plans to coworkers and superiors and run the risk of being dismissed or demoted. Especially in the early days of the emigration movement, and during periods of severe repression, a prospective Jewish emigrant ran the risk of being caught in a state of limbo: unemployed and unemployable because of the desire to leave, and unable to leave due to lack of employment and the necessary references. [Remember the theater director in the introduction to this book who worked as a gravedigger. Unemployed applicants were often arrested for "parasitism."] Of course, a number of other official justifications also were used to deny visas, most notably various reasons of "state security," but in truth the regime did not have to give any explanations at all to disappointed applicants and sometimes refused to do so.[7]

Although less than nine thousand Soviet Jews left in the earliest years between 1965 and 1970, and all against great odds, these emigrants created a lifeline back to the remaining Jews, a lifeline that grew to a huge bridge. Gradually, more and more people could claim relatives in Israel, and in the United States, as Jews began to seek refugee status in America after leaving the Soviet Union. Whether from Israel or America, as well as Canada, Australia, and Western Europe, letters and phone calls opened channels of information, and the Soviet Jewry movement in the West began to send emissaries into what the latter often imagined to be the dark depths of the Soviet Union. I went myself, sweating at the border over whether my bags would be searched and the prayer books or the Passover Haggadahs or even the bottles of children's vitamins would be discovered. Gradually, secret Jewish clubs began to open, illegal Hebrew lessons were given, and smuggled Western literature opened up the world of Jewry and Judaism to Soviet Jews.

For many young Jews, Jewish identity was born not by the scanty news coverage of the Six-Day War, or, later, of the Yom Kippur War in 1973, and not even by first-hand reports from friends and relatives who had managed to escape the "cellar" of Soviet life, but by an ear-worn, often coverless copy of Leon Uris's epic novel *Exodus*, smuggled in and passed around in secret. Several Soviet and ex-Soviet Jews told me of reading the novel from cover to cover in the course of one or two nights, the only time allotted them as the contraband passed from hand to hand.

The early 1970s saw a broad opening of the emigration door in a series of erratic steps by the Soviet government, in reaction to both internal unrest and U.S. pressure. That pressure, in the form of the Jackson-Vanik amendment to the Trade Act of 1974 and the Stevenson amendment to the Export-Import Bank Act, linked U.S. trade with the Soviet Union to the emigration of Soviet Jews.[8]

As already noted, the emigration, even before it reached mass proportions, sparked new antisemitism among other Soviet citizens not given the privilege of leaving for the West, even as tourists. Gilison cites a newspaper account critical of the applicants for emigration: "This was not a group of lovers of easy money come together by chance. It was a criminal syndicate whose goal, to be reached at any price, was to amass capital both here and abroad, since many of its members planned to emigrate [*sic*] to Israel or to some other Western country. . . . They didn't believe that King Solomon's treasures were waiting for them beside the Dead Sea. Therefore, they plundered treasures, here, in the country where they were born, raised and lived."[9]

Clearly, the antisemitic themes had not changed since the time of Stalin's anticosmopolitan campaign, nor even from nineteenth-century Judeophobia, which focused on the insidious economic threat of the Jews to legitimate heirs of the "country where they were born, raised and lived." Ironically, the capital the applicants needed to amass was probably to pay a head tax, instituted in 1972, but later suspended under U.S. pressure, in an effort to require the emigrants ostensibly to repay the cost of their Soviet education.

By the 1980s, emigration was on the lips of virtually all Soviet Jews. I myself attended countless farewell parties for Jews who were emigrating, and talked repeatedly with friends about the reality, and difficulty, of prospects abroad. Although the real number of emigrants fell off after 1979, the percentage of remaining Soviet citizens who applied to leave for Israel was still unprecedentedly high. On a personal trip to Liuban', the once 90 percent Jewish town in Belorus' where my husband's grandparents were born, the two of us found a grand total of four Jews, only one of whom had been from Liuban' before the war. (She had hid in a haystack when the Nazis came through and destroyed the rest of the Jewish population.) The Belorussian city of Bobruisk, which once boasted a huge, thriving Jewish community, had virtually no Jews left by the end of the 1980s as well. Our unofficial guides in Bobroisk, who took us to the decaying shell of a synagogue that had been promised back to the Jewish community, were young adults who all planned to leave soon as well. They knew that mostly the old and infirm would remain to enjoy the new community center that was planned to occupy the rebuilt synagogue building.

Viktor, a poet, resisted leaving the Soviet Union, *because of my literary activities, the language.* But he admitted that: *the idea of emigration was simply everywhere in the air. Many Jews left in the 1970s. Maybe half. Many of my acquaintances, friends. My brother left in 1976. And he wanted me to leave as well.* Emigration was almost a given; Soviet Jews were being reunited with world Jewry at a remarkable rate.

Seryozha, who finally made *aliya* in 1992, felt the same pressure to leave that Viktor had reported feeling fifteen years earlier. His father first raised the subject, and himself moved to Israel in the late 1980s. Seryozha, however, *said that I don't want to. Not because I was such a lover of Russian peasant shoes or so fond of the dialect from the Volga area, or anything like that. I simply didn't understand why you should change geography when what was really needed was to change your soul.* It turned out oddly for Seryozha, however, when he came to visit his father in the land of Israel. He discovered that geography does, indeed, make a difference. Years passed since his baptism, and *I didn't think about Jewishness.* When he decided to make the visit, *I didn't understand the land of Israel, the people of Israel. It all seemed like a museum to me. A reliquary. But when I came and had a look, I saw that the museum was alive. And it was not merely alive. It was so alive that all the other lands by comparison seemed a museum. . . . I didn't come with the intention of staying. I came with a totally different intention. I came with only two suitcases. But I never went back* [to Russia]. Contact with the Jewish land, and the Jewish people, brought back to Seryozha a sense of his own Jewishness. And now, living in Israel, he thinks of it constantly.

What is different, then, for the generation of the 1980s who chose baptism in the Orthodox Church? The mass emigration of the 1970s opened up for them not only the possibility of leaving the Soviet Union "outside," as Father Michael had said. It also brought the possibility of Judaism and Jewishness back to the Soviet Jews, both outside, and, to some extent, inside the Soviet Union. No longer could they say: *Judaism simply wasn't an option.* It might not have been the easiest option, but it was certainly a realistic possibility for courageous Jews who were looking for a sense of spiritual identity to escape the Soviet "vacuum." The choice of Russian

Orthodoxy, then, must be seen as more than simply "easier," Judith's cynical term quoted earlier for the choice of baptism by her fellow Soviet Jews.

A few Jews who later became Christians did, indeed, wander into synagogues. A family in New York admitted: *When we first came to New York, some Jews invited us for shabbos. But the synagogue didn't seem so natural. It disappeared from our life.* Vitya, a wide-eyed parishioner at Father Michael's New York church, related a similar experience, although he was looking for something "mystical," rather than "natural": *I tried at first to reach for Judaism. I went to a synagogue with a Jewish friend of mine, but I didn't feel any mystical experience. I simply couldn't pray there.*

Obviously, although the option existed, the learning and background of most Soviet Jews was insufficient to see beyond their superficial acquaintance about Jewish tradition. Anya, a woman who could have been one of my own older relatives from the "old country," provided this not particularly convincing explanation for her choice of Christianity over Judaism:

> We went to a synagogue, and we spent one evening with religious Jewish people. But, you know, there is an Old Testament and a New Testament. The Old Testament is Torah. The Old Testament is a conversation with small children: "You must do this or that. I don't explain why, but so it is. You must. Separate your plates, and eat from different dishes, and eat only kosher food." And so on. But the New Testament explains why, and solves our spiritual problems. I see that today Judaism offers an old way of tradition and doesn't explain why. Because in old times maybe the different plates were necessary. But now, when we have hot water, it is not connected with our spiritual sides. We cannot serve this tradition. It does not give us light. But the New Testament teaches how to be good.

Anya called her belief *a defense in apocalyptic times,* and in this statement we see a crucial difference between the generation of the 1960s and that of the 1980s. For those of the 60s generation, the Church was the single possible exit from a reality that seemed as though it would never change. But for Anya, her stable Soviet reality was changing all too quickly; the world she had known since childhood, ideologically empty or not, was crumbling in front of her eyes. Her identity as an Orthodox Christian thus became an anchor in "apocalyptic times." For Father Michael and others of the 60s generation, good and evil were two distinct categories. The waters of morality, and identity, were no longer clear as the Soviet Union began to open up to the West—to a large extent because of the Jewish emigration—and then began to fall apart. The "right" way was no longer simply to counter an evil incarnate in the Soviet state around her; she now needed to be taught "how to be good."

And this difference highlights in even greater relief the question of identity for the Russian Jewish Christians who chose baptism in the 1980s. They could, indeed, have chosen Judaism, but did not. At the same time, they were not so much leaving a Soviet identity as it was leaving them. Who were they now? Not Soviets. Not Russians. Not *iudei*, followers of the laws of Judaism. What about their *Jewish (evreiskii)* identity? When I asked, "Would you still identify yourself as Jewish," Anya answered: *Yes. Today I am more Jewish than I was at home. You know Moses' story about the exodus from Egypt? It became my history. We all are descendants of Moses and of Israel. Because it was God's people, God's nation. And we continue this.*

In fact, Jewish *(evreiskii)* identity became even more important than it had been in the 1960s, but in a new way. Not only was religious identity successfully separated from national identity, so that the term "Jewish Christian" did not seem an oxymoron. And not only was religion itself fully divorced from society, so that David, an intense young man who was baptized in the late 1980s in Moscow, admitted: *I was raised on atheism, and religion was a very, well, obscure place, not because I didn't know, but because I didn't, well, want to know.* In addition, *national* identity became an increasingly major topic of conversation. The Soviet Union was disintegrating. The Latvians, the Georgians, the Ukrainians were all reasserting their unique traditions.[10] And Israel was an actual homeland that had already absorbed friends and relatives. Photos, maps, books all attested to a real link to the Jewish people. My interviewees from the 80s generation were not simply Soviet, but decidedly Jewish. Their Jewish identity was now more than a simple point on their passports; it was a ticket to the West. And the West welcomed them, simply because they were Jewish, with money, apartments, host families, English-language instruction, and job counseling. But Judaism was still foreign to them. To join world Jewry had nothing to do with a religion that they did not know.

Not all Russian Jews had such a limited knowledge of Hebrew scripture and tradition as the interviewee above who compared the Old and New Testaments. Avraham, whose depth of self-reflection reminded me much of Father Michael's despite the difference in their ages and experiences, explained his path of faith:

The fact is that we lived in an atheistic society. Young people did not know anything about any religion. We came to it ourselves. I got a copy of the Torah in Hebrew, with Russian translation. My grandfather taught me how to read it. He taught in a high school, and had a Jewish education. That is all I had. But when I began to read Torah, I became a religious person. I don't know how much of my feeling was Judaism (iudeistvo), *but I felt myself part of the Jewish people* (evreiskii narod). *Considering how much cynicism there was then in Soviet society, this gave me the strength to consider myself significant. For me it was both a sort of nationalization and an approach to faith.*

Avraham continued in a second interview: *I was a student, seventeen or eighteen, the age you study in the institute. And I was looking for an exit from my internal, spiritual problems. So I gradually came to my Jewishness* (evreistvo). *I studied Hebrew. From the Bible. Beginning with Moshe Rabeinu. At the same time, I read the Gospels. For me, it was all connected.*

Boris is a quick-speaking Jew with wild, red curly hair, who had been recommended to me by several sources. He turned out to be an artist more than a scholar, like Avraham, and clearly someone in touch with an inner spiritual impulse. Poverty—in Russia as well as in Israel—seemed to have deepened and perhaps altered his faith. He repeated the same motif as had Avraham: *When I read the Gospels, I understood what it meant to be a Jew. . . . This was the first Jewish* (evreiskaia) *book that I ever read. It aroused in me those feelings of childhood. The God of my childhood.* Boris, whose children now attend Israeli state religious schools, was one of the Jewish Christians, like Marina earlier, who reported a positive Jewish role model in childhood. For him, spiritual inspiration came from an elderly neighbor who still practiced some of the rituals of Judaism in Soviet Central Asia. After becoming Christian, Boris brought that man's *t'fillin* with him on *aliya* to Israel. He, like others in this study, saw only continuity and logic in the return of Jewish ritual items to the Holy Land in the hands of an Orthodox Christian. He saw no paradox in the phylacteries of his neighbor, not to mention the *kippah* of his young son, forming part of his life as a Christian in Israel.

Being Jewish, strangely, took on a whole new meaning for these Jewish Christians. As Pasha explained: *You will laugh at this; you won't believe it. In the Soviet Union, I was always shy about being a Jew because it carried with it a mass of inconveniences. External ones. . . . But then, after I was baptized, and we began to study Hebrew—because without that you can't understand*

Christianity—then I began to defend myself as a Jew. And the more I am a Christian, the more I feel myself a Jew.

I heard this line again and again. According to David:

Only after baptism did we feel ourselves to be Jews. Before then, to be a Jew was a negative. When someone in Russia calls you a "Jew," he means to put you down. That is the first point. Secondly, I knew that many famous people were Jews, and, on the one hand I was proud of that, but I also couldn't include myself in that group. Which people? Well, I knew that Christ was a Jew. And Karl Marx. And Einstein. Many. A lot of people from the history of culture, art. And I was from that tribe. It's interesting that in the course of our study of Christianity, of Orthodoxy, we entered deeper and deeper into a different understanding, that Jews are precisely the chosen people. After baptism, we began to feel ourselves more deeply Jewish. Why? It wasn't a kind of pride, but simply an internal feeling.

When I asked a woman who has recently been baptized in New York if she would still identify herself as Jewish, she answered: *Yes. I am today more Jewish than I was at home, when I didn't have any religion at all.*

I am a pravoslavnaia evreika (an Orthodox Christian Jew), claimed the young Elena, with a slight giggle. *I know it sounds funny. And if I said such a thing in Russia, they would kill me.* Thinking back on this line, I am not sure if she recognized the incompatibility of her Orthodox and Jewish identities through the eyes of the Russians or of the Jews. Which group would have been more hostile? Who would have found it funny?

Thus it was religion, although ironically not Judaism, that brought Jewishness as a positive identification back to these cynical Soviet Jews. Mikhail Agursky noted the irony of this in his own case: "It wasn't a rabbi of the Moscow Choral Synagogue, but a graduate of the Kiev Spiritual Seminary, Father Nikolay Glebov, who pushed me, practically forced me to contemplate, to formulate my national philosophy. . . . Such is the dialectic of life. Christianity, which had always seems a mortal threat to the national existence of the Jewish people, can in our day become the source of a new national rebirth."[11]

When emigration became not only an option, but an expectation, the question arose for many whether or not they could continue to be Jews, Christian or otherwise, in Russia. One spoke of the pressure to emigrate, the intensity he felt around others who were preparing to leave, even if he, himself, was not. For Osip, *faith gave me the surety that I could do this, that I could leave for Israel. I think that without my entrance into faith, I would not have left so easily. I would have left in any case, but I would have come to that decision much later. I felt that I could fulfill my Jewishness. I didn't need to fear.*

Felix Svetov enunciated this paradox toward the end of his novel, *Open the Doors for Me.* His main character defends himself in front of a group of former Jewish friends, some of who are preparing to emigrate from Russia. One has just accused him of betraying the "voice" of his Jewish blood. The Jewish Christian responds:

> "And what do *you* hear? The voice of your stomach! If it were the voice of blood, then why don't you know the Jewish language? Why don't you go to synagogue? Why don't you know the Old Testament? Jewish culture? I hear the voice of my blood, and that is why I am an Orthodox Christian. Even more, I am precisely an Orthodox Christian *because* I hear the voice of my blood. Only the Jew who hears the voice of blood, who becomes a Christian, . . . only then does the possibility arise to begin to pay the unpaid bill for spilt blood. . . . For some reason, only the Jews were chosen, a pure race. . . . You aren't even humanists, it is . . . it is. . . ." Lev Il'ich felt, understood, that he was not saying what he meant, that they wouldn't understand. "Well, let it be wrong, not quite right, just so they know." [He continued:] "Yes, my God is the God of Abraham, Isaac, and Jacob, the God of Moses, the Son of David, the Son of Man, of our God Jesus Christ, who spoke with the prophets and apostles, who has lived for ages in the Russian Orthodox Church. And I hear Him—*that* is the voice of blood. It is chosenness.[12]

A number of Russian Jewish Christians enunciated this paradox of the connection of Jewish "blood" to Christian belief. They feel "tribally" connected to their Jewishness, now, in the Church. As Seryozha tried to explain, to be a Christian among the Jews *is very Jewish. To be a Christian here* [in Israel] *is the same as being a Jew among the Christian nations. For me, this is the height of Christianity.* Presumably with no knowledge of the passage from Svetov that I cited above, Seryozha added: *It is chosenness.*

At this point in our analysis, we can clearly see a central paradox of this study: most of the Russian Jewish Christians I interviewed began to feel *more,* not less Jewish after their baptism than before. What is most surprising is that this feeling is *not* consistent with what researchers have found among other Jewish out-converts. According Todd Endelman in *Jewish Apostasy in the Modern World:*

> Most Jews who became Christians were eager to leave their Jewishness behind them and worked assiduously to promote their own and their children's absorption into the larger society. In a few instances, however, converts and their descendants found it psychologically impossible to bury their origins. Their sense of Jewishness would not quietly fade away, relinquishing its hold on them, allowing them to transform themselves effortlessly into gentile citizens. . . . On occasion, the children of converts, much to their parents' horror and confusion, reclaimed attachments that their parents had sought to bury.[13]

Rodger Kamenetz found in American JUBUs not only the desire to leave Jewishness behind, but anger and disappointment with their own heritage.[14] And a study of Jews in the Messengers of the New Covenant, a sect of Messianic Jews, finds that: "much personal testimony centers on alienation from and feelings of anomie toward Jews." Furthermore, "[m]any of these young people, alienated from and scornful of Jews in general, continue to be repelled by the residual Jewishness in themselves."[15]

According to one interviewee, the desire to leave Judaism behind is, indeed, the rationale of a small number of Russian Jews who convert to Christianity after they come to Israel. As cited before: *There are some of these, but precisely in the sense that they* converted [the difference between *perekrestilis'* and *obratilis',* as we saw in chapter 3]. *They left Jewry per se.* As opposed to the majority of baptized Russian Jews who never repudiated their former Jewishness, *It was an exit as much as an entrance.*

We can begin to understand the reasons for the paradox of increased Jewish identity: entrance into the Orthodox Church brought back to virtually all of the Russian Jewish Christians I interviewed a correspondence of their religious and national identities. How did this happen? Earlier in life, Jewishness was defined for these people negatively and externally. Virtually everyone reported feeling what one called "antisemitism of the street." As Zhenya told me, *They would never let you forget that you are Jewish.* David had the same experience: *In Russia it usually happens that others tell you that you are Jewish.* And as Svetov wrote in his autobiography: "I felt myself to be Jewish only because they reminded me of the fact."[16]

Without the Church, according to Glazov, such an understanding cultivates only a philosophy of "offense," with no positive, active outcome.[17]

After baptism, however, Jewishness takes on a positive meaning, so that Pasha told me: *the more I am a Christian, the more I feel myself a Jew.* As we saw, Avraham admitted strangely that: *The deeper I went into the Church, the more deeply I felt myself as belonging to the people of Israel.*

This new understanding of their Jewishness now connects these Jews to an ancient and spiritually rewarding tradition. The identity question is both national and religious. Father Michael told me with an ironic smile: *For me, Judaism was not an issue at all. Until I became a Christian.* This is as true for Father Michael now, in his Orthodox parish of mostly Russian Jewish Christians, as it is for Avraham, a member of the 1980s generation, who perhaps overstated when he claimed that: *I don't consider myself as belonging to Christianity. The fact is that I also always felt myself part of Judaism,* since, he went on to explain, ancient Judaism is the foundation of Jesus' message. Only one interviewee announced that *Judaism is a dead religion,* and I don't even think he realized that he might have said anything offensive. For the rest, the Gospels are a refraction, not a rejection of Hebrew scriptures. They see no incongruity, and only historical and theological logic in this reading.

At least two of the interviewees, one in New York and one in Israel, told me about *an interesting phenomenon.* In the words of one of them: *If some popular, open activist appears in the Church, immediately rumors start in the Church that he is a Jew, that he has some kind of Jewish roots.* There is a frightening parallel here to earlier periods of discrimination both against dissidents in the Church, and against Jews, dating as far back as the Judaizing heresy in fifteenth-century Muscovy. Opponents of the heresy pointed a finger at Jews who had supposedly "infiltrated" the court. According to the historian John Klier, "by enshrining the assumption that real Jews were indeed actively promoting apostasy, a work like Iosif's enormously popular *Enlightener* [ascribed to Abbot Iosif of Volokolamsk] created the spectre of an enduring threat." In the future religious dissidents were easily fitted into the paradigm of "Judaizing."[18]

The Russian Jewish Christians who spoke to me of the association between dissidence in the Church and Jews implied a positive connection, however. Activism, dissent in belief, is, for these intellectuals, associated with ideological vitality. And with Jewishness. When recounting the story of his spiritual father, Pasha told me: *Those who envy him say about him that he seems to be a Jew. He is so spiritual. It is interesting in Orthodoxy, among the high officials, that if a priest becomes very spiritual, then they attach the label "Jew" to him. It is a surprising thing.* Perhaps, however, after hearing the stories of baptism over and over, it is not so surprising. The concepts of "Jewish" and "ideological vitality" or "spiritual strength" are all connected to the understanding of the "true" Church for these baptized Jews, one still an active parishioner, the other having left his own Orthodox ordination behind. Ironically, entrance into the Christian Church gives these Jews an internal and positive, as opposed to a previously external and negative, Jewish identity of their childhoods. As we might say, they feel, now, doubly chosen.

According to Father Pavel, who now leads his flock of "doubly chosen" Jewish Christian Muscovites: *The reality is that a Jewish consciousness has either awoken or been born in practically all the Jews who have begun to live a Church life, thanks to the Church life, and in connection to the Church life.* However, as Father Pavel admits: *For many of them, if not for the majority, this became a problem.*

Reactions to this "problem" bring us to the second categorization of Jewish Christians, and the focus of the next chapter: the directions in which their paths of faith turned. In its simplest terms, the problem is antisemitism in the Church. When confronted with more than simple "street" antisemitism, or with more than benign cold shoulders by ethnically Russian churchgoers, but instead with repeated liturgical references and ecclesiastic pronouncements as well, many of these Jews were forced into a new examination of their Jewishness. Thus the "problem" touches the deepest levels of identity, precisely at the intersection of national and religious self-definition. We will explore the twists of that identity in the following chapter.

CHAPTER FIVE

The Paths Diverge

The Conflict of Identity

But the deeper I went into the Church, the more deeply I felt myself as belonging to the people of Israel.
—Avraham, Jerusalem 1998

Either you are a Christian, or you are an antisemite. You cannot be both.
—Marina, Moscow 1997

In the end my move to Christianity was not an escape
from Judaism but, on the contrary, a way of finding answers to my
problems as a Jew.
—Brother Daniel, in Tec, *In the Lion's Den,* 167

THE RUSSIAN JEWISH CHRISTIANS interviewed for this book moved along their respective paths of faith at various speeds, and to varying destinations. One, at least, has left Christianity completely, although he maintains social ties with other Orthodox believers. Yura, this Jewish Christian "apostate," refused to be recorded, claiming he did not want to talk about himself, but was willing to give general statements about the period, and to help me meet others. He was as curious about why an American Jew (myself) would have an academic interest in Russian Orthodoxy, as I was interested in the Russian Jews (like himself) who had at some point joined the Orthodox Church. When pressed for specifics, he spoke of his former cohort in the Church fondly, but referred to the "blinders" that they wear. It is a group, he claimed, that does not look on Jews as people, but as a concept. They read Berdyaev and Florensky as contemporaries, not seeing that life has changed. Marina had already spoken with me about this naive "misreading" of Berdyaev's use of the term "freedom" by Russian Jewish intellectuals attracted to Orthodoxy. There was sure to be some disillusionment, or reassessment at best, when the Church did not prove to be so existentially free.

For those who begin to see the disparity between their assumptions and hopes for a new life in freedom and the reality of the Church, any retreat can be painful. Marina, perhaps referring directly to Yura, I cannot be sure, confessed that Christianity *is a fire that is very difficult to exit. I know very many people . . . I have a very good friend who has gone through this. A Jew. He was baptized, and then somehow put it aside. I know a lot of such people. . . . The fact is that Christianity does not let you out very easily. It is difficult to enter, and even more difficult to leave. It always remains with you, that feeling of stepping away, of leaving.*

Speaking with Yura, I began to recognize not only the similarities, but the *differences* among my "clients," as he jokingly called them. Those differences, I realized, were most pronounced not at the beginning of their paths, but further along the road; baptism into the Orthodox Church led these Jews in many different directions.

Despite the difficulties, I suspect that quite a few Russian Jews, perhaps even the majority, stepped away from the Church after their initial flirtation with it, and now look at their earlier faith as no more than a youthful phase, confined to a time and place in their and the Soviet Union's past. I was not as likely to know about those "ex-Christians," who have, now, no connection whatsoever to their former Christianity. And because of my interest in the relationship of national and spiritual identity, I would not be as interested in their path. Instead, I have focused on those who passed through a period of intense participation in the Russian Orthodox Church—sometimes serving as lay officials, sometimes, as we saw, even entering the clergy—and now, in Israel, in New York, and even in Moscow, find themselves searching for a new expression of their religious faith that includes, rather than rejects, what they learned of themselves—as Jews—in the Church.

To a certain extent, the degree of distance from or participation in the official Orthodox Church today depends for these Russian Jewish Christians on the ways in which they have come to understand their Jewishness, and how they have chosen to cope with antisemitism within the Church, the latter a factor that virtually every one of my interviewees acknowledged. Not surprisingly, the issue of antisemitism forces their Jewishness back into conflict with their religious identity.

REMAINING TRUE BELIEVERS IN THE RUSSIAN ORTHODOX CHURCH

I spoke with only two Jewish Christians still active in the Church who feel *no* conflict with being a Jew in the Russian Orthodox Church, although they both recognize its existence for others. Seryozha, the particularly introspective believer from the previous chapter who, early in life had *a small inkling of the fact that there is something higher than man,* surprised me by answering my question about antisemitism with the following: *I personally haven't met up with any. But I know that it exists. And I think that it is connected with the understanding that Israel exists, and a misunderstanding of the fate of the Church.* Likewise, Viktor answered: *Strangely, I was free of this. . . . I never met any sense of nonacceptance of Jews. This is strange, because I know that others had a different experience. I simply have not met it.* Viktor still attends the churches of the Moscow Patriarchate in Jerusalem whenever he can manage. Does he know of antisemitism in the Church? Yes, but: *I consider that there's antisemitism everywhere. The Church in Emigration* [in contrast to the Church of the Moscow Patriarchate] *is not pure in this regard. It's everywhere.* Does he feel a conflict from the other end, from being a Christian in a Jewish state? *Well, I didn't anticipate purely technical problems. Sunday, for example, is a work day in Israel.* He chuckled, and added, *But since I am out of work now, I can go to church.*

A month or so later, Viktor invited me to accompany him to the Divine Liturgy at a convent in Ein Kerem, the Gorneny Monastery. What I remember most from that visit, other than the comings and goings of the novitiates in the near empty chapel, was being scolded for crossing my legs as I rested on a lonely bench during a part of the long service. This church, clearly, was not putting on a friendly face to seek converts from among the uninitiated, Jewish or otherwise. Based on my informant's familiarity, we were invited to a meal after the service, and sat with a busload of Russian tourists who were making a pilgrimage trip to the Holy Land. It wasn't clear to me how many of those Russians were actually believers, and how many felt, more simply, culturally connected to the Russian Church. Some of the tourists, most likely, were Jews.

Most of the Russian Jewish Christians still somehow active in the Church feel their "difference" more keenly than does Viktor. An interviewee who now studies early Christianity in the university bitterly agreed: *The Church helps people understand their Jewishness. The Church talks about this constantly. For me the problem was not that the Gospels constantly talk about the Jews, but that the Church constantly talks about the Jews.* For most, the awareness of Jewishness awakened by their new status in the Church created dissonance. They believed ardently in their new Christian life, but heard that *the Church has two understandings of the Jews. One, as a holy nation up to and including Jesus and the apostles, and another people, a rejected people, after Jesus. Rejected by God.* But how can they be with God, many wondered, chosen by God in their newly chosen Church, and rejected by God at the same time?

Russian Jewish Christians justified this conflict in various ways. For some, Father Alexander Men' opened a path of broad-minded ecumenism that leads to participation in selected liberal parishes, in some cases led by Russian Jewish Christian priests, like Father Michael in New York or Father Pavel in his parish outside of Moscow. Many of these ecumenically minded Jews find Orthodoxy *"broad,"* as they described it, able to accept many different kinds of faithful. The quick-spoken, wild-haired Boris claimed: *My priest opened up all the poetic and spiritual riches of Orthodoxy. From him I learned that the Orthodox tradition collects everything. It has room for everything: for the private, individual life of a believer, and for faith in relics. It allows this path, and that path, and a third path.*

Another believer, this time in New York, agreed: *In Orthodoxy there is room for everyone. For the old woman who simply knows that Christ is God, and knows the prayers. She comes to church. And there is also room for someone like the scholar Sergei Averintsev. There is room for everyone; everyone can find his own activity there.*

Some, like Zoya Krakhmal'nikova, have stayed within the Church in terms of ritual and belief, but have vocally broken with the official hierarchy, which she considers tainted by "fascist" and "unchristian" anti-semitism. "True" Orthodoxy for Zoya and these later-day disciples of Men', not to mention of Vladimir Solovyov, is at heart universal. These believers can identify themselves as part of the original, "authentic" Church, even while dissenting from aspects of its contemporary manifestation. According to Viktor, who had come to faith largely through his study of philosophy and history: *What I learned from Men's writings, although not only from his, is that the Orthodox Church is, at essence, ecumenical. What I have in mind is Orthodoxy as a view of the world. There was another element in my historical interests, and that is Byzantium. The history of Byzantium, the history of the Byzantine Church, the history of the Church itself. This was after my baptism. At that time, I saw that authentic Orthodoxy is not exactly what they call Orthodoxy today: an ethnic, narrow faith. But authentic Orthodoxy is, essentially, universal. That view of the Church on the world was completely ecumenical. The contemporary Church is the heir of this, but does not always make use of it.*

When Viktor would meet Orthodox antisemites, he tended to see their distance from Orthodox ecumenism, rather than a condemnation of Orthodoxy per se. *Of course I have encountered Orthodox circles that have a very narrow view, but in that case I don't call them truly Orthodox. On the other hand, maybe they don't consider me to be truly Orthodox. For them, Christianity itself doesn't play the role of real "news"* [nastoiashchie novosti]. *For them it is a religion of laws. . . . For me, Christianity in general, and Orthodoxy in particular, is most of all a religion of "good news," the Gospels* [khoroshie novosti, blagaia vest'].

Pasha, a much younger Jewish Christian, said almost the same: *To show you are a Jew in Orthodoxy is a kind of litmus paper. Jewry is the verification of faith for a Christian. Why? If you take this paper, Jewry, and you immerse it in someone's faith, and the paper changes color, even just a little, then that is a marker that something is not right in his faith.* True Orthodoxy for these Jewish Christians is thus associated with tolerance and ecumenism, with what they see as the true message of the gospels. And any Orthodoxy that does not accept Jews, that flunks the litmus test, must have abandoned its true ecumenical form and become intent only on its own ritualistic laws. Ironically, according to Viktor, it then *does not differ in any significant way from Judaism. Contemporary Judaism. If you fulfill the law, then everything will be okay.*

Men' wrote about the blatant anti-Jewish and anti-Judaic statements that remain in Orthodox liturgy to this day: "Those texts are a remnant of medieval morals; they have already been removed from Catholicism. When it comes time for the review of Orthodox liturgical texts, I hope that these attacks will also be removed there."[1] According to him, as to his followers, the erasing of antisemitic references from Orthodox liturgy will reveal, rather than eliminate the truth from Orthodoxy. Father Alexander Borisov, a popular ecumenical-leaning priest who now leads many of Father Men's "children," expanded on the problem: "The vast majority of Orthodox Christians are neutral about the question [of antisemitism]. As for those who take an active position, I'm afraid that anyone who consciously counters antisemitism would be in the minority."[2] Why is this so? In his words:

Russian society, the Orthodox believers, people who want to come to Christ, are presented with books written in the nineteenth century, put out now in massive copies and only weakly relating to anything happening to us today, one hundred years later. The people who have come relatively recently to the Orthodox Church, therefore, barely have a grip on the very term "Orthodox." For many people, still poorly oriented in Christianity, the Church to which they recently came becomes some sort of symbol that provides a bad service: we are orthodox, and the others are not orthodox, we correctly praise God, and all the rest— incorrectly.[3]

As an outsider who need not try to justify my uncomfortable position within a Church that apparently does not welcome Jews, I cannot help but feel an element of apologetics in these statements. It is easy to distinguish an ideal Church from its current manifestation, but it is a more difficult matter to live and pray, actually, within it.

Men's comment about recent revisions in Catholic liturgical books raises the question of why these Jews sought baptism precisely in the Russian Orthodox Church, despite its historical connection to antisemitism. Marina explained rather nonchalantly: *In this world you need to be a certain denomination. So I will say that I am Orthodox. It's the local religion* [mestnaia religiia].

For many, the coincidence was in meeting deeply spiritual people whom they respected, including Father Men': *Why Orthodoxy?* Avraham repeated my question as he thought. *Because those personalities that I met were Orthodox; they belonged to the Orthodox Church. Now I see it as a coincidence. Then, I just spoke with those I met, as I am speaking with you. . . . Those people became my orientation point. I saw how a religious person can lead a profound life. I had nothing to compare them to on the Jewish side. I think that is one of the main reasons why I went the way I did.*

Yet comments in many narratives attest to the fact that the choice of Church was *not* purely coincidence or a matter of local convenience. Instead, Russian Orthodoxy struck a cultural chord in these Russian Jewish intellectuals. As Marina continued the narrative of her path of faith: *I love a lot that is in Orthodoxy. As though I was born with it. It is my language.* Here the question of Russianness arises; her assertion about language expresses the sense of, or perhaps the search for belonging in the majority culture that I had originally assumed formed the major impetus for baptism. Yet I found that the impulse is not exactly to belong, but to express fully what they feel is already theirs.

Why Orthodoxy? Because the Russian language is my language. I graduated from a Russian school, and I am a teacher of Russian literature. I am educated on Dostoevsky, on Tolstoy. In a communist country, religion was prohibited, but Russian literature was not prohibited. So it influenced us. That is my men-tality, explained a middle-aged émigrée who had sought baptism after find-ing herself adrift in America, where a teacher of Russian literature could find no employment. Pasha responded to my question about the choice of Russian Orthodoxy in similar terms: *Orthodoxy is closer to our roots. It is in the same language. If Catholicism was served in Russian, and Orthodoxy in Chinese, then of course I would have been a Catholic. It is a question of language. But not just of language. Of culture as well. How can you separate language from culture?* Viktor's response was nearly identical: *I was raised on Russian literature. People who lived in the environment of Russian culture had at one time or another to come face to face with ideas of religion. You can't avoid it in Russian literature. Some kind of a relationship to the Church, to faith, to religion. Russian literature was one of the bases of our faith.*

For Boris: *It seems to me that a person brought up on Russian culture, that is Russian, not Soviet, culture—Pushkin, Tolstoy, Dostoevsky, etc.—and into the twentieth century, such a person must come to Orthodoxy. That's what I think. To Christianity first of all, and specifically to Orthodoxy. Russian cul-ture is built on Orthodoxy. Russian culture is Orthodox.*

Another Russian Jewish Christian first claimed that it was neither Russian literature nor culture in a broad sense, but specifically Russian philosophy that struck a chord: *The fact that Orthodoxy is connected to Rus-sian culture did not have an effect on me. But Russian religious philosophy was much closer to me than other religious philosophies.* When asked if Judaism was an option, this philosophically oriented Jew nonetheless responded: *In everything there is an aesthetic element. The synagogue service itself is not aesthetic. And there were only old men. It's true that there are only old women in church, but at least there was the aesthetic element, a feeling of mystery, perhaps.*

The mystery, the "aesthetic element" felt to be absent in Judaism, grew for these Jewish Christians, it would seem, from Russian culture itself. The theology of Russian Orthodoxy rests on a mystical moment. Empha-sis is placed not on Christ the Victim, but on Christ the Victor, and the central icon on most iconostases depicts Christ Enthroned, rather than on the cross. In fact, crucifixes are absent from some Orthodox churches alto-gether. It is the mystery of the incarnation, and the potential for all human deification that the incarnation represents, that captures the imagination of the Orthodox believer.[4] No doubt for this reason did Dostoevsky, so

The Conflict of Identity 107

steeped in Orthodoxy despite his rejection of the Church hierarchy of his day, have Prince Myshkin in *The Idiot* react so sharply to the Holbein picture of Christ being removed from the cross that he sees at Rogozhin's.[5] Myshkin, and his Russian readers, did not recognize such a human, suffering Jesus. Their icons are flat, two-dimensional, or painted in reverse perspective, as a window on the spiritual world. They are concrete representations of transfigured matter, not realistic depictions of a historical scene. The sensuality of the Orthodox service does not point to the mere physicality of this mortal world, but to the mystery of incarnation in its aesthetic splendor.

Vitya came to Orthodoxy as a young man, but claims that he was already *pretty religious as a child* and *always had a clear sense that there is a God. For a while I lost that sense, but not completely. And I was always interested in religious philosophy, but as a purely intellectual activity.* Yet he, like the "philosopher" above, felt the draw of "mystery" in the Russian Orthodox Church, and, conversely, felt its lack in Judaism: *I tried at first to reach for Judaism. I went to a synagogue with a Jewish friend of mine, but I didn't feel any mystical experience. I simply couldn't pray there.*

Why not Protestantism, I asked? A Russian Jewish woman who remains extremely active in ritual aspects of the Church responded: *I have never been happy with Protestantism. I need liturgical satiation. I think their faith, well, their exegetical studies are excellent, but their faith is not existential enough. It's not a matter of living.* Boris, a musician by training, combined the mystical, "existential" attraction of the Russian Church with what others labeled the "aesthetic question" in his narrative: *In Protestantism, everything was very simple, and that never attracted me. There was no musical mysticism.* Marina, too, waxed poetic: *I listen to the music with great love; much is warm and significant for me, and important.*

As we saw, there is indeed something viscerally attractive about a service in an Orthodox church; it is the same attraction supposedly felt by Vladimir's boyars when they visited Constantinople in the year 987, and came back with the report that "God dwells there among men." And it is presumably the same attraction that causes a secular Jewish colleague of mine in New York to announce periodically that if she were to be interested in any religion at all, it would certainly be Orthodoxy. The liturgical music is chanted in several parts of harmony, icons cover all visible surfaces, the priest's entrances and exits through the doors of the iconostasis reinforce the drama not so much of the passion of Christ but of his resurrection and of the very real presence of God. The history of the development of Orthodox liturgy has been one of elaboration, in contrast to a process of simplification and austerity in the Western Church, and the mood of an Orthodox service has been described as one of "warm, exuberant cheer." Even the fact that there are no pews in traditional Orthodox churches—sometimes troublesome to foot-weary and impatient American visitors—can lend the church an aura of pleasant charm about which Timothy Ware writes: "They are at home in their church— not troops on a parade ground, but children in their Father's house. Orthodox worship is often termed 'otherworldly,' but could more truly be described as 'homely': it is a *family* affair. Yet behind the homeliness and informality there lies a deep sense of mystery."[6]

Viktor had some experience with Baptists, but felt: *you could feel their complete separation from tradition. The lack of ritual. And the lack of depth. A kind of narrowness.* It was the ideological "breadth" of "true" Orthodoxy that allowed some Jews to find a place within it, despite the antisemites and antisemitic liturgy that they encountered, and it is apparently also the "breadth" of tradition and ritual, and the theology of mystery, that has kept many coming back for the aesthetic and mystical pleasure that services in an Orthodox church offer.

But the aesthetic pleasure comes with a price, Marina admitted, ever ready to discuss the difficulties as well as the attractions of faith: *But there are also many things that are difficult for me, and always were. It is always a difficult joy for me to be in church. It is an internal requirement, I feel. But, on the other hand, I always feel an internal contradiction.* Even these Jews, who justify their continued participation in Orthodoxy by concentrating on its universal "true" nature and/or by admitting their attraction to the aesthetic, mystical "Russian" aspects of the ritual, even they constantly feel an identity conflict in their chosen Church.

TRANSCONFESSIONAL MOVEMENT

The "internal contradiction" has caused some Russian Jewish Christians to stay within Christianity, but to move into other traditional denominations, where they feel, sometimes, more comfortable as Jews. Yury Glazov joined the Catholic Church after he immigrated to America. Leonid Nikitin, who later changed his name to Arye Barats, wrote of his spiritual and actual journey to Israel intermingled with personal Christian-Judaic *midrash* in a curious book called *The Countenances of Torah (Liki Tory)*.[7] In his search to understand his own identity, he first moved from reading the Zohar of Jewish Kabbalah to the Russian Orthodox religious thinker Father Pavel Florensky's work on cult. He was baptized in the Orthodox Church, but, having spent a year in an ecumenical community in Moscow, he met a Catholic nun in Vilnius, who helped him see the compatibility of his homegrown existentialist philosophy not with Orthodoxy, but with Catholicism. Barats later married another Russian Jewish Christian, embraced Judaism, and immigrated to Israel.

The case of young Ira perhaps is typical of those whose involvement in Christianity began with Orthodoxy, but led her, and her family members, toward a variety of other Churches. Contrary to Marina and Boris and Vitya, as quoted above, Ira never was attracted to the "local" religion because of its relationship to Russian culture. Quite the opposite. Over the phone, she asked me to speak in English, and when we met in her tiny, two-room shared apartment in Jerusalem, she explained that *I don't like speaking Russian. I don't feel comfortable.* She couldn't remember what nationality was listed on her old Soviet passport, but with a Jewish mother, and a father who was half German, and the other half a mixture of French, Jewish, and Russian, she could have chosen just about any nationality for "point five." But, *I always wanted to be anything but Russian in my passport.* Ironically, Ira found herself in the early 1990s without a nationality altogether, since her first step upon reaching maturity was to leave her overprotective family in Moscow, and move to Lithuania, *the most European-like country that I've ever seen.* Shortly after that, Lithuania separated from Russia, and Ira willingly gave up Soviet citizenship (although she did return to Moscow, and to the Orthodox Church, to marry her Lithuanian husband), without being able to gain Lithuanian citizenship. It would be at least three years before she could receive permanent residence status, and, in the meantime, could neither study nor work. Ira is in Israel now not because of any Zionist feelings, but because it was the only country that would take both her and her husband. (They made *aliya* at a time when non-Jewish spouses of former Soviet Jews were automatically given citizenship. This is not always the case now.) Her parents were already in Israel, living, and attending church, in Haifa. Like all these Russian Jewish Christians who made *aliya*, they had to be less than honest on entry questionnaires when asked if they confessed any religion other than Judaism.

Ira's family was baptized, it seems, almost by chance. One summer, her parents were traveling by raft on a lake in northern Russia when the wind blew them toward a church on the shore, and continued to blow so hard that they could not leave for several days. *Wind brought them. Nothing else,* she giggled. *They were just sitting there, you know, being not able to run away from the weather. And then that young priest came to see them. And he talked to my mother and father and as far as they were already, you know, on the way kind of . . . to faith, they made friends first of all with him. And they saw many young people coming there to visit him because he was very young, very charismatic, you know . . . and many foreigners, and artists, and every-thing, they were coming to see him.*

Only six years old at the time, Ira's baptism was not her choice, and therefore not one hundred percent pertinent to the present study. Her memories, however, are vivid, and her parents fit well into the paradigm of the generation of the 1960s. *Well, first of all, well, I remember myself . . . it's not that I remember everything now from those times, but about my per-sonal way to faith, well, I remember myself in the past and my father first teaching us to pray. Which he was quite reluctant to do, but he taught us that first prayer.*

Ironically, Ira's first encounter with her Jewishness came about the same time as her baptism. *About the second day at school, I remember sitting with my girlfriend, or whatever you call her, you know, the girl with whom I wanted to sit during that day at school. And the other kids calling her a Jew, you know . . . and, uh, kind of pushing her. And coming back home, I was ask-ing my father: "What is it to be a Jew?" And he said, "Well, it's exactly what you are." And that's probably when I was first aware of my Jewishness. It meant for me first of all that I have to go and stand by the side of that girl, you know.*

Ira's parents were typical dissidents of the pre-Gorbachev years, or, per-haps, not so typical, more like the "freaks" about whom Father Michael joked, who would jump in the ocean in order to escape. Her father was refused permission to leave the Soviet Union because of prior "secret" employment, and instead took his wife, mother-in-law, and six children by foot across Europe, knocking on various embassy doors for asylum. His trek led, ultimately, to Israel, but disillusionment there, in the "land of the free," forced him, at one point, into a return march. (He did, ultimately, return to Israel.) *My father is a very special person, and he likes to be different from everyone, in all kinds of ways. He was a dissident him-self; most of his friends were in prison at that time, you know. He was telling us all kinds of things and explaining and when I was very small, he explained what Russia is, you know, how bad it is, and what kind of country it is and what kind of life is waiting for us there. He brought his children up, I mean, me and my brother, we were really sure we would go, you know, to the Red*

Square, to tell the communists that they are pigs, you know, the moment we are eighteen, and go to prison for the rest of our lives, which never happened because, uh, well, it was too late. She laughed remembering that her eighteenth year coincided with the disintegration of the Soviet Union.

As a refusnik, Ira's father's life took on a shape that will sound familiar to many American Jews, who made pilgrimages, as it were, to Soviet Jews in the refusnik community, with suitcases stocked with baby aspirin, vitamins, and dual-language prayer books. I met many like him on my numerous trips to the Soviet Union in the 1970s and 80s. But, because of her unique situation, Ira's childhood turned into an odd combination of Christian inner life and Jewish acquaintances. According to her, the Western visitors never noticed: *We had an Israeli flag on the wall, you know, and everything like this. . . . And there was really a flow of Jewish people, mostly young ones, coming to see us from England and from America and, what's strange, it never came to the question of were we Christian or not. I don't know how, because we never hid anything from them, you know, neither the crucifix which we had on the wall just under the flag of Israel, you know, and icons were there, too, as far as I remember. . . . We had priests visiting us, and baptizing people in our house, because, as I told you, you know, so that KGB wouldn't be aware of it.*

Ira's mother preserved the prayer shawl of her grandfather as a family heirloom. *She was coming from the Jewish family, but they never believed in God as far as I know and there was no traditional background, except for something, you know, about her grandfather.* And for Ira, herself, *my Christianity and my Jewishness were never quarreling.* Why? *For me, nationality is nationality still, and Judaism is a religion, you know.* Like all these Jewish Christians, she clearly feels no conflict between her Jewish nationality, and her Christian religion. If anything, she has a sense of Judaism only because it *is the roots of the Christian faith.*

Nonetheless, national questions did indeed affect Ira's path of faith. Her desire to escape the negative associations of Russia and the Soviet Union laid the bed for an attraction to Catholicism: *And then, when I was sixteen, I became Catholic. I stopped being Orthodox and became Catholic. Which happened [on a visit] in Lithuania. . . . I wanted to be really earnest and when we came to Lithuania and there was the national revival, you know, and there was like this, it was so beautiful, people going to church, you know, and praying. . . . And I was just sixteen and I liked it so much.*

Her mother's path also began to diverge from Russian Orthodoxy, leading, in her case, toward Pentecostalism. Like the rest of the family, she concentrated on the aspects that bind the Churches, rather than separate them. In this way, this group of baptized Jews resembles those who have stayed in ecumenical Orthodox parishes. *So, you see,* said Ira, who admitted that she rarely goes to church in Israel, *what I am trying usually, what I believe I should do, I am trying to make peace between Christians, you know. I'm telling Orthodox people about Catholics and Anglicans and Anglicans about Catholics and Orthodox, and trying to explain to them that really they're more or less the same, you know, they don't have to curse each other. Well, in our family we have, well, my mother who is Pentecostal, me, who is Catholic, my father, who believes you have to be Lutheran.*

I cannot say necessarily that Jewishness is the determining factor in a turn toward ecumenism for Russian Jewish Christians, but it would, indeed, be a possible conclusion based on the number of times interviewees, now in or out of a variety of Churches, include a discussion of it in their narratives. They either leave Orthodoxy because it is not universal enough, or they remain in it because they believe in its essential, "true" universality.

ECUMENISM AND FATHER (BROTHER) DANIEL

The Russian Jewish Christians who, it seems to me, have grappled most seriously with their Jewishness have taken a somewhat different path from those who justify their participation in their "local" religion by emphasizing the universal nature of the true Church, as well as from those who have moved to other confessions, seeking distance from the "Russian" aspects of the Orthodox Church, but equally professing universalism.

I had this idea that in Israel, insofar as it is being reborn, stated an interviewee of the 1960s generation who immigrated to Israel at the very beginning of the mass *aliya, that there would be a rebirth of some kind of Jewish-Christian communities outside of the Church. Something new. A reborn apostolic kind of Church.* This Jewish Christian was disappointed, and now feels alone and isolated. *Life doesn't always work out. Especially in Israel. Purely concretely, of course, I was disappointed, but that is my problem. No one told me that it would be such and such a way. It was only I who built up the conception, so I can be disappointed with my conception, but not with reality. No one lied to me. Not Berdyaev, whom I had read with such eagerness, and not Alexander Men' and not the Jewish agencies that facilitated my aliya. I had a conception. If it was naive, that is my problem. Not the problem of God, or of others. I believed in it for quite some time. For many years I believed it was possible. That it would occur in some way.*

What was the "it" of which he dreamed? Many Jewish Christians in Israel who had been baptized in the Orthodox Church, including this disillusioned interviewee, suggested that I meet a particular priest: a Polish Jew who became a Carmelite monk and served as priest to Arab and Jewish Christians in a nontraditional service in Haifa. This Catholic priest was in fact first recommended to me by Zoya Krakhmal'nikova. On a visit in Moscow, she had given me articles written about him in an ecumenically oriented Russian-language religious magazine.[8] I went to Haifa to meet the popular monk, and learn more about his "conception" of an apostolic Church, shared by a number of my interviewees. My three-hour discussion with Father Daniel in his small meeting house, as other visitors—from Poland, Germany, Israel—filtered in and out, speaking in a variety of languages, was, in fact, one of the final interviews he gave, since he died in the summer of 1998, shortly after I left Israel.

This priest and monk is known throughout Israel for the famous 1962 "Brother Daniel" Supreme Court case regarding Jewish nationality, religion, and the Law of Return. Father Daniel was born Oswald Rufeisen to a Jewish family in Poland in 1922, and spent his youth and adolescence active in Akiva, a Zionist youth movement that later became the Independent Liberal Party in Israel. He and his younger brother escaped to Vilna at the beginning of the war, and lived on what Father Daniel called a "preparatory kibbutz": Kibbutz Hakshara, founded by eighty-six refugee members of Akiva. When the Soviets arrived and the kibbutz was disbanded, his brother managed to leave Vilna and settle in Palestine, as had always been his Zionist dream. Oswald was arrested, escaped, and headed east, instead.[9]

What made the "Brother Daniel" case so newsworthy in Israel in the 1960s was the strong, if paradoxical, sympathy many felt toward this converted Jew. It was well known that Oswald had saved hundreds of Jews in a Belorussian ghetto by passing himself off as a Pole and translating for the Gestapo in the town of Mir. *I was passed over to the gendarmerie, the German gendarmerie, because of my knowledge of German. And I was the right hand of the commander of the German gendarmerie for nine months. I was in uniform. I was dressed in the German black uniform.* All the while, however, he passed information, documents, and weapons into the ghetto. And he let the Jews there know that the ghetto was set for extermination on August 13, 1942. Because of his help, more than a third of the eight hundred Jewish inhabitants of Mir were able to escape into the surrounding forest. Forty-five people still alive at the time of our interview continue to see the renamed Father Daniel as their benefactor, even though the humble man confessed to me that *I'm not a very courageous man.*

A disbelieving Jew in the ghetto revealed to the Germans that Oswald was helping the Jews, and Oswald himself felt compelled then to reveal that he was a Jew. His supervising officer, although fond of his translator, was forced to arrest the daring imposter. Nonetheless, the enterprising twenty-year-old managed to escape yet again, and he took refuge in a local convent of the Order of the Sisters of the Resurrection. It was there, in the attic of a barn where the nuns hid Oswald, that he first read a Carmelite publication on miraculous healings and asked for more books from the convent's library on supernatural cures. He was fascinated, perhaps connecting the stories of divine intervention in the tragedies of human life with his own close encounters with horror. As he revealed to an earlier interviewer:

> And so, after I read about these miraculous cures I asked for the New Testament and began to study it. I also read different Hebrew books that I found in the attic. . . . I was full of questions. I kept asking why such tragic things were happening to my people. I felt very much like a Jew, I identified with the plight of my people. I also felt like a Zionist. I longed for Palestine, for my own country. . . .
>
> In this frame of mind I became exposed to the New Testament, a book that describes events that were taking place in my fatherland, the land I was longing for. This, in itself, must have created a psychological bridge between me and the New Testament. . . . In the convent, all alone, among strangers, I created an artificial world for myself. I pretended that the 2000 years had never happened. In this make-believe world of mine I am confronted by Jesus of Nazareth.[10]

Oswald did not look back. As he told me: *I found myself before Jews, Jewish problems, inside, inside problems, not outside. Not Jesus against Jews. . . . And then discussions, then problems between him and the Pharisees or the teachers, interpreters, all the subject of the priests, problems I knew, being a Jew, I knew what they are, because we had also problems with the same questions: Shabbat, ritual prescriptions, interpretations of the Torah. The "fence around the Torah." How far it is obligatory, how far it is divine authority. The Gospels are this.*

Feeling a personal, *Jewish,* connection to what he read, the former kibbutznik was baptized by the nuns, and *since that day Judaism and Christianity have been always at the center of my very existence.*[11] For him, and as

we have seen for many of the Russian Jewish Christians I interviewed: "In
the end my move to Christianity was not an escape from Judaism but, on
the contrary, a way of finding answers to my problems as a Jew."[12] As he
and virtually all my other interviewees revealed to me, *You see now that I
was always a Jew. I saw myself always as a Jew.*

The newly baptized convert soon felt compelled to leave the convent,
since he recognized that his continued presence placed his new spiritual
sisters in grave danger (he could see the gendarmerie through his attic
window), and escaped, once again, to the forest. But he never forgot his
Jewish/Christian revelation there, so that after the war, Oswald entered
the Carmelite order, taking the name "Daniel," in reference to his escape
from the "lion's den." He became a priest in 1952, and applied for a visa
to Israel in 1956, when Poland's borders opened for its Jews.

But Daniel did not receive his visa until 1959. Applying under the 1950
Israeli Law of Return, by which all Jews are entitled to immigrate and
instantly become a citizen of Israel, Father Daniel was told: "But you are
a monk and a priest and therefore not a Jew!" He answered: "This is my
occupation. But I am a Jew and I have a right like all the other Jews."[13]
However, the case was not as simple as it seemed to the young monk. In
fact, his insistence on his continued, even strengthened Jewishness is the
paradoxical, perhaps inexplicable thrust of this current study of Russian
Jewish Christians.

Father Daniel was finally allowed into Israel, and in due time could
have been naturalized as an Israeli citizen, but he decided that he wanted
more: the designation of "Jew" on his identity papers. He took the case
all the way to the Supreme Court, but was ultimately denied. (Later, he
did accept naturalization.) At that time, the Court's position and that of
the Chief Rabbinate was the reverse to what they are today. The Law of
Return originally understood the question of who is a Jew purely halachically, as anyone with a Jewish mother. The rabbinate ruled that the priest
should be given citizenship as a Jew, for a Jew by birth is always a Jew,
a member of *Knesset Israel*.[14] The Court, based on a later, 1958 interpretation of the Law of Return, ruled otherwise, saying that anyone professing
another religion cannot remain a Jew. In other words, Jewishness remained
legally tied to religious identification, not purely inheritance. Since the
Brother Daniel case, the Law has been further amended to include a
"grandparent clause," bestowing immediate citizenship rights and benefits
of *olim* on the child and grandchild of a Jew, the spouse of a Jew, and
the spouse of the child or grandchild of a Jew, but adding, still, "except

a person who was a Jew and willingly converted to another religion." The amendment has allowed in tens of thousands of non-Jewish or only partially Jewish immigrants from the former Soviet Union (including Ira's husband, for example). But Russian Jewish Christians can, and have come, only under false pretenses.

Father Daniel was a short, soft-spoken man with lively, penetrating eyes. I recently heard an acquaintance referred to as "the only man I know other than Santa Claus with eyes that twinkle." I couldn't help feeling that the description would even more aptly apply to Father Daniel, with his Santa Claus–like attraction to wayward believers, and his commitment to providing services, especially a retirement home and burial plots, to all non-Arab Christians in Israel. Or, looking to his Jewish, rather than Christian identity, we might find an even closer comparison in the character of Gedali, Isaac Babel's bespectacled hero of the eponymous story in his cycle *Red Cavalry*. The narrator, a hidden Jew in a regiment of Cossacks fighting for the Bolshevik army in the Polish campaign of 1920, has sought refuge from war and revolution in the Jewish quarter of Zhitomir on the eve of Sabbath. Gedali, the ancient keeper of Jewish values, asks him rhetorically: "'The revolution—we will say yes to her, but will we say no to the Sabbath?' Thus begins Gedali, entwining me in the silken thongs of his smoked eyes. 'Yes, I hail the revolution, yes, I hail her, but it hides from Gedali and sends ahead of it nought but shooting.'" He continues:

> "But the revolution—that is pleasure. And pleasure loves not orphans in the house. Good deeds are done by a good man. The revolution is the good deed of good men. But good men do not kill. That means that revolution is being made by bad men. But the Poles are also bad men. So who will tell Gedali where is the revolution and where is the counter-revolution? Once upon a time I studied the Talmud, I love the commentaries of Rashi and the books of Maimonides. And there are also other men of understanding in Zhitomir. And so we all, we learned men, fall upon our faces, and cry aloud, 'Woe to us, where is the sweet revolution? . . .'"[15]

Like Gedali, Father Daniel yearned for a "good revolution," infused with spiritual learning, with kindness, and with joy. Again like Gedali, he fought seemingly insurmountable hatred in his ceaseless battle for a better future.

When I met Father Daniel, he wore casual corduroy pants, sweater, and sandals, with his white, Gedali-like beard set off against a scarf, and, later, a poncho to guard against the late March chill. He, together with his helper of many years, Elisheva Hemker, served me coffee and animals crackers *(I'm sorry. For children)*, and continually, but humbly, repeated in his excellent, but clearly not native English, that he wasn't sure that he could help me. He was quite wrong, of course. *I'm not the right person*, he claimed several times, but in fact spoke eloquently on all the subjects that concerned me. Later, he repeated, *You are coming too early, you are coming too early to me*, as he confessed that he, too, is still working out issues of the relationship of nationality and religious identity.

Father Daniel spoke many languages, but was at a loss for what to call himself in any of them. He told me that he did not want to be called a Jew: *evrei* in Russian, *żyd* in Polish. The latter term became the derogatory word for Jew in Russian after the Polish partitions and the subsequent inclusion of masses of Jews into the Russian Empire. If anything, Father Daniel would have liked to call himself a Hebrew: *ivri*, following the prefix *notzri*, the Hebrew for Christian: *Notzri-ivri. Christian-Hebrew. I don't understand why some people do not want to call themselves* notzri. Notzri *comes from Nazareth [the land of Israel]. . . . We are Christian Hebrews here.* Although he continued to live in the Carmelite monastery in Haifa until his death, Father Daniel had stopped calling himself Catholic. *I know the Pope, personally*, he said proudly as he pointed to a picture taken during a several-hours-long discussion with the pontiff a number of years ago, *but . . . I cannot call myself neither Roman of the first Rome, neither Roman according to the second Rome, neither Roman of the third Rome.* Why? *Because to call Rome the "Mother" and the "Center" is an abuse. It is an error, a theological error. The Mother was always here.* He pointed to the floor, to the earth, to the land of Israel where I sat together with him. *I told this to the Pope.*

Based on his own firm theology, Father Daniel instead established a small church, or, rather, a religious center, that attracted many Russian Jewish Christians, as well as other displaced Christians in Israel. He served his own liturgy, based on the early Church gathering around a table, not before an altar, once a week in Arabic, and once in Hebrew. (See Appendix B for the text of the Hebrew liturgy.)

Referring to Israel, Father Daniel repeated the term "home" over and over throughout his narrative. This is our Home, he repeated, this is our Center. For him, the diaspora is the biggest problem for Judaism, as well

as for Christianity. And the same is true for Islam, he added. There is a
possibility for the three religions to reconcile, he believed, but *only* in
Israel. *There* is *a possibility to meet. But there is* no *way to ecumenism outside of Israel.* Unfortunately, even in Israel, *we don't know how to live at
home here.*

As I sat in Haifa and listened to Father Daniel repeat his conviction
that the very land of Israel, the geography of Nazareth, holds the only
clue to peaceful coexistence of a plurality of peoples and religions, I
thought back to my cab ride through the congested streets of lower Haifa,
looking for our meeting place near, it turns out, the Spanish Embassy. I
had spent the night with acquaintances in a beautiful home in the hills,
high above the harbor. The ride down was slow, and we got stuck in
traffic at several points, causing my Sephardic cab driver to curse the
(mostly Russian) immigrants who had flooded into his proud city. He
loves the open, secular atmosphere of Haifa, and told how he had once
had the opportunity to move to Jerusalem for a substantial pay increase,
working in an auto shop. He returned north quickly, however. *I didn't
like to get up in the morning and see rabbis.* At this, he took one hand off
the wheel and spiraled it down from his chin to indicate the traditional
long beard of the ultra-Orthodox. As we tried to turn around and find
a less congested route (I was anxious not to make the busy Father Daniel
wait), the driver went on to another area of distress that interested me
greatly. He began to point out doors on just about every street corner that
led, he assured me, into Russian houses of prostitution. *They come here with
no shoes,* he said, *and now look at them dressed up.* Obviously disgusted, he
indicated several women walking down the street, who may or may not
have been Russian Jewish immigrants, and, for that matter, may or may
not have been prostitutes. (I wondered how he would feel about Russian
Jewish Christians, but decided, wisely I think, to avoid the subject.)

I suggested in my inelegant Hebrew that it might, indeed, be a bad
thing to work in a whorehouse, but wouldn't he admit that it is equally
bad to frequent one? Simple economics tell us, after all, that supply follows demand, and the houses of prostitution would close down if no
one rang the bell. So, I asked, who goes there? Don't they bear some
blame along with the prostitutes, allegedly all Russian immigrants? Who
are the patrons? My driver was quick to reply: *Arabs,* he spit out. *And,*
again taking his hand from the wheel, *rabbis.*

Clearly, this particular Jew, no doubt a life-long citizen of Israel, felt
no benefits from the plurality of belief and nationality that Father Daniel

was soon to proclaim to me. I realized with some of my disillusioned interviewees that it would take much more than small gatherings of "Christian Hebrews" to bring *shalom bayit*, peace to this Home.

Oddly, the most tolerant person I was to meet, perhaps even including Father Daniel himself, came into my ken only several hours later, again in a cab, this time on my way to meet my ride back to Jerusalem. Taking note of my hobbled Hebrew, the driver asked where I was from, and what I do. When I told him I am a professor, with a specialty in Russian religious philosophy, he became quite animated. *I am only a driver, but you deal with books. You do the most important work of all.* I usually find that *I* am the one who needs to defend the humanities in this practical world, and here in a cab I found myself wondering with whom I was speaking. It turned out that, with his bare head, he was not at all the secular Israeli Jew that I had assumed, but an Arab Christian. Unlike my previous driver, there seemed to be room in his world for an American Jew studying Russian Orthodoxy, and, I would suppose, for a Catholic monk who celebrates the Eucharist in Hebrew, not to mention a bearded Orthodox rabbi, whether or not the latter visited Russian whorehouses together with Muslim Arabs. His home—the "Home" Father Daniel constantly evoked—was indeed the religiously and ethnically diverse land of Israel.

Father Daniel's ideal home was not just any pluralistic society, however. *It is not so easy. We are like archaeologists who are digging in order to find out what was here two thousand years ago, three thousand years ago. We are a kind of theological archaeologists.* According to him, *the Jewish religion at that time, or I prefer to say the religion of Israel, was pluralistic. . . . What you call, what we all call Judaism is a substitute, created in Babylonia. . . . A genial substitution. . . . It was genial, but it was created in the diaspora, not here.* Somewhat later he explains that, *In the diaspora it had to continue. But Judaism is a restriction of the religion of Israel.* Judaism, the religion of the diaspora, divides rather than unites Jews. *It is dividing the Jewish people. But in Israel it is not dividing. Because we have another factor unifying all of us. It is the state, the idea of Home, of the Holy Land, we are here again at home. The culture, the language.* And later: *I think this is one of the reasons why Ben Gurion called the state Israel and not Judea. We are called for two thousand years, even more, Jews, Yehudim, and now he comes and says, Israel. The twelve tribes. It means larger than Judea.*

For Father Daniel, there is not one, but two diasporas: the diaspora of Judaism and the diaspora of Christianity. *Here you have the quintessence of our problem. . . . Now, with Christianity it's the same. The nucleus, the matter, was the predication of Jesus. Yes? But it seems that he never intended to create a new faith, another faith, another religion, a new religion.* That "new religion" happened only later, in the diaspora, when the Church moved away from the land of Israel and from the Jews who began it. As a matter of fact, some of his discussion with the Pope centered around the errant Father Daniel's insistence that the Church is not the "new Israel," as claimed by the Pope. *It was the beginning of the conversation, and I didn't want to begin to attack him, but a little later, about a quarter of an hour later, I told him: "It seems to me that, according to Paul, speaking about the tree and branches and, well, that tent that had to be enlarged, it is more an 'enlarged Israel,' the Church, an 'enlarged Israel.'*[16] *And he did not react. Only after, we continued to speak. Only after another ten minutes or half an hour, he interrupted me, excused himself, and told me: "I made a mistake. I'm sorry. I made a mistake. I want to correct it. It is not right to call the Church the 'new Israel.'"*

Later, Father Daniel reminded me: *It does not mean to make all the Christianity Jewish. This will be an absurdity. No. No. But you know that in the beginning there was an ecumenism. We forget about that. Because the apostles prayed in the synagogues. They continued to pray in the synagogues, according to the Acts of the Apostles. The apostles. And the first Christians. In the synagogues. And they participated in the sacrifices of the temple. Even Paul.*

In the pluralistic society of two thousand years ago, a society that "theological archaeologists" in Israel might discover, *Christianity was normal, was at home here.* What Father Daniel called the "misunderstanding," the "quintessence of our problem," came as the Church was established apart from the Jews. *Catholic, Orthodox. What is the original meaning of Catholic? It means "according to the meaning of the totality." Totality. Whole. The whole, oui? Is from Greek, yes? And totality doesn't mean the universal "Church" of all nations. No. Absolutely not.* He then used Solovyov's term for the Universal Church: *Vselenskaia tserkov'. No. It is false. If I had the possibility to ask both of them, my greatest brothers, Paul and Peter: "What does it mean, what could it mean in your time?," both would answer me, surely, "Yes, Catholic means not* only *we Jews, also the others." But [it] never [meant] a Church without Jews. And never a Church without gentiles. You see?*

But I was not sure that I understood his quarrel with Solovyov—why did the term Catholic, totality, not suggest Solovyov's Universal Church?— and I pressed him to explain. *It is not vselenskaia tserkov' because vselenskaia tserkov' from the beginning, from Constantine the Great, meant a* Church without Jews. Actually, Solovyov did include a vital role for the Jews in his future Universal Church, and he insisted that it was not coincidental that the majority of Jews in his day lived precisely on the border of Catholic Poland and Orthodox Russia. Ultimately for him, however, the Jews would affect a reconciliation of East and West, would help create the Universal Church of the future, and then the Jews would see the wisdom of baptism in it. They would become Christian, and no longer be Jewish.

You see? Father Daniel repeated. What I did see now was why this Jew, baptized by the Sisters of the Resurrection, no longer called himself a Catholic, for it is an identity he associated with what he would call the Church of the diaspora, a religious establishment, like Judaism, conceived and practiced outside of the land of Israel, in which Jesus himself preached. His ideal Church, instead, was a Church that includes Jews, *as* Jews, in the center or home that is Israel. As he stated: *the basilica in Rome is called Mother and head of all the churches of the town and of the world,* urbis et orbis. *But this is not true. The Mother was never there. It is a historical falsification. The Mother was Israel.*

What I still did not understand in our discussion, however, was Father Daniel's belief in Jesus as the "Son of God," a term he had avoided in our historical and political discussion. Was Jesus of two thousand years ago more than a Jewish teacher to Jews and gentiles, an interpreter of Jewish scripture for a new and more widely flung generation, someone who wished to "enlarge the tent," as he said in his discussion with Pope? Father Daniel chided me: *You must abandon this* goyishe *kind of thinking. This is what I called brainwashing, you know. We are not allowed to rethink the things according to their original meaning.* In his liturgy, he told me, there is no creed, as was established by the very first Church councils: "I believe in One God, the Father Almighty . . . And in One Lord Jesus Christ the Son of God, the only begotten . . . Who for us men, and for our salvation, came down from heaven . . . And was crucified . . . And rose again . . . And ascended into heaven . . . And He shall come again with glory . . . And in the Holy Spirit . . ." Father Daniel no longer incorporates the creed into his worship: *I am not saying the creed at least fifteen years. At least.* Furthermore: *I cannot say in Hebrew "Mother of God,"* theotokos. *I cannot call Mary: "Mother of God."* But does he believe that Jesus was God, I asked? *I don't know. I can't say "Jesus, my God" in Hebrew. . . . The son of God.* He sighed. *It is a problem. You see. "The son of God" was a title of the people of Israel, a title of the king. What it means, there are different interpretations. Somebody who is obedient like a son until the end, somebody who is suffering because he sees in God his father, there are all kinds of interpretations. . . . We, here in Haifa, reached the conclusion that we cannot call Jesus* Adonai: *"my God." Jesus was a servant of God. Of God his father.* Adonai *is only God. The Creator.* So Jesus in the theology of this Christian-Hebrew, this *notsri-ivri*, was not necessarily the Only Begotten. But did he believe that Jesus rose from the dead? Was there a miracle in his Christianity? *No, no. I believe that Jesus was chosen by God. And he remained faithful to this, to this vocation, and to his vocation, personal and messianic vocation, and perhaps, perhaps, well, I do not, well, believe. Perhaps therefore he was called "my son." But "my son" must not be a pre-existing son. . . . But I'm not an Arian. I'm not an Arian or a Unitarian. Because the Arians were also Greeks. And the Unitarians were also Greeks. . . . I am not giving a clear answer.*

Father Daniel's answer, however, was clearer than he suspected. What I understood from his narrative and from a number of my other interviews was a desire to keep their Christianity close to the Judaism from which it was born, and a desire to keep their own Jewish identity central in the religion of Jesus. Father Daniel advocated a kind of apostolic Jewish Christian Church in Israel. He dreamed, perhaps hopelessly, of a Church in which Jewish national identity would be vitally important, as it was before the institutionalization of the Church among the gentiles outside of the land of Israel, as it was when Jesus of Nazareth roamed the land.

He wavered between optimism and pessimism in our interview. *Today, Christianity has an interest to know better its own roots. Ja? Therefore, not only pilgrimages, they are not only coming to see the holy places, but also there is a trend to know the language, to know the people. To know the [Hebrew] Bible. You know, the Bible is read. So, there is a possibility to meet somewhere. With the Jews, because today, for the Jewish people, Israel is the Center. There is no doubt. Israel is the center of the Jewish people. And it seems that in Christianity there is a trend in a similar direction, yes? You spoke about ecumenism.* (Actually, it was Father Daniel who has spoken about ecumenism.) *There is no way that ecumenism outside of Israel can grow. Only through Israel. Because we must find a common platform. The common platform could only be the* first *platform. And then everything went apart. Not immediately, not immediately, but it happened. . . . Now there is a [new] possibility to meet.*

A JEWISH CHRISTIAN CHURCH IN ISRAEL

Avraham, who knew Father Daniel well, also wavered between optimism and pessimism during our two interviews. He was firm, however, in his belief that the Russian Jews who have come to Israel in such numbers will have a special role to play. That is why he is working on a full translation of the Hebrew Bible into Russian, as well as teaching in a study center, to help preserve the connection to Russian culture in Israel. *It is as though we are beginning a new epoch,* he told me. *I don't know if we will succeed. But for me it is very important, because I believe that the million Jews who have come here need to preserve their connection to Russian culture. And for their children. . . . the situation in Israel differs from the "melting pot" of America. There you had a kind of bazaar, but here you have a constant war.*

Avraham protested that *I am not a good example of, as you said, baptized Jews. The fact is that many Orthodox believers would consider me a heretic now. But I don't want to play the ridiculous role of heretic.* In fact, he turned out to be an excellent example of a baptized Jew whose once intense participation in the ritual of the Orthodox Church forced him to confront conflicts in his Jewish identity, but who wanted, still, to reconcile his Christianity with his Jewishness.

Like Oswald Rufeisen forty years earlier, Avraham saw himself in the Christian texts he first read. *The Christianity that Jesus revealed to me is Jewish at its core. Jesus was a Jew from the very beginning. With that kind of Christianity I would be fully at home. Now I see that this is a huge problem for Christianity itself. It needs to solve its problem somehow in our era. Otherwise, I don't know how the Church will continue to survive.* A Jewish Christian in New York remembered the same connection to the time of Jesus during his years after baptism in the Soviet Union: *We organized prayers at first at home. We prayed in Hebrew. We prayed, as we imagined, the first Jewish Christians prayed.* For both of these men, their initial experience of Christianity brought alive their connection to ancient Jews.

Seryozha did not feel that connection until he actually came to Israel. Although he had not planned to make *aliya* when he first visited his father with only two suitcases, *I came and I stayed, because two realities caught up with me. One is sitting in front of you,* he said as he pointed to his wife, *and the other was the land of Israel, also feminine gender, by the way. The land of Israel, and the people of Israel. I felt myself part of that people. In some completely ideal way, I felt as though the sensation that I was an apostle and a Jew was hidden within me. . . . It was a feeling of completeness. . . . Here I understood the directions of my teacher [Jesus]. I understood his words. Because he was more of an Israelite that anyone I had met.*

Seryozha was already Christian at the time of his *aliya,* and Israel brought him to a new level not of his Christianity, but of his Jewishness.

Instead of saying, as was often said, in fact, by Solovyov, that Christianity is the completion of Judaism, Seryozha claimed, when I asked about what it is like to be a Christian in Israel: *This is very Jewish* [po-evreiski]. *To be a Christian here is the same as being a Jew in a Christian country. For me, this is the completion of Christianity.*

There was a common theme here, and one that came together for me as I listened to Father Daniel's dreams—*You have come too soon to me*—and saw the small room where his ad hoc congregants came to celebrate. Again Avraham: *I came to Jesus through those gates as to a Jew. As a representative of the Jewish religion. I related to him as to a Jew. I saw in him a Jew* (iudei). *This sounds strange to you. But the deeper I went into the Church, the more deeply I felt myself as belonging to the people of Israel. Many people are surprised by this. It should be just the opposite.*

I, in fact, was not surprised at all, having heard something similar already many times. Mikhail Agursky had written the same, although I only learned of it after I had completed my interviews: "In the New Testament I immersed myself in a Jewish world, in Jewish history. . . . What is more, in Christianity I first began to acquire a Jewish consciousness that had been denied to me. . . . I began to discern in myself a kind of continuity with my forebears, a continuity lost by my parents."[17]

Avraham continued his narrative about his Jewish identity in the Russian Orthodox Church, and the conflict that it created: *But because of this, I took a stand against much that was happening in the Church. I'm not against the Church. I am against the fact that it is being destroyed from the inside. Not just antisemitism. Hatred to Judaism. Hatred and rejection of Judaism. It is not that the Church is antisemitic. You can be an antisemite or not an antisemite. A Jew or not a Jew. This is universal. But that condemnation of Judaism that has made its way into the theological thought, into the liturgy—I know it well, I studied it—that is suicide for the Church. It is destroying the Church from the inside.*

The rejection of both Jews and Judaism in the Orthodox Church threw many Russian Jewish Christians into a severe identity crisis: *A terrible problem arose,* confessed Boris. *My attitude toward the Church was serious. Without compromise. From that side, I couldn't negate what had simply become my life. But what happened, the spiritual lie, immediately hit me. At first it was very good for me. In the early days I ran to the Church as a child. But the first sermon I heard was about the* zhidy [kikes]. *In the most negative sense. The Jew as Satan. The highest level of antisemitism. Nazism. Orthodox Nazism. That is what hit me. And I entered a crisis.*

Boris saw Israel as the place where he could be a Jew without apology. *I had an idea to come to Israel to live an Orthodox life here. A utopia. . . . Why did I leave? The contradiction between prayer and life is still an unanswered question in the Church. For me it was a principle question. The lie. And a lot of antisemitism has made its way into the liturgy as a mystical element. This contraction is primary. At first I heard it, and I shut my eyes to it. But it was there. It exists in the very liturgy. In the most sacred moments. The Easter service is full of it. I saw Catholic nuns in the Eastern rite,[18] who had simply taken all of that out. They just took the books and crossed out the lines. So that it is clear that the word "Jew" used to be there. They took it out. But there, in the Orthodox Church, there was none of that. Just a contradiction.*

What was the contradiction? *The Gospels yes, the Orthodox Church, in its contemporary form—no. And me? Where am I?*

This Russian Jewish Christian made *aliya* in the mid-1990s, literally on his birthday, hopefully to be "reborn" in what Father Daniel called "Home": *Ultimately, there could be no question. I knew. A monastery for a monk. The priesthood for a priest. And Israel for someone who feels himself to be a Jew. Either you live in your sealed monastery with its golden cupolas, or you live a real life. Crude. And cruel. Without defense. So I decided. The mass of contradictions forced me to leave. . . . On the one hand, I was afraid to leave for Israel. On the other hand, I could not be a full Christian there. With my Jewishness. It would prevent me from being honest in the Church. I am a crude person. Like a spoiled child who swears at his mother and everyone he loves—that was me. My internal spiritual crisis was so great.*

But what happens in Israel, where a Jew can be a Jew, presumably, with no internal conflict? One of Boris's children was enrolled in a religious nursery, and wore a kippah when I met him. Another attended the Tali School where my son also studied for the semester we spent in Jerusalem. Tali provides a Jewish religious education, although not a strictly traditional one. This compromise to Israeli options seemed a common thread in Boris's circle, where, he told me, they still gather together to pray, but do not necessarily go to church. Boris has not baptized his youngest child who was born in Israel, and an acquaintance he wanted me to meet, also a Jewish Christian, could never arrange a time, being too busy preparing for his own son to become *bar mitzvah.* Boris works part time in a Jewish religious institution, albeit a non-Orthodox one. But he still calls himself a Christian. How did he reconcile this? After his severe identity crises: *What remained of the Gospels, of the Truth, is that all questions were posed anew.* I think of Father Daniel's chiding that I pose questions about Jesus as the son of God in a *goyishe* way, unwilling to see things wholly differently. For Boris, who spoke always in an intense whisper, at breakneck speed: *I no longer had the need to call Jesus "God." It is false. The* shekhina *is in me. The* shekhina *is in you. The presence of God is simply a fact of human life. . . . Immaculate conception? The conception of every child is a miracle of God. I quickly and easily rid myself of the Russian Orthodox liturgy. So easy, that you can see a distinct boundary between my life there and here. There was nothing inside me there. I sang those words, and my heart was silent. And here I was free of all that. You understand. I became more myself. Faithfulness to the Church traditions remained, but it was heavy in me. It seemed to me that I was a traitor. To Christ. I am betraying God. Here there was none of that. I can praise Jesus in that he was a very strong teacher. His accent, which he left in his sermons, in fact forbids those things on which the Church lives. . . . It is not in the externals, but inside that you seek God.*

For Avraham, *I feel myself both within and outside all confessions.* He thought this might be a very Jewish position: *Maybe that is my Jewish complex,* he said, and we both laughed. If it is a Jewish complex, Boris has it, too: *Still, and maybe this is a contradiction, I still consider myself a son of the Church. I don't feel that I entered the Church in vain. I feel that I entered because God intended me to. And the Church helped me in its time. Without it, I would have died spiritually. I wouldn't have come to Israel.*

Sounding much like Father Daniel, Boris described his current, "pluralistic" spirit: *Not mysticism, but a direct relationship of man to God. What is that? It is Israel. It is Sinai. It is the giving of the Torah. All of these are Jewish themes.*

For these Russian Jewish Christians, the question of their Christianity is connected tightly to the question of their Jewishness. I heard over and over that the Jewishness of Jesus is central to his very message, and his message is tied to the land of Israel, the land these Jews have taken as their new home. Barats, in his personal *midrash,* unselfconsciously called his emigration from Russia an "Exodus." Avraham firmly believed that *The Gospels have more Jewish than non-Jewish roots. Even though the composition of them was later, you cannot understand them without understanding Judaism. That is why I study the Second Temple. Jesus belongs to Judaism more closely than he does to any of the later manifestations. Of that I am sure. He did not create a new religion. That is my position. And Paul also did not create a new religion.*

In contrast to those Russian Jews still active in the Orthodox Church because of what they call its broad, universal tendencies, Avraham and his cohort focus on the particular "Jewish moment": *This is a personal issue. They might put the emphasis on the universal aspect of the Church. This is what attracts them. It also attracts me. But the Jewish moment is the most important.*

To the ears of this American Jew, some of these statements sounded uncomfortably close to the proclamations of Jews for Jesus, or what are called Hebrew Christians (not Father Daniel's Christian-Hebrews) or Messianic Jews in Israel.[19] Strangely, to a one, every Russian Jewish Christian I spoke with rejected Jews for Jesus, despite their desire to see a reconciliation of Christianity and the Jews. Avraham, who was most articulate about his longing for a Jewish Christian Church nonetheless declared: *I do not wish the Messianic Jews success here in Israel.* Why? Some answered that Hebrew Christians are, in essence, Protestants. If my interviewees had left the Church, they wanted no part in *any* established religious institution. If they had not, they remained loyal to the ritual, and the aesthetic or mystical appeal of their own. Even more, though, it seemed to me, they felt that the understanding of Jesus, and of Israel, was tied, somehow, to their own Russian, Soviet stories, and to their own personal narratives of faith. The very fact that they, as previously nonbelieving Jews, had entered a Church with a strong national identity, and with a strict ritual basis that includes antisemitic under- and overtones, affected their very understanding of Christianity.

For Russian Jewish Christians, Jews for Jesus are unacquainted with the history of the Church, with the raw pleasures of its ritual but also with its tradition of antisemitism. It is as though many of my interviewees felt that no one could understand the truth of Christianity if they had not come through the spiritually debilitating Soviet experiences that they themselves had. Because they had been, or remained a part of the Russian Orthodox Church, they believed they understood the conflict of Jews in a non-Jewish Church in a way unavailable to other Jews, and other Christians. Unlike Jews for Jesus and Messianic Jews, my interviewees were not missionaries. Never did anyone try to bring me to Jesus. They wished instead to bring their Christian religious identities together with their own Jewishness through the Jewishness of Jesus' Christianity.

At first confirming what I had found in the narratives of Russian Jews still in the Church, Avraham stated: *When I talk about Christianity at lectures in Russia now, I see that the more educated people say that Christianity is closer to them than Judaism. That Christianity is more understandable than Judaism. Not that they will convert. But from the ethical side . . . as related to Russian culture. People were brought up on that culture.* But he continued, clearly thinking about his own experience both entering and leaving the Church: *It is a different thing when an obvious Jew enters the Church, and seriously enters it, when he begins to read the Gospels and commentaries on them. Then the "moment" of Israel is "genetically" emphasized. He begins to consider his Jewishness. And if you are at the center of the Church, that makes you think even more about it.* For these Jews, grappling with their Jewishness in the land of Israel, but not willing to abandon the impulse that first led them into the Orthodox Church, Jesus' message expresses the essence of God, before the "diaspora" religions of both rabbinic Judaism and ecclesiastic Christianity. "Their" Jewish Christian Church would be true, authentic, founded on the research of Father Daniel's "theological archaeologists," and enlarging on that of the apostles. In many ways, they were not interested in bringing Jews to Jesus, but in bringing the true Jesus back to the Jews from whence he originally came.[20]

THE MATURITY OF CHOICE

The crisis of identity that most of my interviewees faced as a result of their choice both to enter, and sometimes to leave the Orthodox Church was similar in both generations of baptized Jews. One Russian *oleh* of the 1980s generation spoke of his new attitude to life as "mature"; he claims that he left his *spoiled childhood* behind for the more real struggles of life and identity he has found here in Israel. Another talked of a *crisis of faith, but in the best sense.* An interviewee from the 1960s generation, who now regularly attends the Orthodox church of Father Alexander Borisov in Moscow, talked of a "maturing" of her attitude toward Christianity. And like Boris and his new understanding of the *shekhina* in all of us, her "mature" understanding also brings Jewish, or Judaic, values together with her Christian identity.

It is worth quoting Marina's articulate explanation of the changing understanding of herself at length: She brings back the theme of literature and philosophy for these intellectual Jews, and describes how she moved away from her early bookish understanding of the Church to blend her new identity with the memory of her Jewish ancestry:

> *There was an unbelievable thirst for knowledge. I read books during those years that greatly surpassed my, shall we say, intellectual abilities. We were carried away by Berdyaev at that time. In general, he introduced the theme*

of freedom into our lives. We were rather obsessively focused on that issue. But our understanding of freedom did not at all coincide with Berdyaev's. But at that time we didn't even notice. Now I read him and his books, well, they make me smile, with the arbitrariness of the thought process, the lack of strict thinking. But at that time it was all a mish-mash, but a wondrous mix of all we read. It was very difficult. And Solovyov, of course . . . Three Conversations *. . . We had everything typed and retyped. So, in that sense, we obviously experienced a very interesting youth. My youth was filled with this kind of intellectual food. But quite a few years had passed before it became clear to many of us at least that Christianity didn't consist of this. That this was the spice, very interesting, but not required. What was more real on that path we had chosen was to learn not to quarrel with our mothers. This is a more authentic goal for a Christian. Not to quarrel with your mother, to have patience with your neighbor. To follow certain things that, say, my grandmother, who was not a believer, would do, a woman who had high morals. And now when I am almost her age, I see that I will never reach her higher level of morality, she, a nonbeliever. It was so deeply ingrained in her soul. Now I can tell you this. Everything that she did, that she said, was absolutely, completely noble, truly self-sacrificing. She never served herself, she always served those around her. She never raised her voice. She never spoke out of irritation. But it took a long time in the Church in order to understand what is significant and what is less significant. What is real and what is less real. Now I can tell you that the reading of religious philosophy is less real than the ability to control your behavior at all times, from morning to evening to adhere to certain formulas of behavior.*

Marina's comments confirm much that I heard throughout all the interviews about ecumenism, about "true" Orthodoxy, about the "original" teachings of the apostles in the land of Israel, and about what is wrong now with the Church:

Furthermore, I must tell you that I don't see any insurmountable barriers between Judaism and Christianity. I don't feel at all alienated from a Jew who sincerely feels his Jewishness. Since childhood I have known the theme of Jewish charity. We always helped the poor in my family. Not emotionally. My grandmother did it very severely, coldly, like a Pharisee, in the exact meaning of that word. Tithing. I don't know if she gave exactly a tenth, but it was a mitzvah. I knew that Jewish expression. It is very harsh; but we, today's Christians, in today's world, we need to grow to that—here I am

talking again about Phariseeism, but that means to fulfill that which is nec-
essary. You don't do it out of love, your love might not be sufficient. But you
fulfill the law. But we, without enough love, consider the law dry, dead. If
you don't fulfill the law, and you don't have love, how can you call yourself
a Christian?

So, what does a "mature" understanding of the Church (Marina says *we need to grow to that*) require for many of these Russian Jewish Christians who were baptized as part of their search for meaningful spiritualism amid the vacuum of Soviet reality? Avraham broke out of his *spiritual prison* only to find that he needed to face even larger questions of spiritual identity as a Jew in the Orthodox Church. He needed to understand who he was as a believer and a Jew. And, he and the others found, now, that their hybrid Jewish-Christian identities ironically require more of what they had thought was the Judaism that had never attracted them; it required *mitzvoth* in the strict, "harsh," real-life, often "unaesthetic" meaning of the word. It is the *way of the cross*, said Seryozha ironically, or so I thought. As Father Men' wrote, "We are not in a nursery school, we are in life, life with all its rigours."[21] Still, for these Russian Jewish Christians, baptism did not bring them a return to Judaism per se, but it brought a different, fuller sense of their Jewishness. They found their Jewish identity could be, in fact needed to be, religious and ethnic at the same time.

Thus, Marina attends church on Sundays, but writes on Jewish themes and tries to emulate her righteous Jewish grandmother throughout the week. Avraham sits with his two small children in the impoverished trailer where he lives, wondering how best to bring them up as *menschim* and *tsadikim* in Israel, their new home, embroiled in Jewish, Christian, and Muslim conflict. Osip feels isolated in his desert town, no longer attending church, but remembering that the intensity of his Jewish Christian dreams are what brought him to Israel. Pasha and his wife go weekly to Father Michael's parish, the one place where they feel they can be both broadly universal and particularly Jewish at the same time. For most, baptism was not the resolution, but the beginning of their identity conflicts. But few would trade that conflict for anything. It is, as Seryozha says, *very Jewish.*

CHAPTER SIX

Concluding Thoughts

The Responsibility of Chosenness

༼༽

a vague Jewishness
multicolored prayer.
He spits it out, gets baptized.
And lights [church] candles.
He mixed God up.
And got the expected punishment.

—"Udivlenie," Mikhail Zhvanetskii, 1995,
trans. Alice Nakhimovsky

THE UNIQUE SOVIET SETTING

Despite the desire of the Russian Jewish Christians to avoid the term conversion, or *perekreshchenie*, and despite the truly unique aspects of their experiences, we nonetheless need to recognize the similarity of the phenomenon considered here to other cases of conversion that have become increasingly prevalent in recent years. Many scholars have noted a turn toward religion in general, and connect the modern phenomenon of religious thirst to the problem of disjunction in contemporary life: "The more tradition loses its hold, and the more daily life is reconstituted in terms of the dialectical interplay of the local and global, the more individuals are forced to negotiate lifestyle choices among a diversity of options."[1] A study of American (but not Jewish) converts to Russian Orthodoxy claims that we are all in a transition period, and are engaged in a search for belonging, in quest of a "grand narrative."[2] The desire for tradition brings many converts *to*, as well as *away from*, Judaism in today's postmodern times, of course, as is clear even from the title of an important book on the subject: *Tradition in a Rootless World.*[3]

131

The case of the Russian Jewish Christians explored here is clearly part of the search for belonging in our disjointed times. When asked recently if I am surprised by the fact that some Jews chose baptism in the Orthodox Church during this time period, I have to answer no. But what *is* surprising is the way in which those Jewish Christians now talk about their identities, the way in which they see themselves connected to the "grand narrative" of Jews and Christians and of the history of Western civilization from biblical times to our day. Their own narratives are special, then, not only for the sociological and/or spiritual fact of conversion, but also for the particular historical, linguistic, and cultural context in which their embrace of religion, and of that particular religion, takes place.

The narratives of faith collected here reflect a number of unique aspects of that context. The first, and perhaps most important for the Jews and for the intelligentsia as a whole, is the profound ideological vacuum that existed in the Soviet Union after the revelations about Stalin's Terror. Faith in communism disappeared almost entirely among the intelligentsia, or I should say that it disappeared among those members of the intelligentsia in which it had been able to continue to exist through the Stalin years. Tellingly, when some interviewees talked of their mothers' chagrin over their baptism, they expressed it less as an affront to Judaism and more as a betrayal of the socialist values to which some of the older generation still clung. Other nuanced reactions unrelated to the religious issues were of course also possible. Boris's mother, for example, was upset not because a Jew became a Christian, but *that I was living in such an "uncultured" way. That I didn't have a refrigerator. That it isn't a life. The terrible cold. Poverty. That is what she was upset about. I was her little baby. A "genius," as children are for their mothers.* But Boris found the deprivation of a dissident life in the Church preferable to the "culture," or, rather, lack of culture that surrounded him in the late Soviet period. When even the Marxist-Leninist belief in atheism of the earlier revolutionaries was lost in the younger generation, their response, like Boris's, was to shake off all aspects of "culture" that remained.

The generation of the 1960s thus associated entrance into the Church with a resurrection of idealism in general, not purely as a religious step. As such, it was a political statement of dissent. For the less politically, perhaps more philosophically minded, entrance into the Church was also an expression of the self, of the individual personality, the *lichnost'*, that the Soviet *kollektiv* relentlessly suppressed.

The 1980s generation had a similar response, but to a paradoxically opposite context; for those Jewish intellectuals, the Soviet Union was not a monolithic ideological prison, but a rapidly changing, even disintegrating battleground. As Benjamin Pinkus found in his exploration of the Soviet Jews of the time who returned to Judaism:

> The existence—in the 1980s and on into the 1990s—of an ambiance of disarray and fear of the future in the Soviet Union, along the lines of an "earthquake" or "total disintegration"—created situations that are specifically conducive to quests for solutions and paths, including some of a totalistic nature, such as the return to religion.[4]

From this point of view, the baptism of Russian Jewish intellectuals into the Orthodox Church in the 1960s through the 1980s and early 90s can be seen as a *Soviet*, not a specifically Jewish, and not a specifically Christian, phenomenon. Some Jews found "solutions and paths" in Judaism, while others found them in Russian Orthodoxy. That certain charismatic figures like Fathers Dmitry Dudko or Alexander Men' came along at this time to bring these searching intellectuals into the Church is not purely coincidence, of course. Men' himself, like Marina, Viktor, or Michael, felt the effects of the Soviet context around him. Yet, we must not underestimate the role of these attractive figures who were able to bridge the intellectual gap between religion and science, who could bring worldly historians, engineers, and writers into a mystically oriented, highly ritualistic Church. As Osip told me, he at first felt alone in his search: *An absolute individual path. And, in truth, if I had not met Father Alexander, I wouldn't have traveled it. Both his books and his personality. That combination. And what I said before: Readiness to believe in things that contradict the Soviet reality, insofar as you know that everything is built there on a lie.* Osip had *an internal readiness* because of the arid, antispiritual Soviet context in which he lived. *And then, when you are given information that you can't prove, but by a man that you trust, then that produces a very strong impression.*

Furthermore, as we saw, the "aesthetic element" of the Orthodox Church, its accessibility because of language and culture, and, conversely, the lack of familiarity with Judaism, all played crucial roles in bringing Soviet Jews toward baptism in the Russian Orthodox Church. All of these are understandable stimuli for their choice, and I need not belabor them any more than I already have. Some paradoxes still remain in the narratives, however, and we need to take a step back to examine them now in slightly more detail.

THE UNEASY INTERRELATIONSHIP OF RUSSIANNESS AND JEWISHNESS

In the beginning of this book, in the section dedicated to a brief history of the so-called Jewish question in Russia, I quoted Gitelman as saying that Soviet Jews were "acculturated without being assimilated." Ironically, both Jewish intellectuals and Russian, then Soviet, authorities had succeeded in creating a Jewish Russian strictly *national* identity that excluded religion. The Russian Jews became "Russian" in terms of language and, largely, culture. But, although they were acculturated, they were never fully assimilated, and continued, in fact continue to this day, to feel marginalized as Jews. Thus those Russian Jews who entered the Russian Church spoke frequently of "our" Russian culture, of the choice of Orthodoxy because of the Russian language or Russian literature or religious philosophy.

But the mainstream Russian Orthodox Church, most acknowledge, does not welcome Jews. Unlike many religious groups with strong outreach to searching souls, the Orthodox Church does not immediately embrace those who might wander in from the street. Tentative worshipers are not "bombarded with love." Quite the opposite. They might be scolded for some ritual misstep (like the crossing of my legs in the church in Ein Kerem) or, most likely, ignored, as I have been on many occasions when I entered Orthodox churches in Russia. All the more, if the new faces look Jewish, they might experience what David did when he attended churches without an already established core of Jews: *Before we had our own church, we would go around to different churches, and when we stood in line to receive communion, we heard, "look, Jews have come for the sacraments." They could tell. In Russia they can tell. They always knew I was a Jew. . . . Even here* [in New York], *when we first went to the Russian Church in Exile, the priest almost fainted when we went to confession and he realized we were Jews.*

For the reasons discussed earlier in this study, many of these Jews have nonetheless persevered. (David told me that the fainting priest ultimately came to accept the Jewish parishioners, and made sure that no one else offended them.) The perseverance, again, had much to do with context. Many of the Jewish intellectuals who took the step of baptism saw a special connection between their status, precisely, as *Russian Jews. Nothing happens by accident,* I was told on numerous occasions.

One Jewish Christian, in his heartfelt battle for the reunion of Jesus and Jews that he believes will take place in Israel now that so many Russian Jews have emigrated there, believes firmly that victory can come only through a preservation of *Russian* culture and language. A scholarly translation of the Hebrew Bible into Russian will allow for the beginnings of that reconciliation: Russian culture with Jewish ethnic origins, steeped in the original words of both the Old and New Testaments. This will be the bedrock of their double chosenness.

I was quite struck by Galya's articulation of a specifically Russian Orthodox–Jewish connection. She is extremely gifted both linguistically (she speaks fluent English, Hebrew, and, of course, Russian) and musically; she sings in her parish choir, as well as studies ancient musical arrangements. Her interview with me was peppered with Hebrew words and a discussion of their flexibility, and she expressed her own connection to Christianity mostly through the issue of language and music.

Galya made *aliya* to Israel as a teenager, and only then began her path to faith. She first surprised her parents by beginning to keep kosher. *But my fascination with Judaism,* she told me, *as is common for the Jews, started with the language. It is really amazing the compactness and purposefulness, the beautiful functionality of Hebrew. . . . After a while you realized that the sense of the mystical, not the abstract as with the Greeks, but the mystical and purely physical, is so intimate and self-evident in the Old Testament that faith stops being intellectual.* In short: *I was first hooked on Judaism through the language.* She studied Jewish religious texts seriously: *There were some books in the Old Testament toward which I was naturally more inclined, and that included Isaiah, first and foremost. And just something, some of the Psalms. And suddenly the mention of the anointed one became very concrete.*

The discussion of the concrete and the mystical that Galya *first sensed through the* [Hebrew] *language* might remind us of Solovyov's interest in the Jews as an organic integration of the material and spiritual. Galya, however, cited Florensky, rather than Solovyov at this point: *Remember how Florensky described how a voice called him? . . . For me it was a personal call. And that dimension is present sometimes in the most mundane, but I first sensed it, even before you put it in those terms, I first sensed it through the language. And it impressed me tremendously.*

Why did she turn to Orthodoxy, I asked, for here was someone who had already found a community for herself in Israel among religious Jews? Why not go more deeply into Judaism? On the one hand, as others had confessed, Galya told me that it was because of the particular personalities whom she met. But there was more than coincidence involved, and that "more" grows directly from a relationship that she and other Russian Jews felt exists between Jewishness and Orthodoxy. It is why they feel doubly chosen to be part of both. As Galya expressed in her typically self-reflective way: *Even from the point of view of ritualism, I have been obsessed my whole life with not casting aside or discarding a tradition, but seeing what comes first and what comes second. And for that reason, actually, when I got interested in Christianity or, rather, in Christ, I would first and foremost look into Orthodoxy precisely because liturgically, and so forth, it is tied with Judaism. The framework is all there except that you have the responses, say, to the Psalms and to the Old Testament readings in the Byzantine verses. They would always play for me the same, the same values, especially the way they attack, tackle the antinomial.*

Russian Jews could see a special meaning in specifically *their* attraction to the Orthodox Church, as a kind of new universalism similar to that of Solovyov's. For Solovyov, it was no coincidence that the majority of Jews in his lifetime were settled on the border between Catholic Poland and Orthodox Russia. Those Pale of Settlement Jews for him signified the possibility of the creation of the true and enduring Universal Church, based on the Prophetic values of the Jews, but, as he said, integrating the Kingly principle of Russia and the Priestly principle of Poland. Geography and national identity were no coincidence, just as it did not feel like a coincidence to some of my interviewees that baptized Jews were coming to Israel precisely at this time. As intellectuals and heirs to the utopian dreams of Solovyov, the Russian Jewish Christians of this study believe that the Church was born from Jewish ritual and Jewish "values," as both Galya and Marina felt, no matter how far Orthodox practices might have moved from their origins. The ritual itself proves the mystical connection of identities. For Avraham: *If the Church had not awakened its Jewish beginnings, not a single important incident in the life of Christians in the entire world would have taken place. That is how it was from the beginning. That is its identity.*

As seekers for spirituality, these Russian Jews could find their *lichnost'* or inner personality in their very own home. The Russian Orthodox tradition into which they were acculturated, if not assimilated, was now re-infused with its Jewish meaning.

Galya continued: *For me, the flesh of the covenant tradition is tremendously important. But it is very important to realize what comes first and what comes second. And for that reason, I would choose, theologically, I would choose Orthodoxy over not only Protestantism, but even over Catholicism. But it would be purely theological.* Galya insisted that she did not choose Orthodoxy because of her Russian background: *The question of nationalism would not come into it because it would not come into it in Judaism.* Nonetheless, the liturgy that she sings with such love is chanted in a particular language. When she talked to me of a certain influence on her, *a great liturgist,* the linguistic connection became clear: *He was also very musical, although it was never his speciality. He taught me a lot about early Russian chants and that is how my interest first emerged. And he would be very much interested in asking me to help him find the original Hebrew verses. So that is how I started working on God's liturgical links between Orthodoxy and Judaism formally, and how my musical interests emerged.* And later: *So to some extent I owe them* [the "great liturgist" and his wife] *a strong sense, a very strong sense of continuity between Judaism, musically and liturgically, and Orthodoxy.*

Thus, Galya vehemently rejects any nationalist angle of the Orthodox Church, but still expresses her mystical connection to Orthodoxy through Russian language and liturgical music, the very material, concrete, physical expression of that intangible spirit that she seeks. And, insofar as she is interested in *what comes first and what comes second,* what is primal for her is the connection between Hebrew and Russian Orthodox liturgy. Her status as a Russian Jew, the time she spent in Israel, and her fluency in Hebrew bring her closer to the spirituality that she sought, and that she feels she found in the Church. What I call the paradoxical interrelationship of Russianness and Jewishness continues to play a part in her path of faith.

The relationship of Russianness and Jewishness plays a large role in virtually all the narratives I recorded. As we saw, for Father Daniel, too, the question of national identity played a role in his identification as a Christian throughout his life, although in his case the identities are Polish and Catholic, not Russian and Orthodox: *In the end my move to Christianity was not an escape from Judaism but, on the contrary, a way of finding answers to my problems as a Jew. . . . For me the acceptance of Christianity was a Jewish step. It was a move of a Jew toward a certain historical period of the Jewish people.*[5] As Father Daniel's biographer writes: "Significantly, Oswald insists that in the convent Christianity did bring him closer to Palestine and hence closer to his national Jewish identity. At that point he began to reason that if, for example, a Frenchman, a Pole, and an Italian can be Catholic, so can a Jew. Issues related to the separation between religion and nationality, in his case Jewish nationality and Catholic religion, continue to preoccupy him."[6]

My children already have American culture, but Russian culture is foreign to them, says one émigré in New York. For him, however, Russian culture was part and parcel of his own identity as a Russian Jewish Christian. Another interviewee married a South American Jew in Israel. Their children are secular Israelis, and alienated from religion of all kinds. But this Christian was baptized in Russia, into the Orthodox Church because *I was in Moscow, so it was natural. . . . It was the local Church, and the Church connected to Father Alexander* [Men']. His interview with me was in Russian, the language, after twenty years in Israel, that he is still most comfortable speaking.

Osip told me that he speaks Hebrew at home with his wife and children. And that he has not succeeded in passing on his Russian Orthodox belief to them. I began to be curious about the future of the Orthodox Church in these Russian Jewish families, and struck by how many do not carry on the tradition. It is true that Galya's entire family, including her mother, is now baptized in the Orthodox Church, and Orthodox ritual items are scattered throughout their small home. And the children of my long-time friend in Moscow are Orthodox; I went to the baptism of one of them. But many other Russian Jewish Christians do not share their faith with their children. For her part, Marina *dragged them* [her children] *to church in their childhood, they are baptized,* but neither son is a practicing Christian today. We saw that Father Georgy wanted to share holidays with his Zionist son, but the latter did not follow him to the isolated village church, and entered politics in Israel instead. And Osip's children do not speak Russian, much less Church Slavonic. Entrance into the Orthodox Church was a highly personal choice for these Russian Jewish Christians, connected to their quest for their own personal identities, their *lichnost'* as both Jews and Russians in the post-Stalinist Soviet Union.

Despite the similarities between the baptized Jews and other converts in their search for a "grand narrative" to explain their significance in a "rootless world," as discussed in the beginning of this chapter, we also saw at the end of chapter 4 that these Jews are *unlike* other Jewish out-converts. Rather than being "eager to leave their Jewishness behind them," as Todd Endelman has found among the Jewish apostates he studied, the Russian Jewish Christians feel *more* rather than less Jewish after baptism. Instead of rejecting their Jewishness and trying to fade into the majority Christian world around them, the baptized Russian Jews celebrate a newly found positive sense of their Jewishness that can now coexist with their Russian identity. In contrast to the externally based antisemitism *that* largely defined them as Jews before, ironically, as we found, baptism has brought the Russian Jewish Christians a positive and internally based sense of Jewish, and specifically Russian Jewish identity. They are, as we said, doubly chosen.

HEALING THE CHURCH

Chosenness carries responsibility as well as privilege, of course, and an expression of that responsibility, related to the question of antisemitism, recurred throughout the interviews. Oddly, I felt at first, many of the Russian Jewish Christians used the same metaphor to discuss antisemitism in the Church. *The Russian Orthodox Church is rather sick*, Marina pronounced. *The Church is infected with antisemitism*, Felix complained. Boris felt that, *The Orthodox Church here was suffering from illnesses. The typical illnesses.* Viktor, who claimed that it never affected him personally, nonetheless told me that, *I look on such things in the priests or the parishioners I meet as a kind of illness.* Later in the same interview he repeated: *I relate to it as an illness. Simply as an illness.* Avraham, in his usually dramatic way, pronounced that the Church *is infected by antisemitism.* He developed the metaphor even further: *It is not just a disease in the Church. It is a genetic disease. It is destroying the Church from the inside.*

So what, we might ask, are the Russian Jewish Christians doing in this hotbed of infection and disease? One might assume that they, too, would become infected. And, in fact, such so-called self-hatred is not unheard of among acculturated Jews in Russia as well as elsewhere. As Markish points out, "Russian self-consciousness can lead a Russified Jew even to the point of anti-Semitism."[7] Jewish out-converts to other denominations have been seen to suffer from the illness. In discussing American Jewish participants in the "Messengers of the New Covenant," Isser and Schwartz argue that, "modern Jews who have converted to 'Hebrew Christianity' or 'Jews for Jesus' groups are not only plagued by the 'ineradicable' Jewishness within themselves, but frequently suffer as well from minority self-hate, often manifested in anti-semitic behavior"[8]

The new, positive and internal identification of themselves as Jewish, however, alters the relationship of the Russian Jewish Christians to the disease of antisemitism within the Church. Their special status as doubly heirs to God's chosen people bestows upon them a new mission, a positive and internal role to play within the Church: that of healer. This mission closely corresponds to Father Alexander Men's work in the Church. He saw himself as helping to heal the division between Church and society, between science and religion, between believers and nonbelievers, and between the Orthodox Church and other denominations. The very fact that he baptized so many Jews, and was himself Jewish by birth, also suggested to many of the Russian Jewish Christians a reconciliation of the unhealthy fracture between Christianity and the Jews.

Avraham, like his spiritual mentor, Men', feels *obligated to help*, but he did not sound optimistic when I spoke with him: *Since I have lived here in Israel, my heart is pained both for Israel and for the Church. It is my disease, my constant problem.* He believed that his scholarly work *will have an effect. But not on the official Church.* He went on to say sadly: *I can say this to you because you are a Jew, and not a Christian. The Jews do not have a future in the Orthodox Church. In Russia. America is a different story. But in Russia it has become a big problem among the Jews. It is the same for the Jews who helped make the Revolution, and then the Revolution turned against them. Jews have done a great deal for the Church and for the culture there. They could help mutual understanding between people in the Church. But they will suffer for the fact that they are Jews. If anything happens, "they" will let them know.*

We might understand the fact that many Russian Jewish Christians gravitate toward more liberal, ecumenical churches as a recognition of the progress of the "disease." Some, like Zoya Krakhmal'nikova, have chosen to speak up against antisemitism in the Church, but I know that she felt tremendously alone, and seemed bitter and exhausted when I saw her last. Many of the subjects of this study seek to retrieve a sense of the Jewish Christian community of apostolic times in a possible attempt to steer the Church back toward health, but even Father Daniel felt discouraged when I spoke with him. *You are coming too early to me,* he repeated several times. Thinking back on the many comments about infection I heard, and contemplating Father Men's murder, some say at the hands of antisemites in the Church itself, Father Daniel's comment can sound as pessimistic as it first did hopeful.

∾

As we saw, the reasons for baptism of these Jews are many and largely understandable: a general spiritual longing felt in many societies beginning in the 1960s; the particular spiritual vacuum in Soviet culture; the attachment of Jewish intellectuals to Russian culture in the midst of their detached world; charismatic individuals who drew others to Orthodoxy along a bridge between the secular world of the university and the Church; the unique aesthetic and mystical draw of Eastern Christianity. Russian

Orthodoxy promises a great deal for anyone with spiritual longings. Several of the interviewees talked of spiritual feelings still in childhood. For Boris: *When I was little, God lived with me. Without any question. I had no question about God's existence,* and Seryozha remembered talking to God *very early. Before school or in the first years of school.* Despite the fact that Boris did know a religious Jew, in exile in Kazakhstan for writing to a rabbi in the West, Judaism was not an option toward which to direct his spiritual yearnings. As one former resident of St. Petersburg told me: *The synagogue there was very weak on the spiritual plane. But in the Church there were rather profound people.* The same, we heard earlier, was true in Moscow, where *there were only old men.*

What we have seen, however, is that the baptisms in the late Soviet Union differ on several levels both from earlier waves of baptism in Russia and from other examples of Jewish out-converts, not only because of the historical and social context of the Soviet and ex-Soviet Jews who joined the Orthodox Church, but because of their self-identification as Jews afterward.

The phenomenon explored here differs from previous waves of baptism in Russia on the one hand because the Jews were not forced to convert, as were, for example, the cantonists in the nineteenth-century imperial army. On the other hand, the Jews did not choose baptism because of any hope of promotion, advancement, economic or educational opportunity, or other convenience. In the Soviet period, there was absolutely no convenience to be gained by participation in the Church, and quite a bit of danger, instead. At least three of the Russian Jews I interviewed for this study had spent time in prison because of their Christian beliefs, and one had been confined to a mental hospital, a place from where many dissidents returned utterly broken. One of Father Michael's reasons for emigration was fear that he would be picked up by the KGB and, given his previous "diagnosis," would be institutionalized again, *where they destroy people completely.* As it is, *every six months I had to change apartments. My parents' telephone was bugged.*

In many ways, this late-Soviet wave of baptisms was a continuation of the movement of the pre-revolutionary intelligentsia toward the Church, with an interruption of some fifty years. Solovyov, Florensky, and Berdyaev all turned to Orthodoxy after disillusionment with their youthful enthusiasm for Marxism, and Jewish intellectuals followed suit as well. Semyon Frank was baptized (although his son joined the Anglican Church after immigration to England, and his grandson re-embraced Judaism). Lev

Shestov, though never baptized, was interested in the nonrational aspects of the Church, and often cited Christian sources in his writing.

We might see Boris Pasternak, who grew up with these earlier thinkers, as in intermediate figure, and several of my interviewees cited him. One interviewee pointed to Pasternak's search not only for faith, but also to be part of the larger Russian culture as well. He was not entirely successful: *Pasternak, who was a baptized Jew, a Christian who believed in a kind of personal faith, as I understand it, perpetually wanted to become a part of Russian society. Ultimately he began to complain that he was writing only for the Jewish intelligentsia in Russia. In* Doctor Zhivago, *he tried to negate Jewishness, but in the negation you feel that he couldn't fully pull himself away.* Thus, like the earlier intellectuals of the pre-revolutionary Silver Age, Pasternak was drawn to the mystical spirituality of the Church. But like the later Jewish intellectuals who survived Stalin (as Pasternak did, but only barely), the pull of his Jewishness remained strong. In this sense, he needed to be more committed than the most committed Russian to be accepted in the Church.

A Russian Jewish acquaintance told me a memory from her childhood. Her father was waiting for the arrival of an usually prompt friend, who showed up more than an hour late with this explanation: *I was walking along Klementovsky Alley, past the church, when fate intervened. I bumped into Boris Leonidovich* [Pasternak] *at the gate as he was leaving. You know, when a Jew engages in Russian Orthodoxy, he gets very excited. So, for all this time Boris Leonidovich was retelling me a text from the Gospels. Very heatedly and in great detail. With commentary.* The tone of this story suggests that Pasternak's ardor about his new Russian faith was transparent, at least to this interlocutor and to the young girl who overheard the story, if not entirely to Pasternak himself. He never stopped being "Jewish."

We have noted that the vexing issue of Jews in the Church increased between the two generations of Russian Jewish Christians quoted here, in direct relationship to the emigration movement and, for many, to their attitude toward their new home in Israel. In this way, too, the phenomenon of this study differs from earlier waves of baptism. All ethnic groups in the late Soviet Union felt a growing self-awareness, and the Jews were no exception. Those Jews in the Church faced additional conflicts about their Jewish identity.

In addition, the baptisms of Russian Jews in the 1960s through the 1980s differed from what we saw as the phenomenon of out-conversion of Jews in other times and places and/or acceptance of Messianic Jewry or Hebrew

Christianity. They did not take on Christianity in order to be Russian, and not simply to escape antisemitism. In any case, neither outcome resulted. They also did not join the Church because of a feeling of inclusiveness that Russian members of the parishes they attended directed toward them. Perhaps like other spiritual seekers of the 1960s and beyond, they turned to religion to express themselves in a repressive society, to find a connection to something beyond themselves and beyond the society in which they lived. The result was not a finding of themselves on an individual basis, but a paradoxical return for them to the strength of their Jewish identification.

Thus the path of faith through the Orthodox Church oddly became a path of reconnection to Jewry and, although in a decidedly nontraditional manner, with Judaism. As a Jewish Christian wrote in a poem shortly after his baptism:

I reject you, Israel,
And I am with you now, to the end.

None of the Russian Jewish Christians interviewed for this study knows what the end will be. But all recognize that the unique circumstances of Soviet reality that brought them to baptism, and their intense time within the Church, no matter how short, helped define them now both as Russians and as Jews. They have a dual religious identity, a dual national identity (sometimes now triple, in emigration), and a special sense of chosenness. The small group's impact on the larger course of Russian, and Russian Orthodox, history might be equally marginal, despite small steps toward "healing," but the stories they tell are central to our larger understanding of our own individual narratives of identity.

The stories gathered here speak, and speak for themselves, with the theological and emotional power that generated them. The twinkly eyed Father Daniel, who spoke with the force of Gedali as though of an impossible Third International, repeatedly crossed the seemingly impenetrable borders that define our identities in his beloved Home of Israel. Boris, who first read the Gospels as a "Jewish" book, was ultimately drawn by the visceral attraction of Orthodox ritual to its "musical mysticism." His children live in Israel, and wear *kippot* with his blessing. Vitya claimed he read Russian religious philosophy as a purely intellectual activity, but came to know the "mystery" of the Orthodox Church as well, even in his new home of New York. Marina relearned the lessons of her great-grandfather, who spoke like a character in a Jewish joke, but who taught her the values that underlie her hybrid adult self. All at one point felt the force of spiritual renewal on the borders of Jewish-Christian identity, on the borders of Russian-Jewish identity, on the borders of the secular world of the intelligentsia and the irrational world of faith. Their double chosenness now speaks in the many voices of their narratives.

Appendix A

Sample Transcript:
Interview with "Marina"

In kitchen of her dark, cluttered apartment, as she prepares soup. I sit on a stool at the kitchen table covered with typical oilcloth of Soviet/post-Soviet kitchens. She is cutting, washing vegetables as speaks. She is in a hurry to get to a meeting, and then to accompany someone to airport, then out of the country in a few days to visit her son in New York for several months. Frequent interruptions from phone calls. Short, attractive, graying woman in her fifties.

"If possible, simply tell me a little about yourself and about your path to faith, about how you relate to Jewish . . ."

I should tell you that I come from a good Jewish family, a correct (pravil'naia) *Jewish family.*

"Correct?"

I'll tell you what I mean. I'll explain. The thing is that I had a great-grand-father, who was ninety-three years old when he died. And I was seven. We spent a lot of time together. He loved me very much, and he was a man of faith (veruiushchii).

"Of faith?"

Yes, of faith. And now as I look back on it and can evaluate from this per-spective, he was a righteous person (pravednik). *He was a very small, old man. He was kind and good and bright.*

"He spoke Yiddish?"

He spoke Russian rather poorly, with a strong accent and with mistakes. He talked just like a character from a Jewish joke.

[Laugh]

Of course he was a man who I remember always with a Torah in his hands. I remember these images from childhood, when he . . . Wait, let me finish with this onion . . . When he would pray, he would wear a tallis, *and I would sit by the table and grab onto the fringes. That was my childhood pastime. He was a real authentic Orthodox Jew. I remember very well how he would lie with me on the couch and tell stories from the Bible and Jewish history. He had cancer of the lungs . . . ahhh . . . of the stomach. He would have pains, but apparently not really strong.*

"This was the father of your mother, or of your father?"

He was . . . the grandfather of my mother.

"Oh, of course, the grandfather . . ."

He was my great-grandfather.

"Yes, yes."

So, the two of us would lie there, he with his vodka, which was categorically forbidden to him, but, but it would lessen the pain, and he would tell me stories from the Bible. So, you see, the inoculation was very early, very beneficial, because when he told stories you had the feeling that he was telling stories about one of our relatives. Essentially, that's how it was. That was the beginning of the 1950s. I was born in forty-three. . . . So, that was the time of the campaign against cosmopolitanism, it was, say, forty-nine, something like that. The hardest years for Jewish families, Jewish intellectuals, for Jewish medical families. My mother was a medic. So, difficult to the highest degree . . .

"Yes, yes, especially since . . ."

So, my grandfather died . . . I have a, well, very sharp memory of him from childhood, I have preserved a very sharp . . . So, when I was already a grown girl, and I met with Christians, grown Christians—there weren't so many in my circle—those were Christians of the highest caliber. They weren't of this generation. They were Christians who very consciously, very seriously and with full responsibility related to their Christianity.

"Well, of course, because it had been so dangerous, they had to treat it very seriously . . ."

Yes, of course, of course.

"Who in particular? With whom in particular?"

One of the first people shown to me—I say shown to me because I feel there was nothing accidental, nothing casual in our relations, our connections were quite deep—was a woman, E. V. [name omitted from typescript for privacy]. She was a re-emigrant, in that is she had returned from emigration to France, that is, when she had already returned. A Parisian priest, Father Andrey Sergeenko brought her. He was a priest who had also spent thirty years in Paris and came back to Moscow in 1949, by invitation of the Patriarchate in the postwar years. He was surprised . . .

"He was Orthodox?"

He was Orthodox, had graduated from the Institute in Prague, a very typical story. He had been an officer in the White Guard as a sixteen-year-old, he left Russia through Bulgaria, Yugoslavia, to Prague, the usual path. He finished theological institute, was ordained in Paris. He was close to Father Sergei Bulgakov. That circle. Not in the Church in Emigration. But the Church that maintained ties with the Moscow Patriarchate. He was a particularly enlightened man, without illusions. He fully understood . . . [Wiping away tears . . .] *Here, I'll finish* [with the onions] . . .

[Laugh] "It's okay. I'm not crying."

He fully understood what was going on in the Moscow Patriarchate, in its so to speak highest echelons. When he came in 1949, he saw a tremendous number (they traveled around Russia at that time), a tremendous number of believers. Churches so packed that you couldn't raise your hand to cross yourself on holidays. And he . . . he had a parish in Medon [?] at that time, if I'm not mistaken, yes, he served in Medon, and what kind of parish was that? Only about, well, thirty, twenty or thirty people would come to the parish on holidays. So, when he saw what a large number parishioners there were here, and the monstrously low level of knowledge of the local priests, which he could judge very well, well, he decided to return for good. So he did. They received him very kindly, appointing him Professor of Theology at the Theological Seminary in Petersburg. But he couldn't get acclimated there. The level of culture was so low. It was such new wine in old bottles. He was noticeable there, so naturally . . . [Telephone rings] . . . *they chased him out quickly. Hello?* [Tape off. Tape on.] *Now, where were we? By the way, that* [phone call] *was from the same circle, connected to E. V. So, you understand, that means . . .*

"Here's a question: The circle is tight, it seems to you that . . ."

This week . . .

". . . that is, your group (kollektiv)?"

This week, no, no, of course. This week, a friend of mine died. . . . Among them . . . [skip in tape/unclear] *So, what it means is that it was a "home church"[?], simply put. He had a very complicated biography after that. They chased him all over Russia. Thank goodness they never arrested him. But they chased him out of church after church.*

"I don't understand why they first accepted him kindly."

You know, I think that it was, in part, because he, because they wanted to manipulate him, that they thought, let's say, that he was a different kind of person. Here is a man, so to speak, of unbending beliefs, very firm, and, let's say, well, the Russian Orthodox Church is unfortunately very sick. It suffers from antisemitism. For Father Andrey that was absolutely impossible. For a Christian it is an absolute impossibility. It can never be. I think that might have been the reason. By the way, at that time he brought us an article that perhaps has many questionable aspects, but that at the time provoked a lot of discussion: Bulgakov's article called "The Persecution of Israel" (Gonenie na Izrail'). *At that time the article was brought in manuscript, so I recopied it on the typewriter. It was a valuable jewel. That was one of the topics of discussion. I think there were many. We never discussed that question* [of his persecution?].*You know, it is one of those situations, like oil and water, two substances that just don't mix. So, Father Andrey was very foreign to them, and problems always arose. Still, people were drawn to him. Of course Father Alexander Men' was acquainted with the best of the priests of the Orthodox Church that was then "in the catacombs." At that time he had plenty of quality priests, but, in any case, I saw, I remember that he met Father Andrey as well, in the home of E. V., as a matter of fact. But with all this I have to say that Father Andrey Sergeenko was by no means a revolutionary. He was not at all a man, so to speak, with sharp opinions.*

[Telephone rings]

He simply knew his measure. He was simply a deeply cultured and correct (poriadochnyi) *man. By training I was a biologist. I finished the university in 1968. My dissertation advisor was a man, also a biologist, somewhat older than myself, by the name of Alexander Borisov.*

"Oh, so that was Alexander Borisov."

We both were geneticists, both biologists. We worked together in the same laboratory and we became friends. Borisov's best friend was Pavel Men'. They were students together.

"Pavel?"

So, as you see, the thread that unites us is very short. So you see there were two persons in my life—Father Andrey and Father Alexander—who influenced me the most. Now, that was a time, as they say, of religious crisis. Nothing happens accidentally in our life. Then, there was a feeling of despair, of the senselessness of life. If the world offered no content other than that which was apparent to us, to put it gently, it would have seemed senseless. But, especially, it was a time in the Soviet period that was unusually stifling. So, let's see, it was then that I was baptized.

"In which year?"

I always . . . let's see, I think it was sixty-eight.

"Sixty-eight? When did you finish school?

In sixty-nine. No, I hadn't yet graduated in sixty-eight. I was studying in the university.

"Almost thirty years ago?"

Yes, that was thirty years ago.

[Long pause. Chopping vegetables.]

"At that time did you read a lot about . . . ?"

Of course, I read an awful lot.

"Did you read Solovyov? Bulgakov? Florensky?"

We read Solovyov, Bulgakov, Berdyaev. No, not Bulgakov, I don't think . . . I read through a lot. A. V. had an open library. It was his heavenly kingdom. These were people around whom, so to speak, . . . but . . . They were a kind of twentieth-century apostles. And apostles on a very high level. It wasn't for fisherman then [?]. In those years fishermen didn't need . . . They lent out the books for a night, for a day. There was an unbelievable thirst for knowledge. I read books during those years that greatly surpassed my, shall we say, intellectual abilities.

"Can you say which books struck you most keenly?"

We were carried away by Berdyaev at that time. In general, he introduced the theme of freedom into our lives. We were rather obsessively focused on that issue. But our understanding of freedom did not at all coincide with Berdyaev's. But at that time we didn't even notice. Now I read him and his books, well, they make me smile, with the arbitrariness of the thought process, the lack of strict thinking. But at that time it was all a mish-mash, but a wondrous mix of all we read. It was very difficult. And Solovyov, of course . . . Three Conversations . . . We had everything typed and retyped. So, in that sense, we obviously experienced a very interesting youth. My youth was filled with this kind of intellectual food. But quite a few years had passed before it became clear to many of us at least that Christianity didn't consist of this. That this was the spice, very interesting, but not required. What was more real on that path we had chosen was to learn not to quarrel with our mothers. This is a more authentic goal for a Christian. Not to quarrel with your mother, to have patience with your neighbor. To follow certain things that, say, my grandmother, who was not a believer, would do, a woman who had high morals. And now when I am almost her age, I see that I will never reach her higher level of morality, she, a nonbeliever. It was so deeply ingrained in her soul. Now I can tell you this. Everything that she did, that she said, was absolutely, completely noble, truly self-sacrificing. She never served herself, she always served those around her. She never raised her voice. She never spoke out of irritation. But it took a long time in the Church in order to understand what is significant and what is less significant. What is real and what is less real. Now I can tell you that the reading of religious philosophy is less real than the ability to control your behavior at all times, from morning to evening to adhere to certain formulas of behavior. Which doesn't diminish my continuing interest in intellectual pursuits.

[Pause. Chopping.]

"I have a personal question. How did your mother react to your conversion?"

You understand I had a truly good family, kind, and what's more, we respected each other. My mother treated me with great respect. She related to this as a kind of caprice. She said, "Oh, [Marina] is a believer. It's popular now."

"But she could say that belief is one thing, and Christ is another. A Jewish mother could say, fine, if she wants to believe, let her have her fun, but . . ."

Judith, you see, the thing is that something happens, you see, a process happens at the same time, that you can't take away, that is very characteristic. Seeing a Christian, if you are perspicacious person, who understands life, honest and sincere, a normal person cannot help but feel at least a minimum of sympathy. So my mother, not long before she died, asked me to give her an icon. She wasn't baptized; that would have been wild for her. But she died under the icon of Sergius of Radonezh, the Appearance of the Virgin, on the day of Sergius of Radonezh.

"And so how . . . ?"

That icon hung over her bed for the last two years of her life. And she died on that day. So my mother is connected to Sergius of Radonezh, to one of the Russian saints. And I consider him to be her protector.

[Pause]

So, as I said I had no scenes, no break with my Jewish relatives. Furthermore, I must tell you that I don't see any insurmountable barriers between Judaism and Christianity. I don't feel at all alienated from a Jew who sincerely feels his Jewishness. Since childhood I have known the theme of Jewish charity. We always helped the poor in my family. Not emotionally. My grandmother did it very severely, coldly, like a Pharisee, in the exact meaning of that word. Tithing. I don't know if she exactly took a tenth, but it was a mitzvah. I knew that Jewish expression. It is very harsh; but we, today's Christians, in today's world, we need to grow to that—here I am talking about Phariseeism but that means to fulfill that which is necessary. You don't do it out of love, your love might not be sufficient. But you fulfill the law. But we, without enough love, consider the law dry, dead. If you don't fulfill the law, and you don't have love, how can you call yourself a Christian? That's what is absurd. So my family was in some sense Pharisees, that is, accurate, so to speak . . . but my grandmother did not observe the laws of kashrut, or did so only minimally. Only for the benefit of my grandfather. He would close his eyes. He was a good man. He understood that you couldn't require this extra work, in those times, it was too difficult for a family to observe all the dietary laws. When he would ask if something was kosher, we would say, yes, yes, grandfather.

[Laughs. Pause.]

"You said that you became Orthodox because that was the "local" religion. Do you consider yourself a Christian and not specifically "Orthodox"?"

No, in this world you need to be a certain denomination. So I will say that I am Orthodox. I go to an Orthodox church. It is the local religion.

"But in some sense it is coincidence that you are . . . ?"

Yes, of course. No, I love a lot that is in Orthodoxy. As though I was born with it. It is my language.

"The ritual is beautiful . . ."

Yes, yes. The music is beautiful. I listen to the music with great love; much is warm and significant for me, and important. But there are also many things that are difficult for me, and always were. It is always a difficult joy for me to be in church. It is an internal requirement, I feel. But, on the other hand, I always feel an internal contradiction.

"Actually, to make a generalization, it is a Jewish tendency to struggle with faith."

Yes, yes, of course. That is the story of the patriarch Jacob, beginning with his struggle with the angel. That is a great image.

"Yes, my son's name is Jacob. He struggles all the time."

[Laughs]

And mine is Peter. How can you name a child Peter?

[Laughs]

"Are your children believers?"

It is difficult to answer that question. The fact is that I dragged them to church in their childhood; they are baptized. The younger son is rather indifferent; he is a jazz musician, and all his life is connected with that.

"The one who lives in New York?"

Yes. He lives in an absolutely musical environment. Artistic people in general have a difficult relationship with the Lord.

"That depends on the individual."

It depends on the individual, but it is not at all simple. Creativity is a great and enormous temptation. My older son, well, he doesn't have fully developed relations with the Church, but, nonetheless, he is the kind of person who doesn't miss Easter, who goes two or three times a year, who has an internal relationship to the Church. He doesn't go to church at this time. But he is the kind of person who is no stranger to my problems. He is of course no stranger to the whole complex of ideas that are connected for a person who goes to church, and in general to religious problems.

"Is he married?"

Well, let's say no.

[Laughs]

"Okay, not married. But is she a Christian?"

It would be hard for me to answer you.

"Okay, okay. You don't need to. And your husband? Are you still married?"

Yes, I'm married.

"Is he a Christian?"

Yes, my husband is a Christian, and much more . . .

"Did you meet in the Church?"

No, we didn't meet in the Church. Besides, my husband is not the father of my children. I married him when they were already . . . No, we met when . . . the children were quite young. But let's say that we traveled part of the path together. He was farther along when we met. He is a more intense person, more disciplined. Well, in any case, I know that he has a deep and close relationship with the Church, and we are people who read a lot, who constantly read.

"How do you speak of your nationality? How do you speak about yourself?"

How can I speak about it? I don't have a choice.

"I understand. I understand. But . . ."

We live in a country where there is such a thing as the fifth point; I write "Jew." Moreover, it is often unpleasant to speak about my Christianity. Now there is such an atmosphere in this country, a kind of loud boom of Christianity. It has become a kind of banner of "partiinost'." People who used to belong to the Party, they have a need for belonging [in English], and they have decided to belong to Christianity. That transfer of paradigms is monstrous, and thus I am reluctant to say I am Christian. Not too long ago there was an event, a round table, a meeting of [unclear]. And there was a presentation related to [unclear]. I have something to say about this. The logic of my presentation, it was built around . . . well, as you can clearly see, that, what I had to say, could only be said by a Christian. And I kind of fidgeted before I, well, sort of, took that on, because, well, it is very difficult (ostro) *to be a Christian. If it isn't difficult for you to be a Christian, then you aren't talking about real Christianity. Christianity is a very difficult way of life. There is nothing at all "convenient" about Christianity. And the new Christians of today, they haven't yet become Christians. Understand, they still have a long way to go, because they entered a rather comfortable situation.*

"Yes, that is very understandable."

It goes against my internal sense that Christianity is difficult . . .

"I understand. It is the question of struggle again."

It is a question of the fact that Christianity is not a comfortable way of life. If it is a comfortable way of life, then you should be very concerned and unsettled about where you are headed.

"No, I need to explain a little, because I asked about nationality intentionally. In English, we don't have two words for . . . If a person is a "Jew" [in English] . . ."

Jewish [in English] . . .

"Yes, Jewish, that refers to both religion and nation."

And we have . . .

"I understand. But Solovyov, for example, wrote about the coincidence of nationality and religion. It is a delicate question, because a person can . . . an American Jew can be a nonbeliever, and all the same be somehow closely connected to the Jewish faith . . ."

[End of ᴄide 1]

"I wanted to ask you something. Yesterday an American told me about some gathering of Russian and international journalists, and an Englishman, I think, no, an American, asked about the separation of Church and State. But the Russian who answered didn't even understand the question."

Yes, the illiteracy, the lack of understanding among Russians today is monstrous. Monstrous. At least half of our great Russian nation is convinced that Christ was Russian. Christ was Russian! The Jews crucified our Russian Christ! If you remember in Merezhkovsky's Peter the First, *Charlotte spoke, if I'm not mistaken, about . . . the wife of Alexey, when she came to Russia from Germany, she fell in love with Orthodoxy. It all seemed very alive and attractive to her, but once, when she . . . she spoke about the fact that the Russian nation is so full of faith, so religious, has such a remarkable spirit, and when she asked one old woman believer who are the members of the Holy Trinity, the latter answered: "The Father, the Son, and Holy Nikolai."* [Laugh] *The level of illiteracy is absolutely fantastic. Absolutely fantastic. In some sense, our believing nation is a nation ripe for evangelizing. Missionaries who come find ready soil for anything. In fact, the Orthodox hierarchs who worry about various Western sects are correct. Because, all the same, a Christian should oppose the Krishnas, sectarians of any kind, those with very elementary, crude beliefs. A Christian can oppose this, and a savage cannot. Therefore, they are right, they are right to be anxious about all kinds of dissent, because the people are not prepared; they are ready to seize on anything at all.*

[Pause]

"You are obviously acquainted with Zoya Aleksandrovna Krakhmal'nikova?"

Krakhmal'nikova? Very slightly, but I am acquainted.

"Does she go to your church?"

I'm friendly with her daughter, Z.

"Yes, Z. is my, well, . . . I first met her in seventy-six, so I have known her many, many years."

So that means that you and I . . . I always say there are no longer any people who are strangers. We are very friendly. I said to her that before I leave, we have to . . . Z., I said, you'll have to come over. We agreed that one of these days, we'll get together.

"I'm going to her house tomorrow evening."

That's incredible. So, you see how the world has become? It is just like a little nut. [Pause] Yes, I know Zoya slightly. And I used to read her journals. But I can't say that I am always delighted by what she says. But she is an honest person, sincere and responsible.

"Is she too angry, or something else?"

From my point of view she is too "orthodox." For the most part, I feel comfortable with people of broader interest. She has suffered a lot. She has the pathos of the hero, the spirit of dissidence. It has stayed with her. It is heavy, and makes it difficult to relate to her. Like all heroes. My closest friend from childhood is N. G., so I know about this psycho-physical type, you understand?

"Yes, but it seems to me that this is a character trait of hers, it is not only . . ."

It is a trait . . . it is actually a tragedy, a tragedy, yes.

"Z. understands it like that."

Well, Z. is charming. She doesn't possess these deficiencies, and therefore knows quite well what they are.

[Pause]

"I think that I met Z. through Shragin, it seems to me, because that was the same trip that I met his son."

Boris Shragin?
"No. Boris already was living in America, but I., his son . . ."
Oh, I don't know him.
"Not N.'s son."
N. didn't have any children. I know that . . .
"Yes, that's true. He is the son of his first wife. But he still lived in Moscow, and I met him and, and then he left for America and got married."
Yes, I know. I know it all. There are some children, grandchildren. N. showed me a photograph.
"Well, when I lived in New York, I often saw him, and now, somehow . . ."
And, please forgive my question, but I have a right to ask, do you confess any religion?
"I am a Jew (iudeika)."
An actual religious Jew (iudeika)?
"Yes."
Really? An observant Jew?
"Yes, I am observant. . . ."
You are a rare Jew (evreika). Of course, you study this professionally. But it is always difficult to relate to religious Jews (iudei). Still, it is always unbelievably interesting for me. It is mine, it is what I was born with. I want to know as much as I can about Judaism. I was invited to work in a Jewish theater, just because I seemed to them the most cultured person on the uncultured horizon of Jewish problems. But if Christians *are aggressive, Jews are more aggressive, I simply don't know. I accept that with great difficulty (ochen' ostro), because well, what else can I say, I have an especially strong aversion to that.* [Laughs]
[Discussion of interviewer's history]
I very much understand that. Very much understand. The fact is that we never had a cultured Jewish society. The believing Jews I would see, those like my great-grandfather, I don't know, they were Jews in torn trousers, who couldn't speak Russian, and for a young girl, they were not, well, attractive. There was shame (pozor) of some kind. They would come to our apartment. And I would make as though I didn't know them. So the Judaism that we had in Russia was in the villages, the provinces, of a kind of second tier. Major teachers, thinkers, I just didn't know. I had no experience with them. Although I did have my great-grandfather in my family. But I never went to synagogue. What I saw was not at all attractive.

"Yes, I agree. And it can be a problem with Orthodox Judaism today. It looks like only men, who pray in a closed circle, and what should a young girl do, what should even a grown woman do. It is still a problem for some people."

Yes, yes.

"I'm not going to record more. I think that . . ."

[Tape off. Tape on.]

Alexander Men' was unbelievably important to Moscow Jews. At that deafest, most difficult period, morally religiously speaking, he was very *attractive. And a huge number of Jews who in a healthy society would have used their so to speak Judaic energies—cultural and religious—would have felt themselves absolutely natural in the synagogue, they took on Christianity with Father Alexander out of simple spiritual thirst. Potentially, they were not his flock. It was simply a different situation, Jews who would otherwise have been attracted to Judaism. It is a different story that Christianity is a fire that is very difficult to exit. I know very many people . . . I have a very good friend who has gone through this. A Jew. He was baptized, and then somehow put it aside. I know a lot of such people. I'm not going to name them by name, because their lives then became involved in Judaism, and Jews don't like this very much, and don't excuse it. There is a great cruelty there.*

"Yes, yes, yes."

In that structure. The fact is that Christianity does not let you out very easily. It is difficult to enter, and even more difficult to leave. It always remains with you, that feeling of stepping away, of betrayal. It is very strong. I simply don't know it. No, I don't know it personally, but rather from people who have that experience. . . . But in that sense Father Alexander simply received a flock that otherwise he might not have received in a different situation. He had a huge quantity of young Jews that weren't destined to him, but for whom he built a wonderful life. Those people, who are already grown now, fifty years old, the children of Men's first work, it is a marvelous generation. In the second half of the twentieth century in Russia there were two charismatic figures, comparable because of their influence, although in different spheres: Alexander Solzhenitsyn and Alexander Men'. If the influence, the literary influence of the one grew quieter . . . [Telephone rings] . . . and began to seem somewhat questionable . . . the influence of Alexander Men', on the contrary, has grown even stronger and wider. [Into phone:] Hello?

[Tape off. Tape on.]

Endlessly important, very attractive things. And you know, for the structure of our generation, not of the generation in general, of people who are cut

*off from culture, from true society—Alexander played a colossal role. He was
an apostle in the full meaning of that word. He continues to grow. A huge role.*

"Which Alexander?"

*I mean Alexander Men' of course. No, I was saying that they were compa-
rable figures, they were both of course charismatic. Each had his own type of
charisma. One cleansed the minds of the generation. It was a great, great cleans-
ing, you understand. And the other, so to speak, the other had influence in a
different sphere, a sphere that continues to grow. As it is said in the Gospels,
you know: I will diminish, said the precursor—and he will grow. I need to get
smaller, diminish, and he will grow more and more. His role is huge, actually
speaking, like that of a real apostle. A huge role.* [Telephone rings]

[Tape off. Tape on.]

"It was interesting yesterday, at Sergeev Posad, to see how they are now
taking on Father Men'."

Through their teeth.

"It is possible, but it seems to me that this is something different. They
have opened an exhibit in his name."

You mean at Sergeev Posad? I thought you were at Novaia Derevnia.

"And I was also at Sergeev Posad. They are opening an exhibit in his
name. It is possible, it seems to me, that they are taking him on in the
same way that the Catholic Church took on St. Francis of Assisi. Because
the people are accepting him, so they need to accept him."

It is a very difficult (ostryi) *situation. It is difficult in that, in such a situation, a person speaks totally from within. As a Christian, you can't be an
antisemite. It reaches a breaking point. Either one or the other. Either you are
cross-eyed, or you are blind. Either you are Christian, or you are antisemite.
You cannot be both. Only in illness. Then it is possible. You can suffer from a
serious illness. A Christian antisemite is a sick Christian. You need to heal him.*

"Does it seem to you that the official Church cannot change?"

*I don't see any basis for it. I don't see any basis for it because the society is
now suffering too great a loss, a social loss, the loss of a great country. Orthodoxy is now trying to replace that former greatness, that lost greatness. It is an
absolutely fantastic situation. It is laughable, impossible, but all the same, it
doesn't have . . . When I was a very small girl, then E. V., my late older friend,
would say: Well, that's very simple [Marina]. Problems would arise, the most
varied problems, the most trivial, ordinary problems, about romance, and she
would say: "Well, that's very simple. You should approach Christ, and present
your problem to Him. Some problems will just disintegrate, and it will seem
like they aren't even there." This was very well stated. You understand, there*

are a huge number of problems in Christ's world that we experience very seri-
ously. They simply stop existing. They no longer are. One of these problems is
antisemitism and Christianity. It simply isn't. Despite the full reality of its
existence in the world, in the world of Christ, it simply isn't a problem; it can-
not be, you understand, it could not be.

"Unfortunately, . . ."

When I told you that Christianity is a very difficult (ostro) way of life, this
is exactly what I meant. If you see a Christian who is absolutely content, for
whom all questions are decided, then something is wrong with him. He seeks
comfort and not Christianity.

"I understand that very well. I would like to stay and talk more, but
I'm afraid that I need to go now."

[End of interview]

Appendix B

Father Daniel's Mass

Father Daniel served his Divine Liturgy in Hebrew and Arabic in a small makeshift chapel behind the office in which I met him. The words, which he handed me on a four-page photocopy, are a collation of prayers from the Catholic Mass, the Hebrew prayer book, and Jewish ritual. True to both traditions on which he draws, the service contains a large number of verses from Psalms, but Father Daniel recombines them in nontraditional ways. Significantly, the Creed is not included in this Mass, and the Mother of God is not mentioned. Father Daniel cited only some of the biblical references in notes to his photocopy, indicated below in italics. I have added other significant references, where appropriate. The following is a translation from the Hebrew text, coordinated with common English translations of the prayers and biblical passages.

ORDER OF THE EUCHARIST OF OUR LORD
(Draft)—Haifa 1991, 1994

CANDLE LIGHTING AND BLESSING

PRIEST: The grace and peace of God our Father and of our Lord Jesus Christ be with you.[1]

CONGREGATION: Amen.

(Silent meditation) Psalms 43, 32

SUPPLICATION[2]

READINGS FROM SCRIPTURE (between the readings: a chapter from Psalms or a corresponding song)

159

BLESSING[3]

A:[4] Blessed are You Lord our God, King of the Universe, Creator of heaven and earth.

CONG.: Blessed is the Lord our God, who alone performs miracles.[5]

A: Blessed are You Lord our God, King of the Universe, who created man in his image and likeness.

CONG.: Blessed is the Lord our God, who alone performs miracles.

A: Blessed are You Lord our God, who makes a covenant with Abraham and his descendants.

CONG.: Blessed is the Lord our God, who alone performs miracles.

A: Blessed are You Lord our God, gracious and merciful, who redeems and saves, and who delivered us from Egypt.

CONG.: Blessed is the Lord our God, who alone performs miracles.

A: Blessed are You for the Torah that You gave to us through Moses Your servant.

CONG.: Blessed is the Lord our God, who alone performs miracles.

A: Blessed are You our God, for when the time had fully come You sent to the earth Your only Son, Jesus of Nazareth.[6]

CONG.: Blessed is the Lord our God, who alone performs miracles.

A: Blessed are You our God, for You wanted to renew Your covenant with us through Him, and to share the inheritance of the sons with all the families of the earth.

CONG.: Blessed is the Lord our God, who alone performs miracles.

A: Blessed are You our God, the Father of our Lord Jesus Christ, who with His great mercy caused us to be reborn in the resurrection of Jesus from the dead.

CONG.: Blessed is the Lord our God, who alone performs miracles.

A: Blessed are You our God, who poured out Your Spirit for the forgiveness of our sins and to establish us on the way to inheritance.

CONG.: Blessed is the Lord our God, who alone performs miracles.

A: Blessed are You Lord our God, who is faithful in all His words.

CONG.: Blessed are You Lord our God, God of Israel, who alone performs miracles. And His glorious name will be blessed forever, and His glory will fill the earth. Amen and amen.

PRIEST: The Lord be with you.[7]
CONG.: And also with you.
PRIEST: Proclaim the Lord's greatness with me.
CONG.: Let us glorify His name together.

PRIEST: Let us give thanks to the Lord our God.

CONG.: It is meet and right.

PRAISE (and at the end):

—Holy, holy, holy, the Lord of Hosts, His glory fills the heavens and the earth.[8]

Hosanna in the Highest; blessed is He that comes in the name of God. Hosanna in the Highest.

CONG.: Hear God our supplication and send Your Holy Spirit to unite us in Jesus Christ your Son in the hour in which we prepare this feast of covenant as he commanded us.

REMEMBRANCE

PRIEST: When the hour came, Jesus bowed and his apostles with him. He took the bread, he blessed it, and he broke it and gave it to them saying: "This is my body that has been given for you. Do this in remembrance of me."[9]

Blessed are You our God, King of the Universe, who brings bread from the earth.[10]

CONG.: Amen.

—They break the bread and eat.

PRIEST: Likewise he took a glass after the meal and he said: "Drink of it, all of you; for this is my blood of the new covenant, which is poured out for many for the forgiveness of sins."[11]

Blessed are You our God, King of the universe, creator of the fruit of the vine.[12]

CONG.: Amen.

—They pass the glass and drink.

PRIEST: Every time that you eat this bread and you drink from this glass, you are remembering the death of our Lord until he returns.[13]

CONG.: We announce your death and give testimony of your resurrection until you return. The Lord has come![14]

Or:

PRIEST: Every time that we eat this bread and we drink from this glass,

CONG.: Christ lives in us and we live in him.

THANKSGIVING (based on the blessing after the meal [Birkat haMazon])[15]

—Psalm 23

PRIEST: Let us sing to God a new a song, because He performs miracles.

CONG.: His right hand and His holy outstretched arm give victory to Him.

—Psalm 98 or other verses

PRIEST: Blessed are You our Lord, the Creator and Giver of sustenance to all.

God is great and greatly praised—and His greatness cannot be known.

CONG.: From generation to generation Your deeds are praised—Your greatness is retold.

PRIEST: God is good to all—and He has mercy for all deeds.

CONG.: The eyes of everyone have hope in You—and You give them food at the right time.

PRIEST: Blessed are You, who opens Your hands and gives food to all creatures.

CONG.: Blessed are You Lord our God, King of the Universe, who feeds everyone.

SONG OF THANKSGIVING:

PRIEST: Give thanks to God because He is good.

CONG.: For His mercy endures forever and He is faithful to all generations.

PRIEST: He is mindful of His covenant forever, of the word that He commanded, for a thousand generations, the covenant that He made with Abraham, His sworn promise to Isaac,[16] which He confirmed to Jacob as a statute, to Israel as an everlasting covenant.[17]

You delivered us from Egypt with Your great mercy and You did not abandon us in the wilderness and Lord our God, You gave us manna that we did not know nor did our ancestors know.[18]

We give thanks to You for the bread with which You have satisfied us, and for Your word that You put in our heart.

We give thanks to You our Lord, the Father of Jesus our Lord, who has blessed us in Christ with every spiritual blessing in the heavenly places.[19]

Blessed are You, for the eternal life that You planted in our hearts through Jesus your servant.

Blessed are You, merciful Father, who brought us to the kingdom of Your beloved Son, in whom we have redemption, the forgiveness of sins.[20]

CONGREGATION: (Song) Who could express the greatness of God; who could express all of His glory?[21]

PRIEST: Please be compassionate, our God, with Israel Your people and with Jerusalem Your city.

Spread over it the shelter of your peace, so that all Your sons can live in peace.

Look at the communities of the Messiah. Lead them with Your Spirit

And gather them from the four corners of the earth to Your kingdom that You have prepared for Your sons.

I entreat You, Lord, that You listen to our prayer, and remember . . .[22]
(Meditations)

CONG.: Hear our voice and save us.

PRIEST: In Christ we are called sons of the Lord, and because of that we say together:

—Our Father who are in Heaven, . . .[23]

PRIEST: May the peace of the Lord be with you always.

CONG.: And also with you.[24]

Handshake of peace

PRIEST: May God be gracious to us and bless us and make His face to shine upon us that Thy way may be known upon the earth, the saving power among all nations.[25]

PRIESTLY BLESSING (or other blessing from the Hebrew Bible or from the letters of the New Testament)

Notes

1. Introduction

1. Naomi Shepherd, *The Russians in Israel: The Ordeal of Freedom* (New York: Simon & Schuster, 1993), ix, 185.

2. Henceforth, all quotations from transcripts of interviews are indicated in the text by italics, while citations from published material are set off in quotation marks. Unless the interviewee has published on the subject of his or her Christianity, as a Jew, only given names are used, usually in altered form, and are omitted altogether whenever possible. Many Jews in the Orthodox Church are reluctant to identify themselves publicly for fear of discrimination from both Jews and Christians. Jews who converted to Christianity and then arrived in Israel under the Law of Return have very specific legal and financial concerns as well. All translations from Russian are my own, and often specifically aimed at preserving the flavor of the interviewee's speech.

3. A source of conflict between Russian-Jewish *olim* and native-born Israelis has been the former's assertion of their higher level of "culture," because of the value they placed on going to the Russian ballet, to concerts, and so on.

4. I argue elsewhere that the very title of this book, as well as many of its entries, reveals a very "Jewish" understanding of exile on Shestov's part, despite his strong attraction to the Russian classics. See "Vechnyi zhid: Lev Shestov i russkaia religioznaia mysl'" (The Wandering Jew: Lev Shestov and Russian Religious Thought), in *Russkaia Literatura XX Veka: issledovaniia amerikanskikh uchenykh,* ed. B. V. Averin and Elizabeth Neatrour (St. Petersburg: Petro-Rif Publishers, 1993), 46–57.

5. *The Prose of Osip Mandelstam,* trans. Clarence Brown (San Francisco: North Point Press, 1986), 76–77.

6. We can find a similar flight in the both the life and poetry of Joseph Brodsky.

7. Shepherd, *Russians in Israel,* 184.

8. Statistics are unavailable for the number of Jewish converts in the late Soviet period. Clearly, the movement began very small, in a small circle of friends, but Father Alexander Men' (see chapter 3) wrote of performing "waves" of baptisms in the late 1980s. Father Daniel (see chapter 5) claimed "that at least 70,000 immigrants during the last decades' wave of immigrants from the former Soviet Union came as Jews but were baptized before their departure" (David B. Green, "The Troublemaker," *The Jerusalem Report* vol. 9, no. 1 [1998]: 100). Jewish Christians, particularly in Israel, are often reluctant to identify themselves publicly for fear of discrimination by Jews. In Father Daniel's words, they have to "behave like 'Marranos.'" Still, extrapolating from the ease with which I was able to meet many in Moscow, New York, and Jerusalem, as well as the later contacts I made through earlier ones, I would also estimate the number to be well into the thousands. A recent survey of Russian and Ukrainian Jews undertaken by Zvi Gitelman and two Russian colleagues and discussed in the following chapter found that more than 13 percent of their respondents feel that Christianity is the "religious faith most attractive" to them. If only a small portion of that percentage took the step of baptism, this would still be a large number of Jews in today's Orthodox Church.

9. The display of icons, of course, is not, per se, a sign of religious practice in Russia. Rather, icons are marks, precisely, of *Russian* cultural identity.

10. For statistics and a typology of converts in the pre-revolutionary period, see Mikhail Agurskii, "Conversions of Jews to Christianity in Russia," *Soviet Jewish Affairs* vol. 20, no. 2-3 (1990): 69–84; and Michael Stanislawski, "Jewish Apostasy in Russia: A Tentative Typology," in *Jewish Apostasy in the Modern World,* ed. Todd M. Endelman (New York: Holmes & Meier, 1987), 189–205.

11. For more on the contemporary Church's own attempt to define itself vis-à-vis the Jews, see Judith Deutsch Kornblatt, "Christianity. Antisemitism. Nationalism: Russian Orthodoxy in a Reborn Orthodox Russia," in *Consuming Russia: Popular Culture, Sex, and Society since Gorbachev,* ed. Adele M. Barker (Durham, N.C.. Duke University Press, 1999), 414–36.

12. Boris Shragin, *The Challenge of the Spirit,* trans. P. S. Falla (New York: Alfred A. Knopf, 1978), 134–35.

13. Carl Mayer, "Religious and Political Aspects of Anti-Judaism," in *Jews in a Gentile World,* ed. Isacque Graeber and Steuart Henderson Brit (New York: Macmillan, 1942), 312. Cited also in B. Z. Sobel, *Hebrew Christianity: The Thirteenth Tribe* (New York: John Wiley & Sons, 1974), 256.

14. Aharon Lichtenstein, "Brother Daniel and the Jewish Fraternity," *Judaism* vol. 12, no. 3 (Summer 1963): 269.

15. Mikhail Agurskii, "Epizody vospominanii," *Ierusalimskii zhurnal* 2 (1999): 207, 215, 216. The episodes relating his experiences with Russian Orthodoxy were omitted from Agursky's published memoirs, *Pepel Klaasa: Razryv* (Jerusalem: URA Publishers, 1996). See chapter 3 for more on Agursky.

16. Nikolai Berdiaev, *Samopoznania* (Moscow: DEM, 1990); in English as *Dream and Reality: An Essay in Autobiography*, trans. Katherine Lampert (1950; reprint, New York: Macmillan, 1951) and excerpted in *Russian Philosophy*, 3 vols., ed. James M. Edie, James P. Scanlan, Mary-Barbara Zeldin, with the collaboration of George L. Kline (Knoxville: University of Tennessee Press, 1976), 3:167.

17. See Pavel Florensky, *The Pillar and Ground of the Truth: An Essay in Orthodox Theodicy in Twelve Letters*, trans. Boris Jakim (Princeton: Princeton University Press, 1997).

18. Pavel Florensky, *Iconostasis*, trans. Donald Sheehan and Olga Andrejev (Crestwood, N.Y.: St. Vladimir's Seminary Press, 1996), 71–72.

19. Agurskii, "Epizody vospominanii," 208.

20. Mikhail Aksenov-Meerson, "Solov'ev v nashi dni," in S. M. Solov'ev, *Zhizn' i tvorcheskaia èvoliutsiia Vladimira Solov'eva* (Brussels: Zhizn' s Bogom, 1977), x, xiv.

21. For more on Solovyov and the Jews, see Judith Deutsch Kornblatt, "Vladimir Solov'ev on Spiritual Nationhood, Russia and the Jews," *The Russian Review* 56 (April 1997): 157–77.

22. Nicolas Berdyaev, *Christianity and Anti-Semitism* (New York: Philosophical Library, 1954), 16; this small book is a translation of "Khristianstvo i antisemitizm: Religioznaia sud'ba evreistva," *Put'* 56 (May-June, 1938): 3–18. Continuing Solovyov's emphasis on Jewish reconciliation, but with a decidedly more negative tone, Berdyaev writes that "the Jewish people is a strange people reconciling the most diametrically opposite qualities. Within it the best traits blend with the lowest, the thirst for social justice with the tendency towards gain and capitalist accumulation" (*Christianity and Anti-Semitism*, 5).

23. V. S. Solov'ev, *Sobranie sochinenii Vladimira Sergeevicha Solov'eva*, 2d ed., 10 vols. (1911–14); reprint, with two additional volumes, Brussels: Zhizn' s Bogom, 1966–70), 4:135.

24. Faivel' Gets, "Nekotorye vospominaniia ob otnoshenii V. S. Solov'eva k evreiam," *Voskhod* 63 (13 August 1900): 30–35; 79 (7 September 1900): 18–25.

25. Those who demonstrate the influence of Solovyov and/or cite his work include the scholar Shimon Dubnov, Nikolai Bakst, Rav Avraham Kook, the first Ashkenazi head rabbi of Eretz-Israel, and the poets Hillel Tseitlin and Chaim Bialik. Hamutal Bar-Yosef has written convincingly about the influence of Solovyov on Russian Jews in "Otrazhenie tvorchestva i lichnosti Vladimira Solov'eva v evreiskoi pechati, literature i filosofii," unpublished paper, and "The Jewish Reception of Vladimir Solov'ev," in *Vladimir Solov'ev: Reconciler and Polemicist*, ed. Wil van den Bercken, Manon de Courten, and Evert van der Zweerde (Leuven, Belgium and Sterling, Va.: Peeters, 2000): 363–92.

26. Gauri Viswanathan, *Outside the Fold: Conversion, Modernity, and Belief* (Princeton: Princeton University Press, 1998), 4, 16.

27. Rodger Kamenetz, *The Jew in the Lotus: A Poet's Rediscovery of Jewish Identity in Buddhist India* (San Francisco: Harper, 1994), 112.

28. See Paul Berline, "Russian Religious Philosophers and the Jews (Soloviev, Berdyaev, Bulgakov, Struve, Rozanov and Fedotov)," *Jewish Social Studies* 9 (1947): 271–318; Emanuel Glouberman, "Feodor Dostoevsky, Vladimir Soloviev, Vasilii Rozanov and Lev Shestov on Jewish and Old Testament Themes" (Ph.D. diss., University of Michigan, 1974); Kornblatt, "Vladimir Solov'ev on Spiritual Nationhood"; Walter G. Moss, "Vladimir Soloviev and the Jews in Russia," *Russian Review* 29 (April 1970): 181–91.

29. Michael Agurskii and Dmitry Segal, "Jews and the Russian Orthodox Church: A Common Legacy—A Common Hope," *St. Vladimir's Theological Quarterly* vol. 35, no. 1 (1991): 21–31.

30. *Pravoslavnaia tserkov' i evrei: XIX-XX vv.: Sbornik materialov k teologii mezhkonfessional'nogo dialoga* (Moscow: Rudomino-Bog edin, 1994), 2.

31. Dominique Schnapper, *Jewish Identities in France: An Analysis of Contemporary French Jewry,* trans. Arthur Goldhammer, foreword by Edward Shils (Chicago: University of Chicago Press, 1983), xxvi and xxix.

32. For a discussion of the ambivalence of the Church toward Jewish conversion even in the nineteenth century, see John D. Klier, "State Policies and the Conversion of Jews in Imperial Russia," in *Of Religion and Empire: Missions, Conversion, and Tolerance in Tsarist Russia,* ed. Robert B. Geraci and Michael Khodarkovsky (Ithaca: Cornell University Press, 2001), 92–112.

33. The Orthodox Church in America is, indeed, attracting many converts today, but not so much among Jews. Young people brought up in other Christian faiths are attracted to the ritual and palpable sense of the sacred in the Eastern Church, something they found lacking in their own backgrounds. I met a number of such converts while studying at St. Vladimir's Seminary in Crestwood, New York, where I took several classes in Church history from the late Father John Meyendorff. See also H. B. Cavalcanti and H. Paul Chalfant, "Collective Life as the Ground of Implicit Religion: The Case of American Converts to Russian Orthodoxy," *Sociology of Religion* vol. 55, no. 4 (1994): 441–54, where the authors speak also of the attractiveness for these converts of Orthodox theology, especially the notion of reconciliation and collectivity.

34. See, for example, a series of booklets published in Russian by the Fund for the Messianic Brotherhood *(Keren achva meshichit)* in Jerusalem. Titles include: *Tanakh i Novyi Zavet (Bibliia)* (The TaNaKh and the New Testament [The Bible]); *Nachalo mudrosti: Svidetel'stva ravvinov* (The Principle of Wisdom: Rabbinic Testimony); *Kto istinnyi evrei?* (Who Is a True Jew?); *Chelovek iz Nazareta* (The Man from Nazareth); *Tsar' Iudeiskii* (King of the Jews).

2. THE JEWISH QUESTION IN RUSSIA

1. I use "Russian" here as the adjective for "Rus'," the name of the princedom tenuously united under Prince Vladimir and centered in Kiev. Ukrainians

as well as Russians claim Rus' as their founding state, and have, geographically and historically speaking, good justification for it. I recognize, therefore, that I use the adjective "Russian" with no small amount of ideological risk.

2. Serge A. Zenkovsky, ed., *Medieval Russia's Epics, Chronicles, and Tales* (1963; New York: Dutton, 1974), 66.

3. Zenkovsky, *Medieval Russia's Epics, Chronicles, and Tales*, 67.

4. James H. Billington, *The Icon and the Axe: An Interpretive History of Russian Culture* (New York: Vintage Books, 1970), 11.

5. Moscow was first called the "third Rome" in a letter of an Orthodox monk to Grand Prince Vasily III in the sixteenth century: "Listen and attend, pious tsar, that all Christian empires are gathered in your single one, that two Romes have fallen, and the third one stands, and a fourth one there shall not be." Quoted in Michael Cherniavsky, *Tsar and People: Studies in Russian Myths* (New Haven: Yale University Press, 1961), 38.

6. *Sobornost'*, a word composed of the root for cathedral or gathering and the abstract ending *nost'*, is a term first used extensively by the Russian Slavophile thinker Aleksey Khomyakov to refer to the organic wholeness of the Church. As Khomyakov wrote in his pamphlet "The Church Is One": "The unity of the Church follows necessarily from the unity of God, for the Church is not a multiplicity of persons in their personal separateness, but a unity of God's grace, living in the multitude of rational creatures who submit themselves to grace. . . . The unity of the Church, however, is not illusory; it is not metaphorical but true and essential, like the unity of the numerous members of a living body" (Khomiakov, "The Church Is One," in *On Spiritual Unity: A Slavophile Reader*, trans. and ed. Boris Jakim and Robert Bird [Hudson, N.Y.: Lindisfarne Books, 1998], 31). Modern Russian religious thinkers distinguish sharply between what they see as the monolithic unity of the Catholic Church under the authority of the Pope and the free, interactive wholeness of the many Orthodox Churches.

7. D. Pospielovsky, "Some Remarks on the Contemporary Russian Nationalism and Religious Revival," *Canadian Review of Studies in Nationalism* vol. 11, no. 1 (Spring 1984): 73.

8. To accuse Yeltsin of his alleged lack of loyalty to Russia, his opponents claimed he was part Jewish.

9. See John D. Klier, *Russia Gathers Her Jews: The Origins of the "Jewish Question" in Russia, 1772–1825* (DeKalb: Northern Illinois University Press, 1986), 23–24.

10. The origins and significance of the Judaizing heresy is under some debate in the scholarly community, with some scholars emphasizing that few to no actual Jews were probably involved. Note that, according to Dubnow, Ivan III could not find a Hebrew translator in his court (S. M. Dubnow, *History of the Jews in Russia and Poland from the Earliest Times until the Present Day*, 3 vols., trans. I. Friedlaender (Philadelphia: Jewish Publication Society of America, 1916), 1:35.

For more on the Judaizing heresy, see Charles J. Halperin, "Judaizers and the Image of the Jew in Medieval Russia: A Polemic Revisited and a Question Posed," *Canadian-American Slavic Studies* vol. 9, no. 2 (Summer 1975): 141–55; John D. Klier, "Judaizing without Jews? Moscow-Novgorod, 1470–1504," in *Culture and Identity in Muscovy, 1359–1584*, ed. A. M. Kleimola and G. D. Lenhoff (Moscow: ITZ-Garant, 1997), 336–49; and Klier, *Russia Gathers Her Jews*, 194–95.

11. See Louis Greenberg, *The Jews in Russia: The Struggle for Emancipation*, 2 vols. (New Haven: Yale University Press, 1944–51), 1:6.

12. Klier, "Judaizing without Jews?" 348.

13. Dubnow, *History of the Jews in Russia and Poland*, 1:306.

14. Ibid., 1:391.

15. Following Dubnow, historians have assumed that the policy was created in an effort to eradicate Jews from the empire, but Klier has shown that "the Russian state did not have a continuous, consistent policy of conversion directed at the Jews," suggesting that there was no single, Judeophobic impulse at work. See John D. Klier, "State Policies and the Conversion of Jews in Imperial Russia," in *Of Religion and Empire: Missions, Conversion, and Tolerance in Tsarist Russia*, ed. Robert B. Geraci and Michael Khodarkovsky (Ithaca: Cornell University Press, 2001), 92–112; and Yohanan Petrovsky-Shtern, "Jews in the Russian Army: Through the Military towards Modernity, 1827–1914," Ph.D. diss., Brandeis, 2001.

16. See Michael Stanislawski, *Tsar Nicholas I and the Jews: The Transformation of Jewish Society in Russia, 1825–1855* (Philadelphia: The Jewish Publication Society of America, 1983), 18.

17. Stanislawski, *Tsar Nicholas I and the Jews*, xi.

18. See Klier, *Russia Gathers Her Jews*, xviii.

19. Mendel Beilis was a Jew in Kiev accused of murdering a Christian child in order to use the blood for ancient Jewish rituals. The trial became an international spectacle, and Beilis was ultimately acquitted. For more on the case, see Albert S. Lindemann, *The Jew Accused: Three Anti-Semitic Affairs (Dreyfus, Beilis, Frank): 1894–1915* (Cambridge and New York: Cambridge University Press, 1991); or Maurice Samuel, *Blood Accusation: The Strange History of the Beiliss Case* (New York: Knopf, 1966). The transcripts from the trial were recently translated. See *The Beilis Transcripts: The Anti-Semitic Trial That Shook the World*, trans. and ed. Ezekiel Leikin (Northvale, N.Y.: Jason Aronson, 1993).

20. Nikolai Danilevskii, *Rossiia i Evropa* (St. Petersburg, 1871), 511. Cited in John D. Klier, *Imperial Russia's Jewish Question, 1855–1881* (Cambridge: Cambridge University Press, 1995), 388.

21. Billington, *The Icon and the Axe*, 72.

22. See the preface to Klier, *Russia Gathers Her Jews*, for a review of scholarship on the origins of the Jewish question.

23. Klier, *Jewish Question*, 66, 405.

24. Ibid., 66, xiv, 27.

25. Jonathan Frankel, *Prophecy and Politics: Socialism, Nationalism, and the Russian Jews, 1862–1917* (Cambridge: Cambridge University Press, 1981), 49.

26. T. M. Kopelson, "Evreiskoe rabochee dvizhenie kontsa 80-kh i nachala 90-kh godov," quoted in Zvi Gitelman, *Jewish Nationality and Soviet Politics: The Jewish Sections of the CPSU, 1917–1930* (Princeton: Princeton University Press, 1972), 31; and in Henry J. Tobias, "The Bund and Lenin until 1903," *The Russian Review* vol. 24, no. 4 (October 1961), 344–45.

27. Stanislawski, *Tsar Nicholas I and the Jews*, 108. For more on the Haskalah in Russia, see Eli Lederhandler, *The Road to Modern Jewish Politics* (New York: Oxford University Press, 1989); and Michael Stanislawski, *For Whom Do I Toil?: Judah Leib Gordon and the Crisis of Russian Jewry* (New York: Oxford University Press, 1988).

28. Klier, *Jewish Question*, 82, 104, 105, 122.

29. Will Herberg, *Protestant, Catholic, Jew: An Essay in American Religious Sociology* (Garden City, N.Y.: Doubleday, 1955; Garden City, N.Y.: Anchor, 1960; reprint, with a new introduction by Martin E. Marty, Chicago: University of Chicago Press, 1983), 34 (page citation is to reprint edition).

30. Norman Roth, "Am Yisrael: *Jews or Judaism?*" *Judaism: A Quarterly Journal* vol. 37, no. 2 (1988): 199.

31. Steven M. Cohen, "Religious Stability and Ethnic Decline: Emerging Patterns of Jewish Identity in The United States," unpublished paper for the 1997 National Survey of American Jews, sponsored by The Florence G. Heller Research Center, of the Jewish Community Centers Association.

32. See Bethamie Horowitz, "Connections and Journeys: Shifting Identities among American Jews," *Contemporary Jewry* 19 (1998), where she analyzes the wide-ranging, evolving nature of Jewish identity (8), and uses a "salad-bar" metaphor to explain how American Jews pick among a whole variety of identity markers (23). See also Steven M. Cohen, "State of Our Unions: Geography, Ethnicity and the New American Jew," *Forward* (February 22, 2002): 9.

33. Steven M. Cohen and Arnold M. Eisen, 'The Jew Within: Self, Community, and Commitment among the Varieties of Moderately Affiliated" (Los Angeles and Boston: The Wilstein Institute, 1998), 19. This comment is somewhat more muted in the book that evolved from this study: Steven M. Cohen and Arnold M. Eisen, *The Jew Within: Self, Family, and Community in America* (Bloomington: Indiana University Press, 2000), 101–2.

34. Anthony D. Smith, "Ethnic Identity and World Order," *Millennium* 12 (April 1983): 156, quoted in Charles S. Liebman and Steven M. Cohen, *Two Worlds of Judaism: The Israeli and American Experiences* (New Haven: Yale University Press, 1990), 13.

35. In the 1990 national Jewish population survey sponsored by the Council of Jewish Federations, 47 percent of U.S. Jews said they were Jews "by religion." See *Highlights of the CJF 1990 National Jewish Population Survey*, ed. Barry A. Kosmin, et al. (New York: The Council of Jewish Federations, 1991).

36. Charles S. Liebman and Elihu Katz, eds. *The Jewishness of Israelis: Responses to the Guttman Report* (Albany: State University of New York Press, 1997), xviii.

37. Liebman and Katz, *Jewishness of Israelis*, 31.

38. It is probably true that the large influx of Russian Jews will gradually erode the "tradition."

39. The existence of substantial difference is the premise of a book that asks in its concluding chapter: "Are Two Judaisms Emerging?" See Liebman and Cohen, *Two Worlds of Judaism*. The book clearly does not consider a third option that developed in the Soviet Union over the course of the twentieth century.

40. Cohen and Eisen, "The Jew Within: Self, Family, and Community in America," 19. In *The Jew Within*, they write: "The only way to lose this Jewish birthright is to choose a different religion for oneself" (23).

41. For more on the institution and ramifications of the Law of Return for Russian Jews, see the discussion of Father Daniel in chapter 5.

42. See *Highlights of the CJF 1990 National Jewish Population Survey*, 4. The aggregate includes the categories of Born Jews, Jews by Choice, and Born Jews without a current religion (secular Jews).

43. Zvi Gitelman has recently found that a small percentage of Russian Jews in or from the former Soviet Union would agree that conversion is a "betrayal" of one's Jewishness, although many of his interviewees disagreed strongly with that sentiment.

44. Michael Stanislawski, "Jewish Apostasy in Russia: A Tentative Typology," in *Jewish Apostasy in the Modern World*, ed. Todd M. Endelman (New York: Holmes & Meier, 1987), 190. Stanislawski points out that this fact is not surprising, since Russian Jewry was the largest Jewish community in the world.

45. Stanislawski, "Jewish Apostasy," 195.

46. See *Encyclopedia Judaica* (Jerusalem: Keter, 1971), 14:450.

47. Eli Lederhendler, "Did Russian Jewry Exist Prior to 1917?" in Yaacov Ro'i, ed., *Jews and Jewish Life in Russia and the Soviet Union* (Ilford, Essex and Portland, Ore.: Frank Cass, 1995), 21–22.

48. Zvi Gitelman, "Jewish Nationality and Religion in the USSR and Eastern Europe," in Pedro Ramet, ed., *Religion and Nationalism in Soviet and East European Politics* (Durham, N.C.: Duke University Press, 1989), 67.

49. Benjamin Pinkus, *The Soviet Government and the Jews, 1948–1967: A Documented Study* (Cambridge: Cambridge University Press, 1984), 14. The author then points out that "the Jews were even further downgraded in the Soviet hierarchy of nations after the Six-Day War."

50. Pinkus, *Soviet Government and the Jews*, 16.

51. Zvi Gitelman, "Thinking about Being Jewish in Russia and Ukraine," in *Jewish Life after the USSR*, ed. Zvi Gitelman, with Musya Glants and Marshall I. Goldman (Bloomington: Indiana University Press, 2003), 50. For other studies of late and post-Soviet Jewry, see Mordechai Altshuler, *Soviet Jewry since the*

Second World War: Population and Social Structure (New York: Greenwood Press, 1987); Robert J. Brym, with the assistance of Rozalina Ryvkina, *The Jews of Moscow, Kiev and Minsk: Identity, Antisemitism, Emigration* (New York: New York University Press in association with the Institute of Jewish Affairs, 1994); Valery Chervyakov, Zvi Gitelman, and Vladimir Shapiro, "*E Pluribus Unum?* Post-Soviet Jewish Identities and Their Implications for Communal Reconstruction," in *Jewish Life after the USSR*, ed. Gitelman, with Glants and Goldman; Zvi Gitelman, "The Reconstruction of Community and Jewish Identity in Russia," *East European Jewish Affairs* vol. 24, no. 1 (1994): 35–56; Mikaella Kagan, "Evreiskaia emigratsiia iz byvshego SSSR v SShA: Obzor izmenenii za 70–90-e gody," in *Issledovaniia po prikladnoi i neotlozhnoi etnologii* 99 (Moscow, 1996); Benjamin Pinkus, *The Jews of the Soviet Union: The History of a National Minority* (Cambridge and New York: Cambridge University Press, 1988); Ro'i, *Jews and Jewish Life in Russia and the Soviet Union*; and Rozalina Ryvkina, *Evrei v postsovetskoi Rossii—Kto oni?* (Moscow: Izd-vo URSS, 1996). Michael Paul Sacks gathered much of this bibliography in "Privilege and Prejudice: The Occupations of Jews in Russia in 1989," *Slavic Review* vol. 57, no. 2 (Summer 1998): 247–66.

52. Gitelman distinguishes between "thick culture," which has tangible manifestations such as language, customs, foods, and clothing, and "thin culture": "common and distinct system of understandings and interpretations that constitute normative order and worldview and provide strategic and stylistic guides to action" ("Thinking about Being Jewish," 49); and Zvi Gitelman, "The Decline of the Diaspora Jewish Nation: Boundaries, Content and Jewish Identity," *Jewish Social Studies* vol. 4, no. 2 (Winter 1998). According to Gitelman, post-Soviet Jews have, for the most part, only "thin culture," and he questions whether that is sufficient to sustain the group's distinctiveness on more than a symbolic level.

53. Gitelman, "Thinking about Being Jewish," 51.

54. Ibid., 51–52.

55. Cohen and Eisen, *The Jew Within*, 23.

56. "Θ," "Kak vernee nazyvat' posledovatelei Moiseeva zakona: evreiami, iudeiami ili izrail'tianami," *Evreiskie zapiski* (1881): 54.

57. See Alice Nakhimovsky, "Mikhail Zhvanetskii: The Last Russian-Jewish Joker," paper for conference on "BORDERLINES: Judaic Literature and Culture in Eastern Europe," Syracuse, N.Y., 6–8 April 2002.

58. Brodsky has been quoted as saying: "I am a bad Jew, a bad Christian, a bad American, but I am a good poet." Valentina Polukhina reports that a woman who looked after Joseph during the evacuation to the Urals had the boy baptized without his mother's permission. His mother was later told, and in turn told the story to Natal'ia Grudinina after Brodsky left Russia. Grudinina told the poet Viktor Krivulin, who related the story to Polukhina. Personal correspondence, 1 May 2002.

3. The Path of Faith

1. A discussion of Krakhmal'nikova's views can be found in Judith Deutsch Kornblatt, "'Christianity. Antisemitism. Nationalism': Russian Orthodoxy in a Reborn Orthodox Russia," in *Consuming Russia: Popular Culture, Sex, and Society since Gorbachev*, ed. Adele M. Barker (Durham, N.C.: Duke University Press, 1999): 414–36.

2. For more on Father Dudko's biography, and samples of his writings, see o. Dmitrii Dudko, *Khristos v nashei zhizni: Voskresnye propovedi* (Moscow: Izdatel'stvo zhurnala Khrama, 1992); and Fr. Dmitrii Dudko, *Our Hope*, trans. Paul D. Garrett, foreword by John Meyendorff (Crestwood, N.Y.: St. Vladimir's Seminary Press, 1977).

3. In Jacob Ingerman, ed., *Evreiskii samizdat, Evrei i evreiskii narod: Materialy iz sovetskoi pechati*, (Jerusalem: Hebrew University, n.d.), 6:72. Benjamin Pinkus also quotes this statement in "The *Hazara Bitshuva* Phenomenon among Russian Jews in the Post-Stalin Era," *Jews and Jewish Topics in the Soviet Union and Eastern Europe* vol. 15, no. 2 (Fall 1991): 19.

4. Alexander Men', "Vospominaniia ob Aleksandre Galiche," in *Kul'tura i dukhovnoe voskhozhdenie* (Moscow: Iskusstvo, 1992), 437.

5. The demographer Mark Tolts reminds us that "[s]ince World War II, the Soviet Jewish population has seen a great increase in the numbers of mixed marriages" ("Demography of the Jews in the Former Soviet Union: Yesterday and Today," in *Jewish Life after the USSR*, ed. Zvi Gitelman, with Musya Glants and Marshall I. Goldman [Bloomington: Indiana University Press, 2003], 184). His article includes statistics from 1978 to 1996 in Belorussia, Latvia, Russia, and Ukraine. See Table 11.6, p. 183.

6. Guy Sitbon, "Qui a tué Alexandre Men, pope et juif?" *Le nouvel observateur* (27 September–30 October 1990): 51.

7. In 1920, the Russian Patriarch Tikhon issued a decree authorizing bishops to establish independent organizations of their own, no doubt in fear for his life and foreseeing the possible end of the authority of his office under the Soviets. Although Tikhon later rescinded the decree, a number of bishops who had left Russia met to establish the Russian Church in Exile, sometimes called the Russian Church Outside Russia or the Russian Church Abroad. Antagonism between the two Russian Churches and competition for authority over Orthodox believers around the world has continued even after the breakup of the Soviet Union, in part fueled by accusations of collaboration between the Moscow Patriarchate and the KGB.

8. *Ma'ariv* (2 August 1996). I would like to thank Rachel Keren and her sister for bringing this article to my attention.

9. Stalin's fluctuating attitude toward the Church can be seen as either highly erratic, or shrewdly political. Churches were closed and priests sent to Siberia at

a mass rate during the 1930s. In 1943, however, Stalin invited Church leaders to the Kremlin (the last meeting between the Patriarch and a leader of the Soviet Union until Gorbachev's invitation in 1988) to solicit their support for the war effort. It is commonly assumed that the Soviet priesthood was heavily infiltrated by the KGB, and the post-Soviet Church today is having difficulty shaking off its image as collaborationist.

10. St. Vladimir's Orthodox Theological Seminary in Crestwood, New York was founded in 1938 with a dual mission of theological scholarship and education, and is accredited in New York and nationally as a graduate professional school and a theological seminary. The seminary is unusual for its ecumenical focus, both within Orthodoxy (its Board of Trustees includes bishops of the Orthodox Church in America, the Antiochian Orthodox Christian Archdiocese, the Greek Archdiocese of America, and the Serbian Orthodox Church), and trans-confessionally. It is there where I studied with Father John Meyendorff.

11. The rivalry between the Russian Church in Exile and the Moscow Patriarchate has been felt perhaps most poignantly in Jerusalem, where they have vied for a limited number of parishioners and, until the past ten years, of pilgrims.

12. Christ the Savior Church was founded in 1924, and, in a building on Madison Avenue and 121st Street, became the biggest Russian church in the city in the 1930s and 40s. During that time, it also provided space for classes of St. Vladimir's Seminary. Christ the Savior Church was even granted the status of Cathedral See of New York City, only to see a long period of decline, forcing the sale of the building. The parish was reestablished in its current location, and Father John Meyendorff became rector in 1976, together with Father Steven Plumlee as pastor, who served a new, English-speaking congregation. Father Michael joined to serve as priest for the Russian population, and later, for the whole bilingual congregation. In 1985, he was made rector.

13. Nicolas Berdyaev, "Marx vs. Man," in *Russian Philosophy*, 3 vols., ed. James M. Edie, James P. Scanlan, and Mary-Barbara Zeldin, with the collaboration of George L. Kline (Knoxville: University of Tennessee Press, 1976), 3:156–57.

14. Mikhail Bulgakov, author and nephew of the religious philosopher Sergei Bulgakov, makes the comparison of Stalin and Caesar as explicitly as he safely could in the 1930s in his famous novel *Master and Margarita*. An abridged version of the novel was finally published in 1966–67, but with the deleted passages immediately circulating in samizdat.

15. Simon Markish, "Passers-by: The Soviet Jew as Intellectual," *Commentary* vol. 66, no. 6 (December 1978): 31.

16. One young woman in Israel told me how her father, having been refused a visa for over ten years, took his wife, mother-in-law, and six children by foot through Hungary to Austria, knocking on doors of embassies for asylum. He eventually ended up in Israel, where, for some reason, he had the entire family rebaptized. We will revisit this family in chapter 5.

17. Yuri Glazov, *The Russian Mind since Stalin's Death* (Dordrecht and Boston: D. Reidel Publishing Co., 1985), xi, 116.

18. By contrast, Anton asserted that Father Georgy Edelshtein, with whom he participated in the same underground cell, was a *sincerely religious person.*

19. Mikhail Agurskii, "Episody vospominanii," *Ierusalimskii zhurnal* 2 (1999): 209.

20. Cited in Paul Ritterband, "Jewish Identity among Russian Immigrants in the U.S.," in *Russian Jews on Three Continents: Migration and Resettlement,* ed. Noah Lewin-Epstein, Yaacov Ro'i, and Paul Ritterband (London: Frank Cass, 1997), 331–32.

21. Feliks Svetov, *Opyt biografii* (Paris: YMCA-Press, 1985), 70, 107. It is significant that the "tooting" of trumpets at a Soviet parade on the next page does not elicit the same negative reaction in the young boy.

22. Glazov, *Russian Mind,* 121, 122.

23. See Michael Meerson, "The Life and Work of Father Aleksandr Men'," in *Seeking God: The Recovery of Religious Identity in Orthodox Russia, Ukraine, and Georgia,* ed. Stephen K. Batalden (DeKalb: Northern Illinois University Press, 1993), 14.

24. Vladimir Zelinskii, "Pamiati o. Aleksandra Menia: Slova proshchaniia," *Russkaia mysl'* no. 3845 (14 September 1990): 8.

25. Iurii Glazov, *Tesnye vrata: vozrozhdenie russkoi intelligentsii* (London: Overseas Publications Interchange, 1973), 145 ff. Yakunin had been Men's roommate when both were studying biology in an institute in Siberia, and Men' is credited with bringing Yakunin, who had been baptized as a child, back to the Church. Yakunin, who has moved away from the Russian Orthodox Church to establish his own autonomous community, has overseen the canonization of Men'. It is not recognized by the Patriarch, but has inspired the painting of a number of icons. One forms part of the iconostasis in Yakunin's church.

26. Benjamin Pinkus cites two sources from the 1970s that suggest that Men' was baptized in 1956, at the age of twenty, but more recent biographies attest to the childhood baptism. See "The *Hazara Bitshuva* Phenomenon among Russian Jews in the Post-Stalin Era," *Jews and Jewish Topics in the Soviet Union and Eastern Europe* vol. 15, no. 2 (Fall 1991): 19. Guy Sitbon cites the historian Andrei Bessmertnyi with an interesting story of Men's maternal grandmother, who suffered as a young woman from a permanently hemorrhaging uterus. As a last recourse she visited a priest (Father John, later canonized as St. John of Kronstadt) who told her: "I see your faith. You must remain in Judaism, thus your blood will serve our Church." It is her daughter who was baptized over thirty years later. In Sitbon, "Qui a tué Alexandre Men, pope et juif?" *Le nouvel observateur* (27 September–30 October 1990): 51.

27. Mikhail Agurskii, "Pamiati Aleksandra Menia," *Nasha Strana* (14 December 1990): 6.

28. Meerson, "The Life and Work of Father Men'," 15–16.

29. Agurskii, "Epizody vosponinanii," 231.

30. Elizabeth Roberts and Ann Shukman, eds., *Christianity for the Twenty-First Century: The Prophetic Writings of Alexander Men* (New York: Continuum, 1996), 8.

31. Meerson, "The Life and Work of Father Men'," 22, 23.

32. Ibid., 20.

33. See note 25, above, on Men's canonization. A follower who still considers himself within the Orthodox Church recently confessed to me that he is confident that official canonization by the Russian Orthodox Church will happen soon. We need only be patient. Another said that it will happen at the end of days, but that, who knows, may be soon as well.

34. Roberts and Shukman, *Christianity for the Twenty-First Century*, xi.

35. Glazov, *Russian Mind*, 117.

36. Agurskii, "Pamiati Aleksandra Menia," 6.

37. Meerson, "The Life and Work of Father Men'," 23.

38. Father Men' seems to have been involved in the original drafting of the famous Yakunin and Eshliman letter to the Patriarch, but did not ultimately sign it, and was not dismissed from his pulpit, as were the other two dissident priests. See Roberts and Shukman, *Christianity for the Twenty-First Century*, 12. See Glazov, *Tesnye vrata*, 145–60, for the importance of the "epistolary campaign."

39. Feliks Svetov, *Otverzi mi dveri*, in *Novyi mir* 10 (October 1991): 48–127; 11 (November 1991): 149–218; 12 (December 1991): 89–152; 12:114. The novel was originally published in 1978 by Les Éditeurs Réunis Press in Paris in a longer form, and substantially edited by the author for publication in Russia immediately following the fall of the Soviet Union. The author himself recommended the short version, although the editing has caused some odd narrative jumps.

40. For extensive biographical information, see Yves Hamant, *Alexandre Men: Un temoin pour la Russie de ce temps* (Paris: Editions Mame, 1993), translated into Russian by N. V. Garskaia as Iv Aman, *Aleksandr Men': Svidetel' svoego vremeni* (Moscow: Rudomino, 1994); and Zoia Maslenikova, *Zhizn' ottsa Aleksandra Menia* (Moscow: Pristsel's, "Russlit", 1995).

41. See Mikhail Agurskii, *Pepel Klaasa: Razryv* (Jerusalem: URA Publishers, 1996). Excerpts on Christianity that were removed are published in the Russian-language journal *Studiia* in Berlin, and as "Epizody vospominanii" in *Ierusalimskii zhurnal* 2–5 (1999–2000).

42. Agurskii, "Epizody vospominanii," 2:223, 209, 210.

43. For some impressive memoirs about Men', as well as photographs, see N. F. Grigoren'ko-Men', P. V. Men', T. A. Zhirmunskaia, M. V. Sergeeva, eds., *I bylo utro . . . Vospominaniia ob ottse Aleksandre Mene* (Moscow: AO "Vita-Tsentr," 1992).

44. Agurskii, "Epizody vospominanii," 2:231, 233.

45. Men', in Roberts and Shukman, *Christianity for the Twenty-First Century*, 7. Hamant cites a similar comment from a letter in which Men' discusses the importance of the rebirth of the Optina Pustyn' Monastery for the Russian intelligentsia: "After a long pause, Optina, in essence, began a dialogue between the Church and society. . . . The thought that we mustn't interrupt this dialogue therefore imprinted itself on me for life, and I participated in it to the extent of my own weak powers." In Aman, *Alexandr Men'*, 46.

46. Benjamin Pinkus feels that the influence of a few charismatic leaders was equally influential for the *hazara bitshuva* movement in the late Soviet Union ("The *Hazara Bitshuva* Phenomenon among Russian Jews in the Post-Stalin Era," 30).

47. Pinkus would concur: "The basic principle fueling this search was 'the wish not to live a lie,' to invoke Alexander Solzhenitsyn's phrase, since the crisis was not only ideological or political, but also, and principally, ethical. Nor was it surprising that members of the Jewish intelligentsia, a totally assimilated group with no Jewish cultural baggage and only the vaguest memories of Jewish history, did not turn to Judaism in their spiritual quests" ("The *Hazara Bitshuva* Phenomenon among Russian Jews in the Post-Stalin Era," 19).

48. Cited in Roberts and Shukman, *Christianity for the Twenty-First Century*, 11. In his article, "Vmesto nekrologa" (In place of an obituary,) Averintsev wrote: "As everyone knows, Father Alexander spent special missionary efforts on that peculiar indigenous tribe that calls itself the Soviet intelligentsia. This tribe, with its notions and traditions, with its prejudices . . . is the wildest of all the wild tribes of the world." In A. I. Zorin and V. I. Iliushenko, eds., *Vokrug imeni ottsa Aleksandra* (Moscow: Obshchestvo "Kul'turnoe vozrozhdenie" imeni Aleksandra Menia, 1993), 82.

49. F. Iskander, "On byl svetom," in *I bylo utro . . .* , 320–24.

50. Nikita Struve, "Apostol," in *I bylo utro . . .* , 340–41.

51. Masha Gessen, *Dead Again: The Russian Intelligentsia after Communism* (London and New York: Verso, 1997), 52–53.

52. Glazov, *Tesnye vrata*, 146, 78, 91.

53. Alexander V. Voronel, "Twenty Years After," in *Russian Jews on Three Continents: Migration and Resettlement*, 423.

54. Pinkus, "The *Hazara Bitshuva* Phenomenon among Russian Jews in the Post-Stalin Era," 19, 20.

55. Compare Benjamin Pinkus, "The phenomenon of *hazara bitshuva* was triggered by the emergence of a spiritual-ideological vacuum in the Soviet Union after the collapse both of Marxism-Leninism, which had anchored the legitimacy of the legitimacy of the Communist regime, and of the foundations of the ruling, economic and social order." Pinkus, "The *Hazara Bitshuva* Phenomenon among Russian Jews in the Post-Stalin Era," 29–30.

4. The Path of Faith

1. Yuri Glazov, *The Russian Mind since Stalin's Death* (Dordrecht and Boston: D. Reidel Publishing Co., 1985), 128.

2. Iurii Glazov, *Tesnye vrata: vozrozhdenie russkoi intelligentsii* (London: Overseas Publications Interchange, 1973), 9, 9–10.

3. Zvi Gitelman, "'From a Northern Country': Russian and Soviet Jewish Immigration to America and Israel in Historical Perspective," in *Russian Jews on Three Continents: Migration and Resettlement,* ed. Noah Lewin-Epstein, Yaacov Ro'i, and Paul Ritterband (London: Frank Cass, 1997), 26.

4. Benjamin Pinkus, *The Soviet Government and the Jews, 1948–1967: A Documented Study* (Cambridge and New York: Cambridge University Press, 1984), 19.

5. Cited in Yaacov Ro'i, "Soviet Policy towards Jewish Emigration: An Overview," in *Russian Jews on Three Continents: Migration and Resettlement,* 50–51.

6. Ro'i, "Soviet Policy," 52. Ro'i believes greatest emphasis should be placed on the domestic issues.

7. Jerome M. Gilison, "Soviet-Jewish Emigration, 1971–80: An Overview," in Robert O. Freedman, ed., *Soviet Jewry in the Decisive Decade, 1971–1980* (Durham, N.C.: Duke University Press, 1984), 6. For more on the emigration movement, see other articles in this volume, as well as in the companion volume: Robert O. Freedman, ed., *Soviet Jewry in the 1980s: The Politics of Anti-Semitism and Emigration and the Dynamics of Resettlement* (Durham, N.C.: Duke University Press, 1989).

8. For an analysis of Soviet-U.S. relations in the decade of the 1970s, see Robert O. Freedman, "Soviet Jewry and Soviet-American Relations: A Historical Analysis," in *Soviet Jewry in the Decisive Decade,* 38–67. For the argument that internal ethnic factors more strongly affected Soviet policy, see Laurie P. Salitan, "Ethnic and Related Factors in Soviet Emigration Policy, 1968–89," in *Russian Jews on Three Continents: Migration and Resettlement,* 68–86.

9. Gilison, "Soviet-Jewish Emigration," 9.

10. Pinkus also sees the return to Judaism partly in the context of growing national movements in the late Soviet Union. Pinkus, "The *Hazara Bitshuva* Phenomenon among Russian Jews in the Post-Stalin Era," in *Jews and Jewish Topics in the Soviet Union and Eastern Europe* vol. 15, no. 2 (Fall 1991): 30. See also Pinkus, *Soviet Government and the Jews, 1948–1967:* "Here, it should be noted that the current rise of national feeling among most peoples of the Soviet Union has had a direct bearing on the Jewish national awakening," 19.

11. Mikhail Agurskii, "Epizody vospominanii," *Ierusalimskii zhurnal* 2 (1999): 222, 223.

12. Feliks Svetov, "Otverzi mi dveri," *Novyi Mir* (October 1991): 97.

13. Todd M. Endelman, ed., *Jewish Apostasy in the Modern World* (New York and London: Holmes & Meier, 1987), 16–17.

14. See Rodger Kamenetz, *The Jew in the Lotus: A Poet's Rediscovery of Jewish Identity in Buddhist India* (San Francisco: Harper, 1994), 147–57.

15. See B. Z. Sobel, *Hebrew Christianity: The Thirteenth Tribe* (New York: John Wiley, 1974); quoted in Natalie Isser and Lita Linzer Schwarts, *The History of Conversion and Contemporary Cults* (New York: Peter Lang, 1988), 33, 34.

16. Feliks Svetov, *Opyt biografii* (Paris: YMCA-Press, 1985), 206.

17. See Glazov, *Tesnye vrata*, 91–104.

18. John D. Klier, "Judaizing without Jews? Moscow-Novgorod, 1470–1504," in *Culture and Identity in Muscovy, 1359–1584*, ed. A. M. Kleimola and G. D. Lenhoff (Moscow: ITZ-Garant, 1997), 348.

5. The Paths Diverge

1. Aleksandr Men', in an interview with A. Shoikhet in the journal *Jews in the USSR* in 1975; reprinted in *Pravoslavnaia tserkov' i evrei: XIX-XX vv.: Sbornik materialov k teologii mezhkonfessional'nogo dialoga* (Moscow: Rudomino-Bog Edin, 1994), 71–77.

2. Father Aleksandr Borisov, "Vse liudi—deti edinogo Boga," interview with Mikhail Gorelik for the journal *Shalom* 6 (1990); reprinted in *Pravoslavnaia tserkov' i evrei*, 83.

3. Father Aleksandr Borisov, "O natsionalizme v russkoi pravoslavnoi tserkvi," in Vladimir Iliushenko, ed., *Nuzhen li Gitler Rossii?* (Moscow: Nezavisimoe izdatel'stvo PIK, 1996), 192–93.

4. For an excellent introduction to Russian Orthodoxy, see Timothy Ware, *The Orthodox Church* (New York and Middlesex, England: Penguin Books, 1997), particularly, for the question here, chapter 11.

5. As the Prince says, "Why, that's a painting that might make some people lose their faith!" Feodor Dostoevsky, *The Idiot*, trans. Henry and Olga Carlisle (New York: New American Library, 1969), 238.

6. Ware, *Orthodox Church*, 270.

7. Ar'e Barats, *Liki Tory* (Jerusalem: n.p., 1993).

8. See Ol'ga Agur, "I nazovu subbotu voskresen'em," *Istina i zhizn'* 12 (December 1996): 16–18; and Stanislava Zaremba, "Otets Daniel': karmelit v Izraile," *Istina i zhizn'* 12 (December 1996): 18–20.

9. For those interested in Brother Daniel, see the excellent study by Nechama Tec, *In the Lion's Den: The Life of Oswald Rufeisen* (New York and Oxford: Oxford University Press, 1990). *The Jerusalem Report* included an article on him in their "Israel at 50" edition: "The 'Troublemaker,'" *The Jerusalem Report* vol. 9, no. 1 (1998): 96–102.

10. Tec, *In the Lion's Den*, 166–67 (ellipses in original).

11. Ibid., 169.

12. Ibid., 167.

13. Ibid., 220.

14. For a thorough, but not overly technical discussion of the *halakha* surrounding the Brother Daniel case, see Aharon Lichtenstein, "Brother Daniel and the Jewish Fraternity," *Judaism* vol. 12, no. 3 (Summer 1963): 260–80.

15. Isaac Babel, *Collected Stories*, trans. David McDuff (London: Penguin Books, Ltd., 1994), 117, 118.

16. Although there is no mention of a tent, Father Daniel may have been referring to Romans 11, in which Paul asserts that God has not rejected the Jews, but regards the Gentiles as a wild olive shoot to be grafted on and share the richness of the [Jewish] olive tree. It behooves the Gentiles not to boast: "Remember it is not you that support the root, but the root that supports you" (Romans 11:18). His reference to a tent might point more generally to the metaphor of the people of Israel as the tent(s) of Jacob.

17. Mikhail Agurskii, "Epizody vospominanii," *Ierusalimskii zhurnal* 2 (1999): 209.

18. The Catholic Church of the Eastern Rite is often called the Uniate Church. It was created in 1596 by the Union of Brest-Litovsk, and permitted priests in the heavily Catholic Ukrainian area to continue observing the rites of the Eastern Orthodox Church, while vowing allegiance to the Catholic Pope.

19. There is an extensive bibliography on Jews for Jesus. For two studies of Messianic Jews in Israel, by sympathetic authors, see Kai Kjaer-Hansen and Bochil F. Skjott, *Facts and Myths about the Messianic Congregations in Israel* (Jerusalem: United Christian Council in Israel in Cooperation with the Caspari Center, 1999); and Gershon Nerel, "Messianic Jews and the Modern Zionist Movement," in *Israel and Yeshua*, ed. Torleif Elgvin (Jerusalem: Caspari Center for Biblical and Jewish Studies, 1993).

20. Compare Barats, *Liki Tory*, 160.

21. "Why Be a Christian," in Elizabeth Roberts and Ann Shukman, eds., *Christianity for the Twenty-First Century: The Prophetic Writings of Alexander Men'* (New York: Continuum, 1996), 37

6. Concluding Thoughts

1. Anthony Giddens, *Modernity and Self-Identity* (Stanford: Stanford University Press, 1992), 5; quoted in H. B. Cavalcanti and H. Paul Chalfant, "Collective Life as the Ground of Implicit Religion: The Case of American Converts to Russian Orthodoxy," *Sociology of Religion* vol. 55, no. 4 (1994): 441.

2. Cavalcanti and Chalfant, "Collective Life," 442.

3. Lynn Davidman, *Tradition in a Rootless World: Women Turn to Orthodox Judaism* (Berkeley: University of California Press, 1991).

4. Benjamin Pinkus, "The *Hazara Bitshuva* Phenomenon among Russian Jews in the Post-Stalin Era," *Jews and Jewish Topics in the Soviet Union and Eastern Europe* vol. 15, no. 2 (Fall 1991): 30.

5. Nechama Tec, *In the Lion's Den: The Life of Oswald Rufeisen* (New York and Oxford: Oxford University Press, 1990), 167–68.

6. Tec, *In the Lion's Den*, 169.

7. Simon Markish, "Passers-by: The Soviet Jew as Intellectual," *Commentary* vol. 66, no. 6 (December 1978): 33.

8. Natalie Isser and Lita Linzer Schwartz, *The History of Conversion and Contemporary Cults* (New York: Peter Lang, 1988), 34, 154.

APPENDIX B

1. *Galatians 1:3–5.* This is the opening greeting of the Catholic Mass.

2. The Catholic Mass includes penitential prayers, then the "Kyrie, eleison" and "Gloria" prayers at this point before the Gospel reading. "Supplication" here could be translated as "Petitions."

3. The Catholic Mass follows the Gospel readings with a recitation of the Creed, omitted by Father Daniel, and then the preparation of the altar and the gifts. This section then might be translated as Consecration, instead of Blessing. The words, however, are largely a variation of the introductory prayers in the Hebrew morning service. Furthermore, Father Daniel does not include a ritual of Transubstantiation.

4. The letter "A" does not refer here to the priest, since above and below his readings are indicated by the letter "Kaf," for "Kohen."

5. Psalms 72:18.

6. Galatians 4:4.

7. The following is a variation on the Eucharistic prayer, with some of the lines quite familiar to a Hebrew ear from the service for the taking out of the Torah. The last line of this section is a popular song from the Passover seder.

8. This verse forms part of the Mass, as well as the Hebrew "Kedushah" prayer.

9. Matthew 26:26–29; Mark 14:22–25; Luke 22:15–20.

10. This is the common Hebrew blessing over bread.

11. Matthew 26:28. See Note 9.

12. This is the common Hebrew blessing over wine.

13. *1 Corinthians 11:23–24.*

14. The last words *(marana ta)* are in Aramaic.

15. Only a few of the lines in this and the next section (Song of Thanksgiving) come directly from the *Birkat haMazon*. Many of the others, taken from Psalms, are recited regularly in the Hebrew "Ashrei" prayer.

16. Father Daniel, who was not a native, but nonetheless a very good speaker of Hebrew after over thirty years in Israel, here oddly misspells Isaac.

17. *Psalms 105:7–9.*

18. Deuteronomy 8:3.

19. *Ephesians 1:3.*

20. *Colossians 1:13.*

21. Psalms 106:2. Some people add this verse before the recitation of Birkat haMazon.

22. The ellipses indicate that names of recently departed or those whose deaths are being remembered are inserted here.

23. This indicates the recital of the "Our Father" prayer, which continues in the Catholic Mass with: hallowed be thy name; thy kingdom come; thy will be done on earth as it is in heaven. Give us this day our daily bread; and forgive us our trespasses as we forgive those who trespass against us; and lead us not into temptation, and deliver us from evil.

24. In the Catholic Mass, these two lines are recited before the breaking of the bread and again as greeting after Communion at the very end of the service. Father Daniel has Communion earlier in the service.

25. *Psalms 67.*

Selected Bibliography

Agur, Ol'ga. "I nazovu subbotu voskresen'em." *Istina i zhizn'* 12 (December 1996): 16–18.

Agurskii, Mikhail. "Conversions of Jews to Christianity in Russia." *Soviet Jewish Affairs* 20, no. 2-3 (1990): 69–84.

———. "Epizody vospominanii." *Ierusalimskii zhurnal* 2–5 (1999–2000): 189–234, 161–210, 231–74, 197–240.

———. "Pamiati Aleksandra Menia." *Nasha Strana* (14 December 1990): 6.

———. *Pepel Klaasa: Razryv.* Jerusalem: URA Publishers, 1996.

Agurskii, Mikhail, and Dmitry Segal. "Jews and the Russian Orthodox Church: A Common Legacy—A Common Hope." *St. Vladimir's Theological Quarterly* 35, no. 1 (1991): 21–31.

Aksenov-Meerson, Mikhail. "Solov'ev v nashi dni." In S. M. Solov'ev, *Zhizn' i tvorcheskaia èvoliutsiia Vladimira Solov'eva.* Brussels: Zhizn' s Bogom, 1977.

Altshuler, Mordechai. *Soviet Jewry since the Second World War: Population and Social Structure.* New York: Greenwood Press, 1987.

Ariel, Yaacov. "Philosemites or Antisemites? Evangelical Christian Attitudes toward Jews, Judaism, and the State of Israel." *Analysis of Current Trends in Antisemitism* 20 (2002).

Babel, Isaac. *Collected Stories.* Translated by David McDuff. London: Penguin Books, Ltd., 1994.

Barats, Ar'e. *Liki Tory.* Jerusalem: n.p., 1993.

Berdiaev, Nikolai. *Dream and Reality: An Essay in Autobiography.* Translated by Katherine Lambert. 1950. New York: Macmillan, 1951.

———. *Samopoznaniia.* Moscow: DEM, 1990.

Berdyaev, Nicolas. *Christianity and Anti-Semitism.* New York: Philosophical Library, 1954.

———. "Marx vs. Man." In *Russian Philosophy.* Edited by James M. Edie, James

P. Scanlan, and Mary-Barbara Zeldin, with the collaboration of George L. Kline. 3 vols. Knoxville: University of Tennessee Press, 1976.

Berline, Paul. "Russian Religious Philosophers and the Jews (Soloviev, Berdyaev, Bulgakov, Struve, Rozanov and Fedotov)." *Jewish Social Studies* 9 (1947): 271–318.

Billington, James H. *The Icon and the Axe: An Interpretive History of Russian Culture.* New York: Vintage Books, 1970.

Borisov, Father Aleksandr. "O natsionalizme v russkoi pravoslavnoi tserkvi". In *Nuzhen li Gitler Rossii?* Edited by Vladimir Iliushenko, 191–94. Moscow: Nezavisimoe izdatel'stvo PIK, 1996.

Brown, Clarence, trans. *The Prose of Osip Mandelstam.* San Francisco: North Point Press, 1986.

Brym, Robert J., with the assistance of Rozalina Ryvkina. *The Jews of Moscow, Kiev, and Minsk: Identity, Antisemitism, Emigration.* New York: New York University Press in association with the Institute of Jewish Affairs, 1994.

Cavalcanti, H. B., and H. Paul Chalfant. "Collective Life as the Ground of Implicit Religion: The Case of American Converts to Russian Orthodoxy." *Sociology of Religion* 55, no. 4 (1994): 441–54.

Cherniavsky, Michael. *Tsar and People: Studies in Russian Myths.* New Haven: Yale University Press, 1961.

Chervyakov, Valery, Zvi Gitelman, and Vladimir Shapiro. "*E Pluribus Unum?* Post-Soviet Jewish Identities and Their Implications for Communal Reconstruction." In *Jewish Life after the USSR.* Edited by Zvi Gitelman, with Musya Glants and Marshall I. Goldman. Bloomington: Indiana University Press, 2003.

Cohen, Steven M. "Religious Stability and Ethnic Decline: Emerging Patterns of Jewish Identity in the United States." Paper presented at the National Survey of American Jews, sponsored by The Florence G. Heller Research Center of the Jewish Community Centers Association, New York, 1997.

Cohen, Steven M., and Arnold M. Eisen. "The Jew Within: Self, Community, and Commitment among the Varieties of Moderately Affiliated." Los Angeles and Boston: The Wilstein Institute, 1998.

———. *The Jew Within: Self, Family, and Community in America.* Bloomington: Indiana University Press, 2000.

Danielevskii, N. Ia. *Rossiia i Evropa.* St. Petersburg, 1871; Moscow: Kniga, 1991.

Davidman, Lynn. *Tradition in a Rootless World: Women Turn to Orthodox Judaism.* Berkeley: University of California Press, 1991.

Dostoevsky, Feodor. *The Idiot.* Translated by Henry Carlisle and Olga Carlisle. New York: New American Library, 1969.

Dreizin, Felix. *The Russian Soul and the Jew: Essays in Literary Ethnocriticism.* Edited by David Guaspari. Foreword by Daniel Rancour-Laferriere. Lanham, Md.: University Press of America, 1990.

Dubnow, S. M. *History of the Jews in Russia and Poland from the Earliest Times until the Present Day.* 3 vols. Translated by I. Friedlaender. Philadelphia: The Jewish Publication Society of America, 1916.

Dudko, o. Dmitrii. *Khristos v nashei zhizni: Voskresnye propovedi.* Moscow: Izdatel'stvo zhurnala Khrama, 1992.

Dudko, Fr. Dmitrii. *Our Hope.* Translated by Paul D. Garrett. Foreword by John Meyendorff. Crestwood, N.Y.: St. Vladimir's Seminary Press, 1977.

Edie, James M., James P. Scanlan, and Mary-Barbara Zeldin, eds. With the collaboration of George L. Kline. *Russian Philosophy.* 3 vols. Knoxville: University of Tennessee Press, 1976.

Encyclopedia Judaica. Jerusalem: Keter, 1971.

Endelman, Todd M., ed. *Jewish Apostasy in the Modern World.* New York and London: Holmes & Meier, 1987.

"Θ." "Kak vernee nazyvat' posledovatelei Moiseeva zakona: evreiami, iudeiami ili izrail'tianami." *Evreiskie zapiski* (1881): 54

Florensky, Pavel. *Iconostasis.* Translated by Donald Sheehan and Olga Andrejev. Crestwood, N.Y.: St. Vladimir's Seminary Press, 1996.

———. *The Pillar and Ground of the Truth: An Essay in Orthodox Theodicy in Twelve Letters.* Translated by Boris Jakim. Introduction by Richard F. Gustafson. Princeton: Princeton University Press, 1997.

Frankel, Jonathan. *Prophecy and Politics: Socialism, Nationalism, and the Russian Jews, 1862–1917.* Cambridge: Cambridge University Press, 1981.

Freedman, Robert O. "Soviet Jewry and Soviet-American Relations: A Historical Analysis." In *Soviet Jewry in the Decisive Decade.* Durham, N.C.: Duke University Press, 1984.

Freedman, Robert O., ed. *Soviet Jewry in the 1980s: The Politics of Anti-Semitism and Emigration and the Dynamics of Resettlement.* Durham, N.C.: Duke University Press, 1989.

Gessen, Masha. *Dead Again: The Russian Intelligentsia after Communism.* London and New York: Verso, 1997.

Gets, Faivel'. "Nekotorye vospominaniia ob otnoshenii V. S. Solov'eva k evreiam." *Voskhod* 63 (13 August 1900): 30–35; 79 (7 September 1900): 18–25.

Giddens, Anthony. *Modernity and Self-Identity.* Stanford. Calif.: Stanford University Press, 1992.

Gilison, Jerome M. "Soviet-Jewish Emigration, 1971–80: An Overview." In *Soviet Jewry in the Decisive Decade, 1971–1980.* Edited by Robert O. Freedman. Durham, N.C.: Duke University Press, 1984.

Gitelman, Zvi. "The Decline of the Diaspora Jewish Nation: Boundaries, Content and Jewish Identity." *Jewish Social Studies* 4, no. 2 (Winter 1998): 112–32.

———. "'From a Northern Country': Russian and Soviet Jewish Immigration to America and Israel in Historical Perspective." In *Russian Jews on Three Continents: Migration and Resettlement.* Edited by Noah Lewin-Epstein, Yaacov Ro'i, and Paul Ritterband. London: Frank Cass, 1997.

———. "Jewish Nationality and Religion in the USSR and Eastern Europe." In *Religion and Nationalism in Soviet and East European Politics.* Edited by Pedro Ramet. Durham, N.C.: Duke University Press, 1989.

———. *Jewish Nationality and Soviet Politics: The Jewish Sections of the CPSU, 1917–1930.* Princeton: Princeton University Press, 1972.

———. "The Reconstruction of Community and Jewish Identity in Russia." *East European Jewish Affairs* 24, no. 1 (1994): 35–56.

———. "Thinking about Being Jewish in Russia and Ukraine." In *Jewish Life after the USSR.* Edited by Zvi Gitelman, with Musya Glants and Marshall I. Goldman. Bloomington: Indiana University Press, 2003.

Glazov, Iurii. *Tesnye vrata: vozrozhdenie russkoi intelligentsii.* London: Overseas Publications Interchange, 1973.

Glazov, Yuri. *The Russian Mind since Stalin's Death.* Dordrecht and Boston: D. Reidel, 1985.

Glouberman, Emanuel. "Feodor Dostoevsky, Vladimir Soloviev, Vasilii Rozanov, and Lev Shestov on Jewish and Old Testament Themes." Ph.D. diss., University of Michigan, 1974.

Green, David B. "The Troublemaker." *The Jerusalem Report* 9, no. 1 (1998): 96–102.

Greenberg, Louis. *The Jews in Russia: The Struggle for Emancipation.* 2 vols. New Haven: Yale University Press, 1944–51.

Grigoren'ko-Men', N. F., P. V. Men', T. A. Zhirmunskaia, and M. V. Sergeeva, eds. *I bylo utro . . . Vospominaniia ob ottse Aleksandre Mene.* Moscow: AO "Vita-Tsentr," 1992.

Hamant, Yves. *Alexandre Men: Un témoin pour la Russie de ce temps.* Paris: Éditions Mame, 1993. Russian translation: Aman, Iv. *Aleksandr Men': Svidetel' svoego vremeni.* Translated by N. V. Garskaia. Moscow: Rudomino, 1994.

Halperin, Charles J. "Judaizers and the Image of the Jew in Medieval Russia: A Polemic Revisited and a Question Posed." *Canadian-American Slavic Studies* 9, no. 2 (Summer 1975): 141–55.

Hamutal, Bar Yosef. "Otrazhenie tvorchestva i lichnosti Vladimira Solov'eva v evreiskoi pechati, literature i filosofii." Unpublished paper.

———. "The Jewish Reception of Vladimir Solov'ev." In *Vladimir Solov'ev: Reconciler and Polemicist.* Edited by Wil van den Bercken, Manon de Courten, and Evert van der Zweerde, 363–92. Leuven, Belgium and Sterling, Va.: Peeters, 2000.

Har'even, Gayil. *Ha-sipur ha-amitii.* Tel-Aviv: Zemora Bitan, 1994.

Heifetz, Mikhail. "The Resurgence of Christianity and Russian-Jewish Relations." In *Christianity and Russian Culture in Soviet Society.* Edited by Nicolai N. Petro. Boulder, Colo.: Westview Press, 1990.

Herberg, Will. *Protestant, Catholic, Jew: An Essay in American Religious Sociology.* Garden City, N.Y.: Doubleday, 1955; Garden City, N.Y.: Anchor, 1960; Chicago: University of Chicago Press, 1983.

Highlights of the CJF 1990 National Jewish Population Survey. New York: Council of Jewish Federations, 1991.

Horowitz, Bethamie. "Connections and Journeys: Shifting Identities among American Jews." *Contemporary Jewry* 19 (1998).

Ingerman, Jacob, ed. *Evreiskii samizdat: Evrei i evreiskii narod: Materialy iz sovetskoi pechati.* Jerusalem: Hebrew University, no date.

Iskander, F. "On byl svetom." In *I bylo utro . . . Vospominaniia ob ottse Aleksandre Mene,* edited by Grigoren'ko-Men', N. F., P. V. Men', T. A. Zhirmunskaia, and M. V. Sergeeva, 320–24. Moscow: AO "Vita-Tsentr," 1992.

Isser, Natalie, and Lita Linzer Schwarts. *The History of Conversion and Contemporary Cults.* New York: Peter Lang, 1988.

Kagan, Mikaella. "Evreiskaia emigratsiia iz byvshego SSSR v SShA: Obzor izmenenii za 70–90-e gody." *Issledovaniia po prikladnoi i neotlozhnoi etnologii* 99 (Moscow, 1996).

Kamenetz, Rodger. *The Jew in the Lotus: A Poet's Rediscovery of Jewish Identity in Buddhist India.* San Francisco: Harper, 1994.

Khomiakov, Aleksei. "The Church Is One." In *On Spiritual Unity: A Slavophile Reader.* Translated and edited by Boris Jakim and Robert Bird, 31–53. Hudson, N.Y.: Lindisfarne Books, 1998.

Kjaer-Hansen, Kai, and Bochil F. Skjott. *Facts and Myths about the Messianic Congregations in Israel.* Jerusalem: United Christian Council in Israel in Cooperation with the Caspari Center, 1999.

Klier, John D. *Imperial Russia's Jewish Question, 1855–1881.* Cambridge: Cambridge University Press, 1995.

———. "Judaizing without Jews? Moscow-Novgorod, 1470–1504." In *Culture and Identity in Muscovy, 1359–1584.* Edited by A. M. Kleimola and G. D. Lenhoff, 336–49. Moscow: ITZ-Garant, 1997.

———. *Russia Gathers Her Jews: The Origins of the "Jewish Question" in Russia, 1772–1825.* DeKalb: Northern Illinois University Press, 1986.

———. "State Policies and the Conversion of Jews in Imperial Russia." In *Of Religion and Empire: Missions, Conversion, and Tolerance in Tsarist Russia.* Edited by Robert B. Geraci and Michael Khodarkovsky, 92–112. Ithaca: Cornell University Press, 2001.

Kornblatt, Judith Deutsch. "Christianity. Antisemitism. Nationalism: Russian Orthodoxy in a Reborn Orthodox Russia." In *Consuming Russia: Popular Culture, Sex, and Society since Gorbachev.* Edited by Adele M. Barker, 414–36. Durham, N.C.: Duke University Press, 1999.

———. "Vechnyi zhid: Lev Shestov i russkaia religioznaia mysl' (The Wandering Jew: Lev Shestov and Russian Religious Thought)." In *Russkaia Literatura XX Veka: issledovaniia amerikanskikh uchenykh.* Edited by B. V. Averin and Elizabeth Neatrour, 46–57. St. Petersburg: Petro-Rif Publishers, 1993.

———. "Vladimir Solov'ev on Spiritual Nationhood, Russia and the Jews." *The Russian Review* 56 (April 1997): 157–77.

Kosmin, Barry A., et al., eds. *Highlights of the CJF 1990 National Jewish Population Survey.* New York: The Council of Jewish Federations, 1991.

Krakhmal'nikova, Zoia A., ed. *Russkaia ideia i evrei: Rokovoi spor: Khristianstvo. Antisemitizm. Natsiolnalizm: Sbornik statei.* Moscow: Nauka, 1994.

Lederhendler, Eli. "Did Russian Jewry Exist Prior to 1917?" In *Jews and Jewish Life in Russia and the Soviet Union.* Edited by Yaacov Ro'i, 15–27. Ilford, Essex: Frank Cass, 1995.

———. *The Road to Modern Jewish Politics.* New York: Oxford University Press, 1989.

Leikin, Ezekiel, trans. and ed. *The Beilis Transcripts: The Anti-Semitic Trial That Shook the World.* Northvale, N.Y.: Jason Aronson, 1993.

Liebman, Charles S., and Steven M. Cohen, eds. *Two Worlds of Judaism: The Israeli and American Experiences.* New Haven: Yale University Press 1990.

Liebman, Charles S., and Elihu Katz, eds. *The Jewishness of Israelis: Responses to the Guttman Report.* Albany: State University of New York Press, 1997.

Lindemann, Albert S. *The Jew Accused: Three Anti-Semitic Affairs (Dreyfus, Beilis, Frank), 1894–1915.* Cambridge and New York: Cambridge University Press, 1991.

Lichtenstein, Aharon. "Brother Daniel and the Jewish Fraternity." *Judaism* 12, no. 3 (Summer 1963): 260–80.

Markish, Simon. "Passers-by: The Soviet Jew as Intellectual." *Commentary* 66, no. 6 (December 1978).

Maslenikova, Zoia. *Zhizn' ottsa Aleksandra Menia.* Moscow: Pristsel's, "Russlit," 1995.

Mayer, Carl. "Religious and Political Aspects of Anti-Judaism." In *Jews in a Gentile World.* Edited by Isacque Graeber and Steuart Henderson Brit, 311–28. New York: Macmillan Co., 1942.

Meerson, Michael. "The Life and Work of Father Aleksandr Men'." In *Seeking God: The Recovery of Religious Identity in Orthodox Russia, Ukraine, and Georgia.* Edited by Stephen K. Batalden, 13–27. DeKalb: Northern Illinois University Press, 1993.

Men', Alexander. "Vospominaniia ob Aleksandre Galiche." In *Kul'tura i dukhovnoe voskhozhdenie,* 434–37. Moscow: Iskusstvo, 1992.

Moss, Walter G. "Vladimir Soloviev and the Jews in Russia." *Russian Review* 29 (April 1970): 181–91.

Nakhimovsky, Alice. "Mikhail Zhvanetskii: The Last Russian-Jewish Joker." Paper presented at conference on "BORDERLINES: Judaic Literature and Culture in Eastern Europe," Syracuse, N.Y., 6–8 April 2002.

———. *Russian-Jewish Literature and Identity: Jabotinsky, Babel, Grossman, Galich, Roziner, Markish.* Baltimore: The Johns Hopkins University Press, 1992.

Nerel, Gershon. "Messianic Jews and the Modern Zionist Movement." In *Israel and Yeshua.* Edited by Torleif Elgvin. Jerusalem: Caspari Center for Biblical and Jewish Studies, 1993.

Petro, Nicolai N., ed. *Christianity and Russian Culture in Soviet Society.* Boulder, Colo.: Westview Press, 1990.

Petrovsky-Shtern, Yohanan. "Jews in the Russian Army: Through the Military towards Modernity, 1827–1914." Ph.D. diss., Brandeis, 2001.

Pinkus, Benjamin. "The *Hazara Bitshuva* Phenomenon among Russian Jews in the Post-Stalin Era." *Jews and Jewish Topics in the Soviet Union and Eastern Europe* 15, no. 2 (Fall 1991): 15–30.

——. *The Jews of the Soviet Union: The History of a National Minority.* Cambridge and New York: Cambridge University Press, 1988.

——. *The Soviet Government and the Jews, 1948–1967: A Documented Study.* Cambridge and New York: Cambridge University Press, 1984.

Pospielovsky, D. "Some Remarks on the Contemporary Russian Nationalism and Religious Revival." *Canadian Review of Studies in Nationalism* 11, no. 1 (Spring 1984): 71–85.

Pravoslavnaia tserkov' i evrei: XIX-XX vv.: Sbornik materialov k teologii mezhkonfessional'nogo dialoga. Moscow: Rudomino-Bog edin, 1994.

Ritterband, Paul. "Jewish Identity among Russian Immigrants in the U.S." In *Russian Jews on Three Continents: Migration and Resettlement.* Edited by Noah Lewin-Epstein, Yaacov Ro'i, and Paul Ritterband, 325–43. London: Frank Cass, 1997.

Roberts, Elizabeth, and Ann Shukman, eds. *Christianity for the Twenty-First Century: The Prophetic Writings of Alexander Men.* New York: Continuum, 1996.

Rogger, Hans. *Jewish Policies and Right-Wing Politics in Imperial Russia.* Berkeley: University of California Press, 1986.

——. *National Consciousness in Eighteenth-Century Russia.* Cambridge: Harvard University Press, 1960.

Ro'i, Yaacov. "Soviet Policy towards Jewish Emigration: An Overview" In *Russian Jews on Three Continents: Migration and Resettlement.* Edited by Noah Lewin-Epstein, Yaacov Ro'i, and Paul Ritterband. London: Frank Cass, 1997.

Ro'i, Yaacov, ed. *Jews and Jewish Life in Russia and the Soviet Union.* Portland, Ore.: Frank Cass, 1995.

Roth, Norman. "Am Yisrael: Jews or Judaism?" *Judaism: A Quarterly Journal* 37, no. 2 (1988): 199–209.

Ryvkina, Rozalina. *Evrei v postsovetskoi Rossii—Kto oni?* Moscow: Izd-vo URSS, 1996.

Sacks, Michael Paul. "Privilege and Prejudice: The Occupations of Jews in Russia in 1989." *Slavic Review* 57, no. 2 (Summer 1998): 247–66.

Safran, Gabriella. *Rewriting the Jew: Assimilation Narratives in the Russian Empire.* Stanford: Stanford University Press, 2000.

Salitan, Laurie P. "Ethnic and Related Factors in Soviet Emigration Policy,

1968–89." In *Russian Jews on Three Continents: Migration and Resettlement.* Edited by Noah Lewin-Epstein, Yaacov Ro'i, and Paul Ritterband, 68–86. London: Frank Cass, 1997.

Samuel, Maurice. *Blood Accusation: The Strange History of the Beiliss Case.* New York: Knopf, 1966.

Schnapper, Dominique. *Jewish Identities in France: An Analysis of Contemporary French Jewry.* Translated by Arthur Goldhammer. Chicago: University of Chicago Press, 1983.

Shafarevich, Igor'. "Rusofobiia." *Nash sovremennik* 6 (1989).

Shepherd, Naomi. *The Russians in Israel: The Ordeal of Freedom.* New York: Simon & Schuster, 1993.

Shragin, Boris. *The Challenge of the Spirit.* Translated by P. S. Falla. New York: Alfred A. Knopf, 1978.

Sicher, Efraim. *Jews in Russian Literature after the October Revolution: Writers and Artists between Hope and Apostasy.* Cambridge: Cambridge University Press, 1995.

Sitbon, Guy. "Qui a tué Alexandre Men, pope et juif?" *Le nouvel observateur* (27 September–30 October 1990): 50–51.

Smith, Anthony D. "Ethnic Identity and World Order." *Millennium* 12 (April 1983).

Sobel, B. Z. *Hebrew Christianity: The Thirteenth Tribe.* New York: John Wiley, 1974.

Solov'ev, V. S. *Sobranie sochinenii Vladimira Sergeevicha Solov'eva,* 2d ed., 10 vols. (1911–14); reprint, with two additional volumes, Brussels: Zhizn' s Bogom, 1966–70.

Stanislawski, Michael. *For Whom Do I Toil?: Judah Leib Gordon and the Crisis of Russian Jewry.* New York: Oxford University Press, 1988.

———. *Tsar Nicholas I and the Jews: The Transformation of Jewish Society in Russia, 1825–1855.* Philadelphia: The Jewish Publication Society of America, 1983.

———. "Jewish Apostasy in Russia: A Tentative Typology." In *Jewish Apostasy in the Modern World.* Edited by Todd M. Endelman, 189–205. New York: Holmes & Meier, 1987.

Struve, Nikita. "Apostol." In *I bylo utro ... Vospominaniia ob ottse Aleksandre Mene.* Edited by N. F. Grigoren'ko-Men', P. V. Men', T. A. Zhirmunskaia, and M. V. Sergeeva, 340–41. Moscow: AO "Vita-Tsentr," 1992.

Svetov, Feliks. *Opyt biografii.* Paris: YMCA-Press, 1985.

———. *Otverzi mi dveri.* Paris: Les Éditeurs Réunis, 1978.

———. "Otverzi me dveri." *Novyi mir* 10 (October 1991): 48–127; 11 (November 1991): 149–218; 12 (December 1991): 89–152; 12:114.

Tec, Nechama. *In the Lion's Den: The Life of Oswald Rufeisen.* New York and Oxford: Oxford University Press, 1990.

Tobias, Henry J. "The Bund and Lenin until 1903." *The Russian Review* 20, no. 4 (October 1961): 344–57.

Tolts, Mark. "Demography of the Jews in the Former Soviet Union: Yesterday and Today." In *Jewish Life after the USSR*. Edited by Zvi Gitelman, with Musya Glants and Marshall I. Goldman. Bloomington: Indiana University Press, 2003.

Viswanathan, Gauri. *Outside the Fold: Conversion, Modernity, and Belief.* Princeton: Princeton University Press, 1998.

Voronel, Alexander V. "Twenty Years After." In *Russian Jews on Three Continents: Migration and Resettlement.* Edited by Noah Lewin-Epstein, Yaacov Ro'i, and Paul Ritterband London: Frank Cass, 1997.

Ware, Timothy. *The Orthodox Church.* New York and Middlesex, England: Penguin Books, 1997.

Zaremba, Stanislava. "Otets Daniel': karmelit v Izraile." *Istina i zhizn'* 12 (December 1996): 18–20.

Zelinskii, Vladimir. "Pamiati o. Aleksandra Menia: Slova proshchaniia." *Russkaia mysl'* (14 September 1990): 8.

Zenkovsky, Serge A., ed. *Medieval Russia's Epics, Chronicles, and Tales.* 1963; New York: Dutton, 1974.

Zorin, A. I., and V. I. Iliushenko, eds. *Vokrug imeni ottsa Aleksandra.* Moscow: Obshchestvo "Kul'turnoe vozrozhdenie" imeni Aleksandra Menia, 1993.

Index